THE GM

THE
GM

A FOOTBALL LIFE, A FINAL SEASON,
AND A LAST LAUGH

TOM CALLAHAN

THREE RIVERS PRESS

NEW YORK

Published in the United States by Three Rivers Press, an imprint of the
Crown Publishing Group, a division of Random House, Inc., New York.
www.crownpublishing.com

Three Rivers Press and the Tugboat design are registered trademarks of
Random House, Inc.

Originally published in hardcover in the United States in slightly different form as
The GM: The Inside Story of a Dream Job and the Nightmares That Go with It by
Crown Publishers, an imprint of the Crown Publishing Group,
a division of Random House, Inc., New York, in 2007.

Library of Congress Cataloging-in-Publication Data

Callahan, Tom.
The GM : a football life, a final season, and a last
laugh / Tom Callahan.—1st ed.
p.   cm.
1. National Football League. 2. Football—United States.
3. Accorsi, Ernie. 4. New York Giants (Football team)—Biography.
I. Title. II. Title: General manager.
GV955.5.N35C35 2007
796.33206'9—dc22   2007024069

ISBN 978-0-307-39461-3

Printed in the United States of America

Design by Leonard Henderson

10 9 8 7 6 5 4 3 2 1

First Paperback Edition

For Ernie Accorsi

Setting no conditions,
asking nothing in return,
he let me in

The acknowledgment is also singular.
Thank you, John Mara, president of the
New York Football Giants, for tolerating such
a conspicuous fly on the front office wall.

CONTENTS

PREFACE: THE ESSENCE OF SPORTS   1

1   THE MEADOWS GAME   5

2   MANNING VS. MANNING   15

3   RED LICORICE   29

4   PLAXICO   39

5   THE BALTIMORE COLTS: DRAFTING JOHN ELWAY   49

6   THE CLEVELAND BROWNS: STEALING BERNIE KOSAR   65

7   THE NEW YORK GIANTS: SIGNING KERRY COLLINS   81

8   SHOCK   93

9   THE DRAFT   105

10   RONNIE   117

11   THE CAP   125

12   PARCELLS   137

13   OFF THE STREET   147

14   REESE   157

15   GOODBYE, TOOMS   167

16   TIME-OUT, GIANTS   175

17   "IT'S A FABULOUS GAME"   185

18   *TITANIC, HINDENBURG,* JOE PISARCIK . . .   189

19   K BALLS   197

20   "NUMBER SIXTY-NINE IS REPORTING . . ."   205

21   STILL WATCHING FOOTBALL GAMES ON TV   213

22   DOUBLE SAFETY DELAYED BLITZ   217

23   REAL LIFE IN THE SPORTS WORLD   225

24   "THERE'S A CHAMPIONSHIP IN THIS ROOM"   237

25   COUNTDOWN   247

26   SUPER BOWL XLII   259

EPILOGUE BY ERNIE ACCORSI   275

AUTHOR'S NOTE   280

INDEX   283

PREFACE:

THE ESSENCE OF SPORTS

TEN OR TWELVE GAMES into the New York Giants' 2006 season, I turned to head coach Tom Coughlin during a players' lunch and said, "You probably haven't heard this for a while, but I like your team. It's a nice-watching football team."

"You're right," Coughlin said with a smile. "I haven't heard that for a while."

Ernie Accorsi, the Giants' general manager, had invited me inside for his farewell season. Accorsi and I go back more than forty years, to August 13, 1964, when we spent five hours in each other's company but didn't know it at the time. He was a twenty-two-year-old sportswriter for the Baltimore *Evening Sun,* tramping after Joe Louis in a local golf tournament. I was an eighteen-year-old college student on the brink of sophomore year, caddying for the former heavyweight champion. Ernie and I formally met in the late 1960s—or was it the early '70s?—by which time *I* was at the *Sun* and he had moved into the football business. In 1987, when I was working for *Time* magazine and Ernie was serving the Browns, I went to Cleveland to write a piece on Accorsi, the fans' "Dog Pound," and quarterback Bernie Kosar. At old Municipal Stadium, Ernie and I talked and laughed away a long afternoon in his office overlooking the field. "I've known Ernie Accorsi forever," I used to say, and that was true enough. But now I really know him.

We had Johnny Unitas in common. "You bull-crappers in the media" was Unitas' usual salutation to me, especially on the telephone, but he loved Accorsi and Ernie loved him. In 2005, reporting my book *Johnny U,* I spent a bit of time in the Giants' front office talking with Ernie. Luckily, I met Wellington Mara there. He didn't hold 1958 and 1959 against Unitas. The Giants' owner didn't hold very much against very many.

"You should think of writing a book yourself," I told Accorsi in parting, and that was the beginning of this project. Months later, in a badminton game of e-mails, I said, "If you want to write a book by Ernie Accorsi as told to somebody, I can find you somebody. But it can't be me. I can only write in my own voice." He responded, "I'd rather you do it your way."

"First, we have to get John Mara's permission," Ernie said, and Mara gave it cheerfully. "Are you up to the seventies yet?" he'd kid me when we'd bump in the hallways. "Are you up to the sixties at least?" I asked Ernie, "Don't we need Coughlin's blessing, too?" "Coughlin," he said, "works for me. I'll tell him about it." Tom was gracious to me throughout. In fact, when it comes to graciousness, Coughlin is the most underrated football coach I've ever been around.

I moved to Belmar, New Jersey, for the fall and winter to be nearer the ocean than the Meadowlands. I bought an E-ZPass and commuted to Giants Stadium on the Garden State Parkway and New Jersey Turnpike three or four days a week. Pat Hanlon, the Giants' communications czar, found me a working space in the front office and made a place for me in the press box at all of the games, home and away. Curiously, my affiliation on the media badge and out-of-town seating charts read "Random House." Thanks to the Giants' director of public relations, Peter John-Baptiste, I was able to get one-on-one time with the ten or so players I wanted to know better than the others. None of them was exactly sure who I was, but they all knew I had some connection to Accorsi. "Are you the guy who owns Callahan Auto Parts?" Jeremy Shockey asked. I'll leave it to the reader to judge if Eli Manning, Plaxico Burress, LaVar Arrington, and others were more open with me on the side than they would have been with someone trawling the locker room for the *Washington Post* or *Time.*

I think of this as Ernie's book more than mine. I tried to get out of the way as much as possible and let him talk. The 2006 Giants season is really just a scaffolding for the life in sports Ernie has led at a post that is suddenly in vogue. Today's magazine stands are crowded with titles like *World Championship of Fantasy Football, Winning in Fantasy Football, Fantasy Football Draft Book, Fantasy Football Guide, Fantasy Football Cheat Sheet, Fantasy Sports, Fantasy Analysis, Fantasy Forecast* . . . In this era of make-believe football, not only fans but players and even sportswriters are thinking and acting like general managers, like Ernie Accorsi.

The GM isn't a biography of Ernie. If it were, it might contain a lot of embarrassing personal information, like the fact that he plays the accordion. ("Lady of Spain," what else?) It's closer to a biography of a job, or maybe just a long look at an inner sanctum behind the door of the front office.

Three days after the Giants' last regular-season game, Accorsi went to the Orange Bowl in Miami on his own hook, not as a scout, as an alumnus of Wake Forest University, as a fan. He didn't sit in the press box. He bought a ticket for a normal seat in the grandstand, where he fell in with Wake Forest's famous stable of golfers: Curtis Strange, Lanny Wadkins, Jay Haas, Billy Andrade. They were all there, including Arnold Palmer. Palmer from Wake Forest and Muhammad Ali—sort of from the University of Louisville—were the honorary captains, decked out in game jerseys. Ali wore Unitas' number, 19, which pleased Ernie, although he knew that John's Louisville number was 16. Arnie wore 66, six under par. "I don't think that's for the 1966 U.S. Open," Ernie said, "when he blew a seven-shot lead to Billy Casper in the last nine holes."

Though Wake lost the game in a downpour, 24–13, its supporters couldn't stop smiling. Tens of thousands of them, half a stadium full, in gold! Where did they all come from? At one point Strange turned to Andrade and said excitedly, "Billy, Billy, did you ever believe we'd be here?" "That's a two-time U.S. Open champion talking," Ernie said of Strange, "standing like a student in the rain, so thrilled to be at a football game that he could hardly stay still. There, right there. Isn't that the essence of why we love sports?"

About a year later, Andrade and Accorsi would be in the stands again—this time at a Super Bowl. More than any football plays, the lasting memory for Andrade would be the look in the eyes of Ernie's daughter and two sons as they watched their father at the game's end.

1

THE MEADOWS GAME

F IT'S TRUE THAT THE olfactory is the keenest of the senses, the most evocative, the best one at recalling the past, then it is little wonder that a man born and raised in Chocolate Town—Hershey, Pennsylvania—can reach back for his childhood whenever he wants. Just a few days ago, on an unofficial and unremarkable playing field called the Meadows, retiring New York Giants general manager Ernie Accorsi returned to November 13, 1954, when he was thirteen. "Smell that air," he said, breathing in. It smelled like fudge bubbling on a stove.

Standing just five foot eight, Accorsi might be described as unremarkable, too, except for one thing: he is the only man in the history of sports who ever set out to be a general manager. Even Branch Rickey, the ultimate GM, didn't set out to be one. He set out to be a major league catcher, as Ernie first read in the *Sporting News* and later confirmed at the Hershey library. George Weiss of the New York Yankees represented another Accorsi study, but Rickey of the Brooklyn Dodgers was his ideal. When Ernie grew old enough to smoke cigars, he smoked only Rickey's brand, and still does. From college age on, he wielded the cigar like a baton, using it to conduct conversations.

Naturally, Accorsi set out to be a baseball general manager—football GMs were never mentioned in the *Sporting News*—but circumstances and an old college quarterback, George Welsh, redirected Ernie first to the Baltimore Colts, then to the Cleveland Browns, and finally to the Giants for the last decade of a thirty-five-year National Football League career. Now that he had time to look around a little, Accorsi wrote out a list of places he wanted to go and things he wanted to see, like the "Field of Dreams" in Dyersville, Iowa; the Negro Leagues Baseball Museum in Kansas City, Missouri; maybe a small college football game or two along the way, perhaps at Wabash or DePauw. Then there was the leaning tin barn in Commerce, Oklahoma, where father Mutt, a righty, and grandfather Charlie, a lefty, made a switch-hitter out of Mickey Mantle. But at the top of Ernie's list, a way of going back to the very beginning, was Rickey's grave in Rushtown, Ohio.

A whip-armed catcher with just an average glove and bat, Branch slipped through the systems of the Cincinnati Reds and the Chicago White Sox before reaching the big leagues with the St. Louis Browns in a June game versus Philadelphia with its managing owner, Connie Mack, squinting out from under his skimmer into the bright sun of old Athletic Park. Though Rickey should have been giving spitball pitcher Cy Morgan his full attention, he couldn't resist shooting an occasional glance Mack's way. Management fascinated Branch. Not just management of the game, management of the sport. Later, on barnstorming excursions, when both teams often rode the same train, he sought out Mack in his private Pullman car, just to sit quietly by as the "Tall Tactician," a former catcher himself, held forth on general managing.

Nearly every lesson began "Now, lookit . . ." and ended with an aphorism like "Don't ever get rid of a player until you're as sure as lightning that you have somebody just as good or better to take his place." On the other hand, "Now, lookit. Anesthetic players will absolutely ruin your team." An "anesthetic player" was defined as a subtly declining veteran whose past is so storied that it has lulled the organization into thinking at least one position is safely taken care of. Rickey converted this into his own aphorism: "Better to trade a man a year too soon than a year too late."

During off-seasons, Branch returned to his college, Ohio Wesleyan, and later to the University of Michigan, to help with football and the other sports, to see to all of the duties in the athletic department that didn't have titles then but do now. Scheduling, scouting, sports information directing, merchandising, marketing, ticketing, recruiting, and of course romancing—players and newspapermen alike. Along the way, Rickey, who enjoyed putting words together, collected a few bylines of his own. Not so long ago a sportswriter, Ford Frick for instance, could actually end up the commissioner of baseball. These were all roads to where Rickey was going, the same ones Accorsi would take as well.

More than playing, more than managing, Branch loved finding, gauging, and championing talent. Rickey could spot athletic ability, people said, from the window of a moving train. Though he specialized in beating the bushes for material, among Branch's most memorable discoveries was an eighteen-year-old freshman engineering student "with dark brown hair, serious gray eyes, and good posture" who just walked up to him one day in Ann Arbor. His name was George Sisler. Though freshmen weren't usually considered for the varsity, something in Sisler's bearing persuaded Rickey to ignore his own order and pitch the kid for seven innings in an intrasquad game. George struck out twenty men. On top of that, Sisler hit so well that in subsequent games when he wasn't pitching, he played first base and batted cleanup. Years later, while Rickey was running the St. Louis Cardinals, he sensed the same quality in a skinny twenty-year-old pitcher who had permanently wrecked his throwing shoulder in a fall. When the Cardinals' Springfield farm club was about to put the wounded boy on its drop-dead list, Branch said, "No, let's hold on to him awhile. Try him in the outfield. See if he can hit his way to Rochester." That was Stanley Musial. Of course Rickey had his misses, too. They all did.

Walter Wellesley "Red" Smith, the prince of the press box, rattled off Rickey's final record like an official scorer closing a pitching line: "Player, manager, executive, lawyer, preacher, horse-trader, innovator, husband and father and grandfather, farmer, logician, obscurantist, reformer, financier, sociologist, crusader, sharper, father confessor, checker shark, friend, fighter." General manager. "And, Judas Priest, what a character!"

The Brooklyn Dodgers today purchased the contract of
Jackie Roosevelt Robinson from the Montreal Royals.
He will report immediately.
                                    Branch Rickey

That defining transaction in 1947 may have been grounded less in sociology than in just a simple, lifelong reverence for talent. But as far as young Accorsi was concerned, breaking the color barrier pushed Rickey over the top. Not that Ernie knew so much about black people. In 1960, the year after Accorsi left Hershey for college, a federal census taker counted six African Americans in all of Derry Township. The Italians were Hershey's minority, most of them Catholics to boot. Vowel-ending names dominate the headstones at the bottom of the town cemetery, far below the Methodists and Mennonites at the top of the hill, where the grandest marker is for Milton Snavely Hershey.

Both Ernie's grandfather, Joe Nardi, and his father, also Ernie, knew Mr. Hershey personally. Just about everyone in town had at least the illusion of being acquainted with the founder, who in this luxuriant valley, surrounded by bush-league mountains and Pennsylvania Dutchmen, built a milk chocolate factory with all of the trimmings. Including, at astonishingly affordable prices and mortgage rates, most of the homes of his employees, as well as a hospital, a stadium, an arena, an amusement park, a theater as acoustically well fitted as any on Broadway, an ornate and splendid movie house, a school, a pool, a library, a life.

Milton turned over the first floor of his mansion to serve as a clubhouse for the Hershey Country Club golf course, a handsome layout sporty enough to attract resident professionals the likes of Ben Hogan, the country's ultimate playing pro, and Masters and PGA champion Henry Picard. The ablest teaching assistant during Picard's tenure was a courtly Oklahoman, Jack Grout, who moved on to a head job in Ohio to show a precocious ten-year-old how to hit the ball left to right. Barbara and Jack Nicklaus honeymooned in Hershey.

Joe Nardi, who spoke only broken English (his grandson spoke sprained Italian), worked at a conveyor belt in the factory, molding chocolate with a mallet. He shipped over, twice, from Pitigliano in Tuscany, first to find a job and a grubstake, then to return with his family. Living on pasta and bread—meat maybe twice a week, often from rabbits he hunted himself—Joe meticulously grew a savings account to $5,000, enough to purchase a modest home in the 1920s. Carrying a note from a son-in-law spelling out the transaction in English, Nardi went to withdraw the five grand from his bank. But the teller handed him six. Several times Joe tried to point out the error, but the counterman was impatient. "Get out of here, you dumb Wop," he said.

In those days, Mr. Hershey knew his longest-serving employees by name, and by more than just their names. That afternoon, as the boss made his regular tour of the plant, Nardi approached him with a worried look. "What's the matter, Joe?" he asked. Together, in a chauffeur-driven limousine, Hershey and Nardi returned to the bank. When the smoke had cleared, the teller was fired and Nardi was told to keep the thousand, a fortune. Joe continued to be a world-class scrimper, but thereafter put his pennies into Hershey stock. Though Nardi's high salary was $21 a week, when he died he left each of his four children $11,000 in cash and a little Hershey house, fully paid for.

Ernie's father quit school in the eighth grade to begin a life of work. He also started at the chocolate factory, but after about a dozen years he went out on his own, opening a beer distributorship in a backyard shed. The first customer to drive up was Mr. Hershey. "I like my beer, Ernie," he said. "Run a clean business, and I'll be here every week to purchase a case. I'll make a big show of it, too, which won't hurt your bottom line. But become a hangout for rummies, and I promise you, I'll run you out of town." Because there weren't many beer distributorships in the area, Accorsi and son now and then loaded a small delivery truck and made a run through the Dutch country, testing their German on beer-loving customers. They knew how to say three things: "hello," "how are you doing," and "goodbye."

Like so many immigrants, Ernie's dad drew a particular joy from sports, maybe for the slight relief it seemed to offer from hard work and prejudice. He made an early pilgrimage to the Baker Bowl in Philadelphia, where a night game was never played, to see the Dean brothers, Dizzy and Paul, and the rest of St. Louis' Gashouse Gang. But he preferred the New York Yankees. They had Lazzari and Crosetti, later DiMaggio, Berra, and Rizzuto. Young Ernie saw his first major league baseball game at Philadelphia's Shibe Park in 1950. Jackie Robinson stole home, but the Phillies beat the Dodgers, 6–4. That year, every Philadelphia victory was critical, especially against the Dodgers. On the final day of the regular season, Dick Sisler, George's son, hit a tenth-inning home run to beat Brooklyn and win the pennant.

The Accorsis didn't have to go looking for pro football; it came to them in 1949 in the form of an exhibition game featuring quarterback Bobby Layne and the New York Bulldogs. In 1951, the Philadelphia Eagles established a regular training ground at the Hershey stadium, and that first summer, the New York Giants won a game there, 21–6, wearing striking red jerseys that stuck with Ernie. Someday he would retrieve those red jerseys from antiquity and dress the Giants in them once a year. In 1952, Ernie saw the Eagles and Steelers play to a scoreless tie that was memorable in its own way, and by 1956 Ernie was firmly on the side of whoever opposed the Eagles. That year the Hershey public address man mispronounced the name of a visiting quarterback making his professional debut, "Johnny YOU-knee-TASS." Come the finish of Unitas' career in Baltimore, he would present his last Colts jersey not to the National Football League Hall of Fame but to Accorsi. Ernie would feel entitled then to pass the number 19 on to a fledgling quarterback in Cleveland.

Two years before Unitas came to Chocolate Town, on a Saturday afternoon in November, the eighth-grade boys of Hershey staged a game of tackle football, without equipment, that turned out to be the game of the century. In the days ahead, players on both sides of that field, including Accorsi, would team up to miss qualifying for the Little League World Series in Williamsport by about a millimeter. Some would make all-city or all-state in baseball, football, basketball, or golf. A few would excel athletically at college. One would participate in two Super Bowls, a victory and a defeat. But of all the games of their lives, the Meadows Game is the one they still talk about when any two of them get together today.

It isn't precisely true that the sons of the town's workers took on the sons of the men they worked for, but it was pretty close to that. Maybe surprisingly, then, the game wasn't a desperate or bitter showdown. It was just sports. No class or religious wars were brought into it. No hatreds were played out. All of the players were schoolmates and, within reason, pals. But while it may have been just sports, it was serious. Especially after Paul Hummer of the other side "stole" Ernie's cousin, Gary Ponzoli, a year younger than everyone else but an all-around athlete bound eventually for West Point. "All bets are off," Accorsi told Hummer, proclaiming the dawn of free agency. In his first job of general managing, Ernie reached out to the farm areas and a couple of other distant neighborhoods for additional players. Hummer couldn't keep up, but he wasn't worried. His side already had the unstoppable Billy Myers, star of the town.

Accorsi's best recruit was a quarterback named Jimmy Warfield (Ernie would always be quarterback-oriented; all of the milestones in this story are quarterbacks) who lived over by the stadium and went on to play second base to Accorsi's shortstop all through high school and American Legion ball, and to have an honored life in baseball as a beloved trainer for the Cleveland Indians. "He was as well thought of as anyone in the game," said third baseman Travis Fryman on the day Jimmy died of a cerebral hemorrhage. "Where are we going to find a church big enough to hold everybody who loved him?" Ernie would deliver the eulogy at Jimmy's funeral. ("Somehow today, I have the feeling that my childhood is slipping through my fingers . . .")

The Saturday morning of the Meadows Game, there was a funeral as well. Joe Nardi had died of a heart attack. Because a cousin had to make his way home from the Navy, the services fell on game day, and Ernie's father was adamant: Italian mourning traditions did not allow for after-burial football games. For a loud while, a Puccini opera was sung through the house. Until, during a pause for breath, the cousin, Ron Gramigni—who knew that nobody was more brokenhearted than Ernie, and that nobody loved Joe more—pointedly informed his uncle, "If you don't let Ernie play in this game, you might as well sell the business and move to Iowa. Because he won't be able to live here anymore."

Ernie played. On a ten-yard run by halfback Bill Rollins, crossing the two goal line trees on the factory end of the field, the sons of the workers scored first. For hours then, they held on. Accorsi didn't do much on offense, but he intercepted three Gary Hinebaugh passes on defense. Hinebaugh wore a Brown University sweatshirt. (His big brother went to Brown.) Ernie wore one of those blank blue football jerseys, so popular at the time, with golden shoulders that described shoulder pads although there were no shoulder pads. No helmets, either. The days of wine and bloody noses.

They had agreed to play from the stroke of noon until the whistle signaling the ten-of-four shift change at the chocolate factory, and it was pretty late in the game when the great Billy Myers ran a sweep to the right, took off down the sideline, and sped the full length of the drainage ditch to tie the score, 6–6. By the way, a parent or two were in attendance that afternoon but none of them was a part of it. At one point, Terry Garman's father, Francis (of the bosses' team), charged the edge of the field to double-check an out-of-bounds call or to weigh in on a late hit. "Dad, stay out of this," Terry said. "We're fine." Those were the days.

With the whistle about to blow, Accorsi's team was at the five-yard line, looking sure to score the winning touchdown, when quarterback Warfield scrambled toward an opening and was bumped into and knocked down by his own halfback, Rollins. "Bill, you tackled me," he said. And the whistle blew. By that time, Chocolate Avenue had filled up with townspeople applauding. Shaking hands, Hummer and Accorsi said almost simultaneously, "We shouldn't play again." As it was, it was perfect.

That night, like the Sharks and Jets with a happier ending, they went to the dance at the "juvenile golf course" with its little log cabin clubhouse that Mr. Hershey had built. But they were too sore to dance and too excited to sit down.

Golf became Accorsi's game for a time. This was one of the elements that attracted him to Wake Forest University, Arnold Palmer's school, in Winston-Salem, North Carolina. But Ernie didn't require all eighteen holes of a practice round with another young aspirant, Jay Sigel, to realize that he wasn't nearly good enough for Wake Forest. Though Accorsi's first impulse was to run home, his father talked him out of quitting, not just Wake Forest, but anything else he started. Ernie and Hinebaugh, the bosses' quarterback in the Meadows Game, became fraternity brothers.

By Ernie's count, Wake Forest had a Roman Catholic population of "about five," one of them a freshman football player, Brian Piccolo. Together Ernie and Pic regularly hitchhiked to Sunday Mass. It seemed that the same family stopped for them every week. A tough runner, adept at lowering a shoulder just before he crashed into the line, Piccolo wasn't anything like the wisecracker actor James Caan would portray him to be in the weeper *Brian's Song*. "In that movie, Caan wasn't like Piccolo in any way, shape, or form," Accorsi said. "Brian had this wit, but it came across with Caan as a smart-ass wit. With Piccolo, you'd hear these great lines, but he always delivered them dropping his head looking into his shirt. Most of the time he was quiet. He was always humble. Hell, he was saintly." A couple of days after Piccolo sprained an ankle in a Friday frosh game at Chapel Hill, Accorsi dropped into Pic's room to see how he was mending. "Ernie," he said, "it's my own fault. In the pregame meal, I ate meat on Friday for the first time in my life. That's why I got hurt. I took one look at those fish sticks and I just couldn't bear to touch them."

Years later, at the Americana Hotel in New York, the pro football writers held a gala dinner honoring Piccolo's Chicago backfield mate Gale Sayers for an inspired comeback from injury. Ernie was in the audience. "Sayers asked all of us," he said, "when we hit our knees that night, to please pray for Brian Piccolo, who was sick. Gale said he was going to take the award he received at the banquet and hand it over to Pic in his hospital room the next day. I had no idea how bad it was until I heard the words 'Sloan-Kettering.' Gale said, 'I love Brian Piccolo. I want you to love him, too.'"

Ernie started to walk up to Sayers as the crowd was milling out, but Vince Lombardi got there first. Accorsi heard Lombardi say, "Gale, you're a great American," and decided not to follow that. He wasn't sure he could manage any words anyway.

2

MANNING VS. MANNING

FOR THE FIRST TIME in sixteen years, the New York Giants were perfect in the preseason, beating the Ravens, Chiefs, Jets, and Patriots.

By contrast, the New Orleans Saints and their rookie head coach, Giants castoff Sean Payton, were 1 and 3. Obviously these were two teams going in opposite directions in the National Football Conference. "I have no idea where we're going," Giants head coach Tom Coughlin said. "I'm not the great philosopher."

New York opened the regular season on a Sunday night at home in a game against Indianapolis that was inevitably dubbed the "Manning Bowl." For the first time in NFL history, brothers were starting at quarterback against each other in a real game. Hours before the kickoff, on different patches of the field, Peyton and Eli Manning were loosening up with their respective teammates, tossing the ball around lightheartedly. Everybody wore comically baggy shorts that went way past today's basketball bloomers almost all the way back to the boxer Archie Moore. Archie Manning, once a very good quarterback for very bad New Orleans teams, looked down from the press level high above. He was the picture of crossed signals and mixed emotions. "This feeling of dread may be a Saints hangover thing," he said, "but I know how, if it gets going bad, how really bad it can get—for the quarterback." Archie and his wife, Olivia, had accepted invitations to watch their sons from the Reebok box upstairs. "Peyton says I like to get to the games in time to see the cheerleaders stretch," Archie said, "but the truth is, I just like watching warm-ups. I'm completely nuts."

This night, more than ever. "Inside of me, I'm not sure what I'm sup-posed to be hoping for," he said. "Usually you can relax a little bit during the parts of the game when your boy is off the field, but what am I going to do tonight? Olivia and I didn't mean to raise quarterbacks, I swear to God. Like all parents, we just wanted them to be well rounded, go to school, grow up to be good people, do the right things. Believe me, I never tortured them on practice fields. Heck, I didn't mold them or anything. I just watched them have a dream that I understood, that I remembered having myself. I watched them work their rear ends off to attain it. Olivia was always a good sport and only pretended to get mad about spending her whole life cleaning up after football players. 'And another thing,' she'd shout, 'I'm sick and tired of washing jock straps!' Both Olivia and I mostly stood off to the side and smiled, or moved a little further away and cried."

Earlier that Sunday, Archie had told each of his sons the same thing, what he always told them before games: "I love you. Play hard. Have fun."

The New York GM, Ernie Accorsi, also stood off to the side, in one of the end zone tunnels at Giants Stadium, the one nearest both the home and the visitors' locker room, the position he had long since staked out as his game-day headquarters and bunker. Ernie was too nervous to watch from the press box and too appalled by the modern press box in any case. Those gentlemen sportswriters of sentimental memory, most of them decked out in suits, neckties, and fine felt fedoras, have all died off. They have been replaced by a convention of class clowns, some of them dressed like sharecroppers. After every play, three or five or ten or twenty of them yell out strained witticisms, the first things that pop into their heads—absolutely everything that pops into their heads—as though they were auditioning for sports talk radio, which perhaps they are. Though press box wags have existed since the Roman Colosseum, they used to have a drier style. At an early Super Bowl, when streaking was in fashion, a naked woman who ran onto the field was trundled off by four policemen. "And they took her away," someone in the press box said with a sigh, "two abreast."

"Ron Sellers was this big, tall receiver from Florida State," Ernie said, "who was constantly on injured reserve. He typified the futility of the early-seventies Patriots, who couldn't get anything right. He was always hurt. So now he's coming back again, this big bastard with all that talent. Jim Plunkett drops back to pass, and here comes Sellers over the middle. He leaps into the air—the ball is this far from his hands, left safety Jerry Logan is this far from his shoulders, right safety Rick Volk is this far from his legs—and, a split second before the crash, Will McDonough of the *Boston Globe* yells out, 'Eight to twelve weeks!' You had to laugh."

One of the Giants exercising in shorts was twenty-three-year-old Mathias Kiwanuka, New York's first pick in the most recent college draft, a six-five, 262-pound defensive end from Boston College. His grandfather, Benedicto Kiwanuka, became Uganda's first elected prime minister in 1961 and was assassinated by Idi Amin eleven years later. Only once, when he was a grade-school student, was Kiwanuka ever in Uganda. He was really from Indianapolis. With three and a half preseason sacks, Kiwanuka had made a more than promising start. In the final exhibition game against New England, he shrugged off 320-pound tackle Wesley Britt to bring about a tip and force an interception.

In the draft room, Accorsi had been the last one to come aboard for Kiwanuka, which was unusual. "I was thinking of maneuvering to get the University of Miami corner Kelly Jennings, who ended up going to Seattle. But Jerry [player personnel director Jerry Reese] and Tom both wanted another pass rusher, and I liked Kiwanuka, too. I decided to let them have their way. A GM shouldn't always be heavy-handed. The front office is a team, too. This was good for the team. And, obviously, it wasn't a franchise-changing decision. If it had been a franchise-changing decision, I'd have ignored everybody and insisted on having my own way. If it's a quarterback, absolutely, I'm making the call."

Just then, the franchise-changing decision Eli Manning passed

Accorsi in the tunnel on his way back to the locker room to get suited up for the game. "Hi, boss," Eli said.

Ernie first saw Eli in person at an Auburn game Manning's junior year at Mississippi, November 2, 2002. The word then was that Eli might come out of school early. He did not. But the scouting report Accorsi typed out in bold capital letters didn't change the next year and, to Ernie's way of thinking (although to almost no one else's), it hadn't changed in the years since.

WEARS LEFT KNEE BRACE . . . DURING PREGAME WARMUP, DIDN'T LOOK LIKE HE HAD A ROCKET ARM . . . AS GAME PROGRESSED, I SAW EXCELLENT ARM STRENGTH UNDER PRESSURE AND THE ABILITY TO GET VELOCITY ON THE BALL ON MOST THROWS. GOOD DEEP BALL RANGE. GOOD TOUCH. GOOD VISION AND POISE.

SEES THE FIELD . . . IN A SHOTGUN ON MOST PLAYS AND HIS ONLY RUNNING OPTION IS A DRAW . . . HIS OFFENSIVE LINE IS POOR. RED-SHIRT FRESHMAN LEFT TACKLE. ELI DOESN'T TRUST HIS PROTECTION. CAN'T. NO WAY CAN HE TAKE ANY FORM OF DEEP DROP AND LOOK DOWNFIELD. WITH NO RUNNING GAME (10 YARDS RUSHING THE FIRST HALF) AND NO REAL TOP RECEIVERS, HE'S STUCK WITH THREE-STEP DROPS AND WAITING TIL THE LAST SECOND TO SEE IF A RECEIVER CAN GET FREE. NO TIGHT END EITHER. NO FLARING BACK. SO HE'S TAKING SOME BIG HITS. TAKING THEM WELL. CARRIED AN OVERMATCHED TEAM ENTIRELY ON HIS SHOULDERS. I IMAGINE, EXCEPT FOR VANDERBILT, HIS TEAM IS OVERMATCHED IN EVERY SEC [SOUTHEAST CONFERENCE] GAME . . . HE'S BIG, NEVER GETS RATTLED. RALLIED HIS TEAM FROM A 14–3 HALFTIME DEFICIT BASICALLY ALL BY HIMSELF. LED THEM ON TWO SUCCESSIVE THIRD QUARTER DRIVES TO GO AHEAD, 17–16. THE FIRST TOUCHDOWN, ON A 40-YARD STREAK DOWN THE LEFT SIDELINE, HE DROPPED THE BALL OVER THE RECEIVER'S

RIGHT SHOULDER. CALLED THE NEXT TOUCHDOWN PASS HIM-
SELF, CHECKING OFF TO A 12-YARD SLANT . . . MAKES A LOT OF
DECISIONS ON PLAY CALLS AT THE LINE OF SCRIMMAGE, BUT
THEY ASK TOO MUCH OF HIM. THEY DON'T LET HIM JUST PLAY.
THIS IS A GUY YOU SHOULD JUST LET PLAY . . . WHEN HE'S
INACCURATE, HE'S USUALLY HIGH, BUT RARELY OFF TARGET
TO EITHER SIDE . . . PLAYS SMART AND WITH COMPLETE CON-
FIDENCE. DOESN'T SCOLD HIS TEAMMATES [DID ACCORSI WISH
HE DID?], BUT LETS THEM KNOW WHEN THEY LINE UP WRONG
OR RUN THE WRONG PATTERN [AT LEAST] . . . THREW THREE
INTERCEPTIONS. TWO WERE HIS FAULT. TRYING TO FORCE
SOMETHING BOTH TIMES. HE COULD HAVE RUN ON ONE OF
THEM, A FOURTH DOWN PLAY. HE HAS A LOT TO LEARN.

SUMMARY: I THINK HE'S THE COMPLETE PACKAGE. HE'S NOT
GOING TO BE A FAST RUNNER, BUT A LITTLE LIKE JOE MON-
TANA, HE HAS ENOUGH ATHLETIC ABILITY TO GET OUT OF
TROUBLE. REMEMBER HOW ARCHIE RAN? IN THAT DEPART-
MENT, ELI DOESN'T HAVE THE BEST GENES, ALTHOUGH I
NEVER TIMED MOM OLIVIA IN THE 40. BUT HE HAS A FEEL FOR
THE POCKET. FEELS THE RUSH.

THROWS THE BALL, TAKES THE HIT, GETS RIGHT BACK
UP . . . HAS COURAGE AND POISE. IN MY OPINION, MOST OF
ALL, HE HAS THAT QUALITY YOU CAN'T DEFINE. CALL IT
MAGIC. AS [FORMER BALTIMORE COLTS DEFENSIVE BACK]
BOBBY BOYD TOLD ME ONCE ABOUT UNITAS, "TWO THINGS
SET HIM APART: HIS LEFT TESTICLE AND HIS RIGHT TES-
TICLE." . . . PEYTON HAD MUCH BETTER TALENT AROUND HIM
AT TENNESSEE. BUT I HONESTLY GIVE THIS GUY A CHANCE TO
BE BETTER THAN HIS BROTHER. ELI DOESN'T GET MUCH
HELP FROM THE COACHING STAFF. IF HE COMES OUT EARLY,
WE SHOULD MOVE UP TO TAKE HIM. THESE GUYS ARE RARE,
YOU KNOW.

                                        ERNIE ACCORSI

"I remember everything about that day," Eli said. "It was a heart-breaker. I threw an interception on the last play to lose the game, actually. It was fourth down. I tried to scramble—maybe I could have run it in. I probably should have tried. The receiver was crossing, but he turned away just as I threw it. The ball went flying right by him. That one hurt for a long while. Still does."

Following Eli up the tunnel, Jim Finn, almost the rarest animal in the league—a fullback from the University of Pennsylvania—offered his own scouting report on the Mannings, and on the night. "Peyton always shows his excitement and always shows his disappointment," Finn said. "He walks off the field with his head shaking one way or the other. Eli doesn't show anything. A touchdown and an interception look the same. That's who Eli is. He keeps it inside."

"Yeah," quarterback coach Kevin Gilbride said, "but I think there's something in there that would like to show his big brother a thing or two."

"Any little brother has to be tough," offensive left tackle Luke Petitgout said, "but Eli is Peyton Manning's little brother. He has to be tougher."

At school—Tennessee and Ole Miss—Peyton was the antisocial one, the football geek tethered to a film projector. Eli was the one who liked the night, music, and beer. Who wouldn't have guessed the opposite? Peyton at thirty, the omnipresent pitchman from Madison Avenue, was the oil-painted portrait of a commander in chief who, up close, appeared taller even than six-five. Eli at twenty-five, with permanently tousled hair, stood only an inch shorter, but somehow it seemed a foot. No NFL quarterback was in more extreme need of black stubble on his chin, a jagged scar across one cheek, or at least a misspelled tattoo.

"I've been playing nine years," Peyton said. "Eli's beginning his second season as a starter. Let him breathe, will you?"

He said this after the game. Before it, the Colts' quarterback reappeared in Ernie's tunnel ahead of any of his Indianapolis teammates, helmet on but with the chin strap unsnapped, standing completely still. Not ten feet separated them, but Peyton didn't seem to see Accorsi or anyone else. "Look at him," Ernie said, not bothering to whisper because Peyton couldn't hear him, either. "He isn't moving a muscle. He isn't bouncing from one foot to the other the way they do. He's come to a stop. He's calm. *Now* does he remind you of Unitas? The best ones all have this same moment of serenity just before the storm. There he is. Tiger Woods on the first tee."

Adam Vinatieri, the most dependable placekicker in the NFL, opened the scoring with a couple of field goals that Peyton stretched to a 13–0 lead in the second quarter with a short touchdown pass to tight end Dallas Clark. Near the end of the first half, beginning at his own fourteen-yard line, Eli finally replied.

GIANTS

1-10-G14 (out of the shotgun) Eli passes to Tiki Barber
  for 17

Two-minute warning

1-10-G31 (shotgun) Barber runs for 11

1-10-G42 (shotgun, no huddle) Eli passes incomplete

2-10-G42 (shotgun) Barber runs for 11

1-10-C47 (shotgun) Eli passes to Amani Toomer for 6

2-4-C41   (shotgun, no huddle) Eli passes to Barber for 7

1-10-C34 (shotgun) Eli passes to Plaxico Burress for 34
  yards and the touchdown; Jay Feely kicks the extra point

Indianapolis 13, New York 7

But twenty-eight seconds remained for rebuttal, enough time after a nice kickoff return for Peyton to push the Colts back inside Vinatieri's range.

COLTS

1-10-C38 Peyton passes to Marvin Harrison for 16

1-10-G46 (shotgun) Peyton passes to Harrison for 5

Time-out (:15)

```
2-5-G41   (shotgun) Peyton passes to Harrison for 9
Time-out (:10)
1-10-G32 Dominic Rhodes runs for 1
Timeout (:05)
2-9-G31   Vinatieri kicks a 48-yard field goal
```
Indianapolis 16, New York 7

Up in the Reebok box, Archie Manning said, "They aren't football players out there. They're my little boys."

Receiving the third-quarter kickoff, New York spent nearly eight minutes moving sixty-nine yards on eleven plays to close within two, 16–14, on Eli's fifteen-yard touchdown pass to tight end Jeremy Shockey. "Shockey reminds me of Ted Kwalick," Ernie said, recalling a Penn State tight end from the 1960s. Of course, nearly everything reminds Ernie of Penn State. "Looking at Kwalick once, Joe Paterno said, 'What God had in mind here was a football player.'"

Two points were still the difference, 23–21, with about five minutes to go in the game, when everything was resolved on a four-play Giants possession. "The reason I've always preferred baseball," Ernie muttered in his tunnel, "is that their umpires can't just blow a whistle and take away a three-run home run."

GIANTS

```
1-10-G10 Eli passes to Toomer for 6
2-4-G16   Barber runs for 2
3-2-G18   Eli passes to Tim Carter for 17
But Carter is called for interfering with defensive back
   Nick Harper, a venial sin all but invisible in the replay
3-11-G9   Eli's pass to Toomer is intercepted by Harper
```

Vinatieri made another field goal, and the final score was 26–21, Colts. "Good game," Eli told Peyton at the center of the field. "I love you," Peyton said. "I'm proud of the way you competed."

To the media in the Giants' locker room, Eli admitted forthrightly, "I think I was throwing to the right guy on the interception, but it was definitely the wrong kind of pass. You can't float that one. It has to be a line drive." Some days later, alone in a small classroom just off the club-house, Eli said, "Peyton is one of the best quarterbacks in the NFL, if not *the* best. In my opinion he is the best. He's the benchmark not just for me, but especially for me. He always has been.

"I'm five years younger than Peyton, seven years younger than our older brother, Cooper. When they were growing up, my dad was still play-ing. Cooper and Peyton hung around the locker rooms, got to know all of the players. They went along to Hawaii when Dad made the Pro Bowl. They were around it. They saw it. I just heard about it. On family car trips, Cooper and Peyton were always playing this numbers game. They would pick out a uniform number at random—eighty-four. Then, back and forth, they'd name all of the players in the NFL who wore eighty-four—sometimes college players, too. Sometimes high school players! They knew everybody. They knew everything. I was more than a little bit behind."

After Peyton elected Tennessee over Archie's alma mater, Ole Miss, "our whole family was harassed," Eli said, "especially my dad. There were death threats and everything. People expected him to force Peyton to go to Ole Miss, because he had starred there. But they didn't know Dad. 'I'm not doing that,' he said. 'It's not my job. He's a grown man. It's his decision.' Those fathers you hear about who force their kids to play sports, who hang over them at school and try to be their coaches, my dad was never that. Never. He had lived his own athletic life. He'd already had his high school days, his college days, his pro days. He didn't have to live it through us. He said, 'You know what? I went my way, you go yours. If you love football, heck, go ahead. I did. But if you don't love it, don't worry about it. It's not that important.'" It's just sports.

In 2004, when overall number one draft choice Eli maneuvered his way out of San Diego and into New York, Chargers fans consid-ered Archie the puppet master. "The heat he took in San Diego wasn't deserved," Eli said. "It was my call, it was always my call. I did what I thought was right for me. He actually got involved only to take the pressure off me, because I asked him to. I wanted him to kind of speak for me at one point, but I told him what to say. 'No problem,' he said, 'I'll draw the fire.' He did it to protect me, as always. It's like, it was entirely my decision to go to Ole Miss. I could have gone to Texas. There were other places where I might have had a shot at a national championship. But I had to do what I thought was best. And, whatever I decided, Dad was going to back me. I can't tell you what it's meant to me to have his support, and Peyton's."

When Eli signed with Ole Miss, Peyton presented him a thick notebook he had been filling out all season on airplanes to and from Colts games. "Full of protections, plays, and reads," Eli said, "pages and pages and pages. He sat down with me and tried to teach me all of these things. I didn't ask him to do it. At the time I hardly knew what was going on. Everything in that book was new to me, and it all came into play. Now Peyton and I talk every week, a couple of times. Right after the game, I might call him just for a minute. Often I'll catch him on the team bus. Then, on Monday or Tuesday, we'll talk a bit longer. We'll actually talk some football. If we didn't see each other's games, we'll go over them a little, you know, a series here and there. I may have seen a highlight of a pass to Marvin [Harrison]. 'Hey, what was that? Take me through that, will you?' You can't have conversations like these with everyone. Not even with your closest friends. 'Yeah, yeah, they were playing a cover two, so we ran, you know, the end thing, and got a great look until they shifted the strong safety, and we had to slide the protection, and . . .' Only another quarterback really understands. I'll tell you, it's lucky to have somebody to talk to who knows exactly what you're saying, exactly what you're feeling, exactly what you're going through, without having to spell everything out."

Statistically their final passing marks were twenty-five of forty-one for Peyton, twenty of thirty-four for Eli, 276 and 247 yards. Peyton threw one touchdown pass, Eli two. They both had a solitary interception, though Peyton bounced a few incompletions off Giants defenders' chests. A two-time NFL Most Valuable Player, the only man ever to throw forty-nine touchdown passes in a season, Peyton likely wasn't halfway through his career, but he was more than halfway to Dan Marino's all-time passing record of 61,361 yards. Of course, the Indianapolis quarterback was also married to Marino at the top of the list of statistically accomplished quarterbacks who had never won a Super Bowl. In Peyton's case, he had yet even to play in the ultimate championship game.

Eli, meanwhile, was still pretty fresh out of the egg. The year before, his first as a full-time starter, he led the Giants to an 11–5 record and a division title before showing his age in a 23–0 play-off loss to Carolina at home. Bart Starr was in his fourth pro season before he got out from behind Lamar McHan and Joe Francis in Green Bay. At Eli's stage, Jim Plunkett hadn't yet been run out of New England, let alone San Francisco, on his long way to Super Bowl titles with the Raiders. At that juncture, coaches Dan Reeves and Chuck Noll were losing patience with John Elway and Terry Bradshaw. Noll was about ready to take a harder look at "Jefferson Street Joe" Gilliam.

Obviously New York isn't the kind of town that wants to hear any of that when its twenty-five-year-old quarterback throws an interception on what was supposed to be the winning drive. At the same time, wide receiver Plaxico Burress, known for a mastery of jump balls and an economy of language, made a quiet suggestion: "Shouldn't four hundred and thirty-three yards of total offense have been enough?"

Coach Coughlin was steely in the locker room. "We have to stop talking about being good," he said, "and get good." When Coughlin was hired two years earlier, Accorsi presumed Tom was going to run his own offense. "I'm not saying you're going to call every play," Ernie told him, "but it's going to be you, right? That's what we're buying, right?" Instead, hardworking, well-traveled offensive coordinator John Hufnagel was at the wheel. "He's a former Canadian League quarterback," Ernie said coolly, "and he thinks like a Canadian League quarterback. Only three downs in Canadian football, you know." At the close of the 2005 season, Accorsi tried to talk Tom into calling Hufnagel a cab and taking over the play calling himself. But Coughlin resisted. "'Okay,' I told him, 'have it your way. You won the division. But I warn you, it's at your peril.'"

Accorsi expected Tom and Eli to be much closer by now. To Ernie's way of thinking, the coach and the quarterback have to be connected tighter than everyone else. "[Pittsburgh Steelers patriarch] Art Rooney told me that years ago," Ernie said, puffing on his cigar, Rooney-like. "He said, 'The most significant relationship in all of sports is the one between the head coach and the quarterback.' How one goes, so goes the other. Come the end of this season, we won't be saying Tom had a good year and Eli a bad one, or vice versa. They're going up or down together."

Sitting in his office, Coughlin said, "Eli's such a good person, such a good kid, so dedicated. When we went to Baltimore and Washington his rookie year and we lost both of those games pretty big, he came up here and sat down in that chair right there. 'I played awful, Coach,' he said, 'but I'd like you to know something. I want to be the quarterback of the New York Giants. I want to be as good a quarterback for this team as I can possibly be.'"

Now, with the Giants standing 0 and 1, a daunting schedule looked even worse. Next up were the Eagles in Philadelphia, followed by the Seahawks in Seattle. From beneath the blackened cloud that follows most GMs everywhere, Ernie murmured, "We could be oh and three. Then we get the Redskins here, Atlanta on the road, and Dallas on the road. Somehow, someway, we've got to get to three and three."

Running back Tiki Barber, defensive end Michael Strahan, and linebacker Antonio Pierce—the Giants most corporate players, the leaders among the ones who walked around the clubhouse like stockholders instead of employees—had already declared for the Super Bowl. "I didn't like that," Accorsi said. "Tom's right about that. Say it to yourselves, but don't say it out loud."

The Monday after losing to Indianapolis, Ernie wrote what he knew was a pointless letter to Mike Pereira, the NFL's head of officials, invoking the name of Wellington Mara, the Giants owner and NFL pioneer who died in the middle of the 2005 season. It began, "Mike: Wellington Mara had a great saying. 'I say this more in sorrow than anger . . .'"

3

RED LICORICE

AFTER HE WAS graduated from Wake Forest, before he had a cup of coffee with the Air Force, Ernie rolled out Branch Rickey's blueprint and began plotting his way to the front office. Looking up newspaper addresses in *Editor and Publisher* magazine, he papered the East with writing samples. "Only two responses came back," he said. "One was from Jerry Isenberg in Newark, who took a red pen to my copy and butchered me, killed me, shattered me, demoralized me. Can you believe it? He cared enough to do that. It was the first time I ever heard of a split infinitive. 'What in the hell is a split infinitive?'" The second response was a job offer from the *Charlotte News*.

Like other sports executives who started out this way—like Frank Cashen, like Harry Dalton, like Pete Rozelle—Accorsi dabbled in sportswriting for a few years at the *Charlotte News,* the Baltimore *Evening Sun,* and the *Philadelphia Inquirer,* enjoying the experience hugely, but never intending to make a life in dangling participles. Others in the sports department had stronger syntax, but few of Ernie's colleagues could touch him for instinct or luck, that mysterious reporter's knack for regularly pulling up and parking in the vicinity of news. He just happened to be in attendance at the Polo Grounds in 1963 on the day the New York Mets (né Boston Red Sox) iconoclast Jimmy Piersall hit his one hundredth home run and ran the bases backward.

That same year, when the minor league Charlotte Hornets baseball team was on a thirteen-game losing streak, Ernie came across an eighty-two-year-old retired physician who in the middle of his medical studies had helped the Hornets win twenty-five straight games in 1902. "The NCAA was not around then to play traffic cop," Accorsi wrote in the *Charlotte News,* "and whistle down every violation. 'They didn't care in those days,' the grand little gentleman related. 'Why, to show how lax rules were, while studying medicine at the University of Maryland I played halfback for the Terps in the fall and professional baseball in the summer. Today you can't even accept a free Lifesaver while you're playing college athletics.'"

The old doc hit what Accorsi termed "a lusty .323" in Charlotte and then moved up from the North Carolina League to the Eastern League to win a batting championship in Scranton. "That's when I got my shot at the New York Giants," he said, referring to the 1905 baseball team that delivered manager John McGraw to his first World Series title, "but I didn't get any breaks there." Unless you count, as Ernie reported, a broken leg. After two innings in right field and just one unofficial trip to a major league plate, he cracked a bone and was finished. His lifetime record in the big leagues stands forever as a lonely 1 under "games played," followed by a desperate string of zeroes.

So, more than a quarter of a century before Burt Lancaster, Kevin Costner, and millions of moviegoers across America and around the world, Accorsi discovered Dr. Archibald "Moonlight" Graham, the spectral figure from *Field of Dreams.* "During our win streak," Graham told Accorsi, "we used to march around the flagpole before games, which really burned the other ball clubs. That Eddie Ashenback was a fine manager, and poor old Dan McGann, our first baseman, he committed suicide, and . . ." The *Charlotte News* declared Dr. Graham to be just the syringe the Hornets had their sleeves rolled up and waiting for, and of course the losing streak was snapped—as Ernie concluded his story— "in front of 588 howling fans last night."

In Baltimore, Accorsi was assigned to write an advance on an all-black golf tournament formally called the Three-Ring Charity Open (after the logo of its sponsor, Ballantine beer) but meanly referred to around town as the "Three-Ring Circus." For an afternoon Ernie watched the old champ Joe Louis, about a five handicapper, being skinned in a practice round by markedly better playing partners. Louis' wife rode along in a cart, guarding a black medical bag stuffed with cash. After every hole, Joe dipped into it with that great fist, pulled out a bird's nest of bills, and held it out to the hustlers. As soon as everyone had plucked what he was owed, they moved on to the next tee.

"I interviewed Jackie Robinson later," Ernie said. Cash was a melancholy part of that story, too. "At the end of the interview he indicated a slight bitterness about money. There was just this tone in his voice that, I don't know, disappointed me. I think I left that out of my piece, I can't remember. But I remember feeling a little let down." ("If I had it to do all over again," Robinson said, "I would never have played a game of football." He starred at halfback for UCLA. "I loved the game in college but the money is in baseball, and don't forget that counts. Everybody plays sports for money. If the door had been open in baseball when I was very young I would have concentrated on it alone. As soon as the game got a little tough for me and I could see there was money elsewhere, I got the heck out.")

Everybody plays sports for money.

At the *Philadelphia Inquirer,* pro basketball was Accorsi's beat. Working the night desk, he took a call from a diner at a downtown restaurant who overheard a 76ers executive talking about trading Wilt Chamberlain to Los Angeles. Ernie contacted the team's GM and its public relations director. Both laughed off the possibility, but they stammered a little first. Ernie put it to Frank Dolson, the paper's star columnist. Turning away from his column, Frank picked up the phone and began sounding out his sources. Accorsi and Dolson worked the tip together right up to the hour of the deadline, and when they couldn't knock it down, they believed it. Lakers center Darrall Imhoff would have to be a part of the deal, they reasoned—correctly. "You better be right," the managing editor told Ernie, copywriting the story and putting it on page one, "or you're going to be covering softball games the rest of your life." Accorsi knew he was right even before the bulldog edition hit the streets. The PR man called back to whisper, "I'm sorry I lied to you, but please, please, don't quote me." The straightforward copy that Ernie had batted out and handed in was headed "By Ernie Accorsi and Frank Dolson of the *Inquirer* Staff." But when the page proofs came upstairs from the composing room, Ernie saw that Frank had scratched out his own name. Accorsi threw a puzzled glance at Dolson, who couldn't have looked more uncomfortable. Generosity has always made hard-bitten newspapermen uncomfortable. "You take this one," Frank muttered.

And yet, even the exhilaration of a front-page scoop, a narcotic for most young reporters, didn't alter Accorsi's ambition. Words and public relations might seem wishful paths to front office careers now, but they were the established routes then, even for those who took that turn accidentally. In the early 1970s, when the NBA was about a hundred times smaller than it is today, commissioner Walter Kennedy sat in his boxer shorts in a Los Angeles hotel room to deliver the state-of-the-league message to ten or twelve reporters at the All-Star Game, including me. "You know something, Leonard?" the commissioner said to Leonard Lewin or Leonard Koppett or one of the other New York basketball writers, all of whom were named Leonard. "I started out to be a sportswriter. What the hell happened?"

As Rickey had Ohio Wesleyan and Michigan, Ernie would have St. Joe's in Philly and Penn State, especially Penn State. His salary as St. Joe's sports information director amounted to a Jesuitic vow of poverty, but there were intangible compensations. The basketball seasons were glorious. For watching a college basketball game, there really has never been a building quite like Philadelphia's Palestra. "I grew up loving St. Joe's for all of the craziest reasons," Ernie said, "because my grandfather, Joe Nardi, was Joseph; because Joseph was my confirmation name; and because when I was thirteen I saw a Big Five doubleheader, and St. Joe's came from way behind to win its game. I couldn't believe that I was actually working there. And Jack Ramsay was the basketball coach, the first great coach of any kind that I was ever around. When Ramsay was on one knee in front of the team, I just knew we had an edge. I was mesmerized by him."

Though he was far from a natural publicist, Accorsi's old luck remained in force. Humoring a dotty priest who came up with the dreary idea of publishing a Latin-to-English, English-to-Latin dictionary, Accorsi dashed off a press release to Frank Brookhouser of the *Bulletin*. And the next thing Ernie knew, it was a best-seller. Forty-one years later, he would stumble across a copy in Barnes and Noble.

Because Penn State had football and, as Ernie said, "was bigger and more in line with my front office quest," he accepted a job as sports information director Jim Tarman's assistant. "Penn State is where everything changed. That's when I stopped being a baseball guy and started being a football guy. Because that's when I met George Welsh."

Welsh isn't remembered as a college football player, but he ought to be. He was a rollout quarterback, about the size of a dollar and a quarter's worth of liver, who played for the United States Naval Academy when the Midshipmen could really play. At the end of George's junior season, Mississippi wasn't just upset by Navy in the 1955 Sugar Bowl, it was swamped and capsized, 21–0. "I don't think I was that good," Welsh said, typically, "but we had a pretty good team." The following year, he led the nation both in passing and in total offense and finished third in the Heisman election behind Howard "Hopalong" Cassady of Ohio State and "Swanky Jim" Swink of Texas Christian. Michigan State quarterback Earl Morrall and Notre Dame junior Paul Hornung followed Welsh, who barely noticed where he placed.

"Nah, I didn't even think about it, I'm serious," he said. "It wasn't like it is today. I suppose I would have had a chance if we'd beaten Notre Dame and Army. We were six and oh at one point, throwing the ball all over the lot, especially for that era." Sonny Jurgensen was averaging about eight passes a game for Duke when Welsh completed sixteen of twenty versus

Penn State and twenty of twenty-nine against Army. But fumbling six times
against the Cadets didn't help. The Midshipmen fell, 14–6. "Football is a
simple game," Welsh always said, "but it ain't easy."

For a decade as an assistant coach at Penn State, George worked first
for Rip Engle and then for Paterno. Accomplishing one of the rarest
feats in sports, Paterno replaced a legend and became a bigger legend.
Basketball coach Dean Smith brought this off after Frank McGuire at
the University of North Carolina, and football coach Tom Osborne stood
pretty close to Bob Devaney at the end in Nebraska, but usually there's at
least one Phil Bengston somewhere in between. Before Welsh moved up
to his own commands at Navy and the University of Virginia, he learned
much from Rip—"that old winged T, boy, that stuff was good, still is"—
and even more from Joe. "Joe knew what he was doing, and he worked
his ass off. There's a certain culture at Penn State that's different from
ninety-nine percent of the colleges. A certain way of doing things. A
pride. It preceded Joe, but he embellished it. I tried to install it at
Virginia. I'm not sure I succeeded. I was tough, too, but not like Joe. He
was a mean sucker, boy, on the field. That's why some kids couldn't
appreciate him until after they left. From Joe I learned how to motivate
players, how to practice. Many things."

As far as Paterno was concerned, Ernie's most vital function wasn't
keeping the media informed, it was keeping a bowl in the coaches' office
filled with red licorice. But Ernie managed to bootleg a number of life
lessons and football lessons from Joe. Tarman schooled Accorsi on the
rudiments of organization and started him on the road to being an executive. Jack Ham, Franco Harris, Lydell Mitchell, and Mike Reid showed
him what football players looked like. But the game of football itself,
and the love of the game, he learned from Welsh. Without knowing he
was doing it, George nudged Ernie off the base paths onto a gridiron.
Now Accorsi was bound to be an NFL GM.

"It seemed we were always sitting next to each other, everywhere,"
Welsh said. "We'd talk football coming and going, into the night. Ernie
soaked up everything. He was a great confidant, a great friend. I didn't

know I was having any particular influence on him, though. I was just answering his questions, telling him what I thought."

"I peppered George," Ernie said, "with millions of questions. 'What did Joe mean by this, that, or the other?' George translated everything for me. He interpreted this new language I was trying to learn. He'd laugh and say, 'Pay very close attention to this,' or 'Completely, utterly ignore that.' In 1969 we opened the season at Navy and killed them, then beat a pretty damned good Colorado team, twenty to nothing. I was really into it. But we had to go to Kansas State next. They had Mack Herron and Lynn Dickey, and speed all over the field. We had never played on Astro-turf before, and we certainly didn't have anything like that kind of speed. They had just blown out Oklahoma, scoring over forty points. Paterno didn't have a particularly good feeling—at least he didn't seem to. 'Holy cow!' he kept saying, studying film. 'Holy cow! Holy cow! This is the quickest college football team we've ever faced!' Naturally, by the time I got on the plane to Manhattan, Kansas, I was sure we had no chance. I said that to George, who of course was sitting beside me. He just smiled.

"'Ernie,' he said, 'they can't beat us. First of all, watch them when we come out on the field. They'll stop what they're doing and look at us. I guarantee you. They might move the ball early. They probably will, while we're adjusting to their quickness. But they'll get anxious and turn the ball over, you'll see. Then we'll make a big play and that will be that. Their balloon will burst.'"

Like in a movie script, the home team did stop and gawk at the visitors. Twice Kansas State drove deep into Penn State territory only to fumble. "The third time," Ernie said, "linebacker Jack Ham made the greatest interception, to this day, that I've ever seen. Coming on a blitz, he caught a Dickey fastball—Dickey had a rifle for an arm—at point-blank range. The next play, Lydell Mitchell ran a sweep, the first time we ever used that particular sweep."

Before the season, at Vince Lombardi's Redskins camp in Carlisle, Pennsylvania, Paterno told Welsh, "While I talk to Coach, you find out everything you can about that sweep." "You know," Accorsi said, "Joe and Vince were great friends. The only game Paterno's high school, Brooklyn Prep, lost his senior year was at St. Cecilia's, coached by Lombardi." Well, Mitchell swept seventy yards for a Penn State touchdown. "We built a seventeen-nothing lead," Ernie said, "before they scored late, too late. Then, following an onside kick, they got a meaningless second touchdown as time ran out. We won, seventeen-fourteen."

Those seven points weren't entirely meaningless. As a matter of fact, they may have meant everything. That same day, Texas routed Navy, jumped the Nittany Lions in the rankings, and stayed just ahead of them the rest of the year to win the national championship. For the second straight season, Penn State was unbeaten and not number one. Football is a simple game, but it ain't easy. "It's intelligent," Welsh said. "It's scientific. It's mathematical. It's artistic. It's musical. It's everything."

It's like a bowl in the coaches' office overflowing with red licorice.

"The funny thing is," Ernie said, "Paterno wasn't going to be a lifetime football coach. He promised his father he'd only coach the one year and then he'd go on to law school, Boston University. For years Joe's dad had worked during the day and gone to law school at night. He didn't take the bar exam until he was forty-four. Joe intended to stay with the team just long enough to help Rip put in the T formation. So, he's single—he's probably had about two dates his whole life—and he moves in with the O'Horas. Jim O'Hora was the equivalent of the defensive coordinator. Fifteen years later, Joe's still in the upstairs bedroom. The O'Horas have raised their entire family, all of the kids are gone, and Joe's still up there. Finally, they called him down into the living room and said, 'Joe, it's time.'" Eventually Joe met Sue, and they had five children, but their marriage constituted a kind of bigamy, because Paterno was already wed to Penn State. In 2006, fifty-six years later, the O'Horas were long gone, and eighty-year-old Joe was still the head coach, and still unable to understand why anyone would ever leave Happy Valley of his own volition.

When the Baltimore Colts summoned Accorsi in 1970, Ernie knew it wasn't just a PR job. NFL front offices were so sparse in those days that everyone—even the equipment men—scouted. And the Colts were the thinnest of all at the top because their original GM, Don Kellett, famously believed that "if there are too many workers in a front office, nothing gets done." After hearing all that, Paterno still refused to accept Ernie's resignation, at least for a day. "Go back to your roots," Joe said. "Have your wife make you a plate of spaghetti. She's Irish, I know, but can she do that?" "Yes, she has my mother's recipe." "And go get yourself a bottle of Bolla Valpolicella."

"You know Pennsylvania," Ernie said, "I had to go looking for a state store, halfway to frickin' Pittsburgh. When I got back home, my son Mike, who was just starting to walk, came toddling outside and I dropped the wine. It smashed on the sidewalk. Was this an omen? Figuring I better do it right, I drove all the way back for more Bolla Valpolicella. 'Did you already drink that first bottle?' the salesman said."

Though full of spaghetti, Ernie nonetheless had an empty feeling, the same one everyone has when leaving a place like Penn State. Don Klosterman, the Colts' GM, could hear the blues in Ernie's voice on the telephone, and upped the offer from $13,000 to $14,000. "He went to his grave thinking he bought me for a thousand dollars," Accorsi said, "but money had nothing to do with it. I loved Penn State, but I had to go." In years to come, he would wash down many hard decisions with Bolla Valpolicella. "It's good stuff," he said, "imported from Italy."

4

PLAXICO

YOU CAN'T SEE or know anybody in this league at a glance," said Eli Manning, off to the side. He was talking about the wide receiver Plaxico Burress, who came over to the Giants from Pittsburgh before the 2005 season. Plax had a sleepy manner and a penitentiary face. Noting how balletic he was in a basketball sense and how physical he wasn't in the football way of speaking, many of the New York writers considered Burress to be an NBA type out of water. The reporters who were there every day, though, liked him. That is, they appreciated the fact that, in contrast to some other stars, Burress always made himself available at his locker for a few words. A very few words. He didn't give them much. He didn't seem to have that much to give. But they could count on Plaxico not to join the crowd soaking and sulking in the training room.

"Plax is smarter than what you think, or what he shows you," Manning said. "In meetings, he doesn't say a lot. When he does say something, the coaches kind of look at him and wonder if he's taking it in or not. 'Is he half asleep?' 'Is he daydreaming?' But one time I couldn't find—this will sound bad—my playbook. So I grabbed Plax's book off the stool in front of his locker—our lockers are close by—to look up a formation or something. And when I opened it, I couldn't believe my eyes. He had written all of these little notes in the margins—in beautiful handwriting. 'I'm the hot receiver here.' 'I go here.' 'I go there.' 'I do this or that.' 'Somebody else does whatever.' All in perfect penmanship. You know, it shouldn't have shocked me. If no one else knew Plaxico was in tune with

the offense, I did. I knew how hard he worked. But I guess I didn't realize how committed he was to understanding exactly what he has to do
on each play. It's almost like he doesn't want anybody to know he knows,
but he does. As I say, you just can't see a player at a glance."

Catching balls over the middle, the six-foot-five Burress was good at
diving under the wave at the very last instant, so that most of the force
would crash over him instead of into him. But when necessary, he was
willing to go up for balls in traffic and be hit with sledgehammers. He
had courage. "He's a terrific big receiver," Ernie said. "When he became
an unrestricted free agent, we heard that Philadelphia was trying to sign
him. I told Tom Coughlin, 'If we have to defense Terrell Owens *and*
Plaxico Burress twice a year, how much are we going to enjoy that?' Tom
has had trouble with him. Tom keeps trying to change him. I said, 'Tom,
Holy Cross was not one of the schools Plax was considering when he
went to Michigan State, okay? If you don't want to coach these kinds
of kids, then go to Holy Cross.'"

Burress wasn't the renegade he appeared to be, but he had idiosyn-
crasies. "For instance," Ernie said, "he doesn't like being touched. Don't
touch him. Tom made the mistake of patting him once. 'Get your hands
off me!'" Incidentally, Accorsi tended to agree that Plax cut a pro basketball player's sort of figure. "A lot of the stylish athletes in our league,
what you might call the artists, find their role models in the highlight
films of the NBA," Ernie said. "That's just the modern circumstance of
sports. The 'performers,' the Allen Iversons, are their idols. Obviously in
pro football now, pass receivers have become the 'look at me' guys, too.
Terrell Owens. Randy Moss. Chad Johnson. Keyshawn Johnson. [The
humble Art Monks and Paul Warfields and Raymond Berrys and Del
Shofners were all long retired.] But the Steelers didn't get rid of Plaxico
for any reason. They would have loved to have kept him."

If Pittsburgh was going to keep Hines Ward, club president Dan
Rooney didn't want to put all of the team's money into receivers. "When
Plax's contract was almost up," Accorsi said, "I started doing homework
on him. People I trusted there told me he was a good kid, which is

exactly what he is. A little eccentric, a little moody, a little mercurial, but a good kid. We scouted him, watched him, observed him. We knew the thing he was most of all: a dynamic big-play receiver who probably had been underused a little bit in five years with the Steelers. And he had an agent that none of us had ever heard of. So we brought him in here, took him to dinner, hauled Tiki up to my office to help sell him on what a great place this was, blah, blah, blah. [Ironic, having Barber vouch for Coughlin's Giants.] But the agent was an amateur and shooting for a record. Minnesota was their next stop. In free agency, if you have them in your office and let them out, you're going to lose them. But after I'd thrown in the kitchen sink, and the agent still wanted to price others in the market, I decided to put out a statement. I'd never done that before. It wasn't meant as a tactic. I was actually being sincere. But it turned out to be a hell of a tactic. I announced we were no longer interested in Plaxico Burress at any price and he couldn't use our offer as a lever with the Vikings or anybody else. We were out of it."

All general managers say that the only misery worse than a famous agent is an unestablished one who is trying to use a single client to make his name. But, it turned out, Burress had wanted to say yes to New York all along. He fired his man and hired Drew Rosenhaus. "Now there," Accorsi said, "is the definition of mixed emotions. No, Drew's okay. He is what he is. We had to wait out the seventy-two-hour grace period between agents, but then we signed Plax in one hour." That was March 17, 2005, St. Patrick's Day. "Considering all of the big plays he made for us last year," Ernie said, "at just the right times to win games, I wonder if we wouldn't have been eight and eight without him, instead of eleven-five with him."

"Do you know why I wear the number seventeen?" Burress asked, lingering in a film room after everyone else had gone. Seventeen *is* rather an odd number for a receiver.

"No," I replied, "all I know about you is that you don't like to be touched. Ernie said, 'Don't touch him.'"

He laughed uproariously. "I wore eighty in Pittsburgh," Plaxico said, "but I wanted seventeen here because I signed on the seventeenth. That's how much it meant to me to be a New York Giant."

Was it true, as linebacker LaVar Arrington had whispered aside, that Plax had named a son after Eli Manning?

Burress laughed again, this time gently. "No, it's not true," he said. "My son is Elijah for my high school coach."

"My name is Elisha also," Manning said, "but it's spelled differently than Plax's boy. When he told me he just had a son, I asked, 'What's his name?' 'Elijah,' he said, and I puffed my chest out for just a moment. Elijah wasn't named for me, though."

"But he could have been," Plaxico said. Told that a number of 1950s and '60s Giants had christened their children Kyle after the revered receiver Kyle Rote, Burress said, "Someday there could be a lot of little Elis running around here, too. In five years at Pittsburgh, I had four different quarterbacks. This is the first one I'm really coming to know, and who's really coming to know me. We have a long, long way to go, but I think we're going to get there eventually. When Eli reaches his full potential, he's going to be much better than good. He's going to be absolutely great."

Was Plaxico an artist, a performer, a "look at me" guy whose role models could be found in the highlight films of the NBA?

"No, but I have a gift," he said. "The reason I know it's a gift is that I don't always understand it. Sometimes I'll reach out to touch a ball that really isn't catchable, and all of a sudden I've got it in my hands. I don't know how. I wasn't trying to catch it. I couldn't catch it. But I've got it all the same. It's amazing to me sometimes."

Though a little vain about this gift, he still sounded more blessed than boastful. While his skills mystified Plaxico, Plax was the mystery to the Giants fans. Not wanting anyone to know you know is cool, but not wanting anyone to know you care is cold. In professional sports—maybe in every other line of work, too—openly caring about what you do goes a long way with the customers. Especially in sports, it's the all-purpose antidote to venality, cynicism, even money. Fans who had no idea why

Plaxico wore number 17 sized him up as a player who simply didn't care as much about the Giants as they did. If he had opened the book to them and showed them how committed he was to understanding exactly what he has to do on each play, in perfect penmanship, he would have had a better chance to be liked. You just can't see a player at a glance.

Taking their 0–1 record to Philadelphia for a Sunday afternoon game at Lincoln Financial Field, the Giants had the general manager worried. "This is the earliest must-win situation I can ever remember," Accorsi whispered. Coming off an easy victory over Houston, meanwhile, the Eagles were on the muscle and in a bright mood during the pregame warm-ups, grateful to be rid of Terrell Owens and anxious for the subject to change. Philadelphia quarterback Donovan McNabb and New York sack king Michael Strahan wouldn't figure to be buddies. On Michael's long list of celebrity sackees, including Brett Favre, Troy Aikman, Tom Brady, Steve Young, Randall Cunningham, John Elway, Doug Flutie, Dan Marino, and Jim Kelly, Donovan was a clear number one. He had bit the dirt a dozen times, more than anyone else by at least four. But Strahan and McNabb nodded and smiled at each other like the best of friends. "T.O.! T.O.! T.O.!" Strahan sang across the field. "Oh, no! Oh, no! Oh, no!" McNabb sang back.

After kickoff returner Chad Morton got them started on the thirty-three-yard line, the Giants went directly down the field to score.

GIANTS

1-10-G33 Manning passes to Amani Toomer for 9
2-1-G42 Barber runs for –2
3-3-G40 Barber runs for 5
1-10-G45 Manning passes incomplete
2-10-G45 Barber runs for 2
3-8-G47 (shotgun) Manning passes to Burress for 16
1-10-E37 Manning passes to Toomer for 37 and the
    touchdown; Jay Feely's extra point is good

Giants 7, Eagles 0

But, from a much worse starting point, courtesy of that seemingly unavoidable illegal-block-above-the-waist penalty, Philadelphia did the same.

EAGLES

1-10-E8   Brian Westbrook runs for 3
2-7-E11   McNabb passes to L. J. Smith for 30
1-10-E41   Westbrook runs for 0
2-10-E41   McNabb passes incomplete
3-10-E41   (shotgun) McNabb passes to Smith for 24
1-10-G35   McNabb passes to Westbrook for 11
1-10-G24   McNabb passes to Westbrook for 8
2-2-G16   McNabb passes incomplete
3-2-G16   Correll Buckhalter runs for 4
1-10-G12   (shotgun) McNabb passes incomplete
2-10-G12   Westbrook runs for 12 and the touchdown;
       David Akers' extra point is good

Giants 7, Eagles 7

After which the game turned into a romp and a sackfest for the Eagles, who tackled Manning behind the line of scrimmage no fewer than eight times. With less than four minutes to go in the third quarter, New York was losing emphatically, 24–7. "All these sacks," said the right guard, Chris Snee. "I mean, that's embarrassing. I had this talk with myself when we were down by seventeen points. 'We just can't go oh and two. We can't. We can't. We just can't do it.' Maybe, at that exact moment, everybody on the team was having that same talk, you know?"

GIANTS

1-10-G12   (shotgun) Manning passes to Sinorice Moss
       for 5; offside Philadelphia, negating the play
1-5-G17   Barber runs for 4
2-1-G21   Barber runs for 2

1-10-G23 Manning passes to Barber for 10
1-10-G33 Manning sacked for –9
2-19-G24 (shotgun) delay of game, Giants
2-24-G19 (shotgun) Brandon Jacobs runs for 6
3-18-G25 (shotgun) Manning passes to Burress for 20
Third quarter ends
1-10-G45 (shotgun) Barber runs for 5
2-5-G50   Manning passes to Jim Finn for 11 yards
1-10-E39 (shotgun) Manning passes for 23 yards to
   Burress, whose fumble is recovered by Tim Carter in
   the end zone; Jay Feely kicks the extra point
Eagles 24, Giants 14

Afterward, most of the Giants would say this was the play of the game. "Lobster or steak?" Plaxico said with gratitude to Carter, figuring Tim was owed an expensive dinner at the very least. "Don't mention it," Carter replied, grinning. But there were other big plays to come. For instance, with 4:11 on the clock, Eagle running back Westbrook fumbled the ball away to Giants free safety Will Demps.

GIANTS
1-10-E33 (shotgun) Manning passes incomplete
2-10-E33 (shotgun) Manning passes to Toomer for 11 yards
1-10-E22 (shotgun) Manning passes incomplete
2-10-E22 (shotgun) Manning passes to Toomer for 22 and
   the touchdown; Feely kicks the extra point
Eagles 24, Giants 21

When next the Giants had the ball, they had fifty-eight seconds and no time-outs.

GIANTS
1-10-G20 (shotgun) Manning passes to Barber for 8 (:51)
2-2-G28   (shotgun) Manning passes to Toomer for 10 (:35)

1-10-G38 Manning passes to Carter for 22 (:16)
1-10-E40 Manning spikes the ball to stop the clock (:15)
2-10-E40 Manning passes to Jeremy Shockey for 8,
    plus a 15-yard personal foul called on Eagles defensive
    end Trent Cole (:10)

Maybe those penalty yards were the biggest in the game. Offensive right tackle Kareem McKenzie thought so. "I was actually helping Cole up," he said, "when he tried to kick me somewhere. He missed what he was aiming for. You can tell he doesn't play darts."

1-10-E17 Feely kicks 35-yard field goal
Eagles 24, Giants 24

On the Giants' second possession in overtime, they began the game's final drive on their own fifteen.

G I A N T S

1-10-G15 Barber runs for 9
2-1-G24   (shotgun) Barber runs for 7
1-10-G31 (shotgun) Manning passes to Toomer for 10
2-1-G40   (shotgun) Manning passes to Toomer for 5
1-10-G45 Barber runs for 0
2-10-G45 (shotgun) Manning passes to Visanthe
    Shiancoe for 9
3-1-E46   Barber runs for 4
1-10-E42 Barber runs for 5
2-5-E37   Manning passes to Toomer for 7
1-10-E30 Jacobs runs for 9
2-1-E21   Jacobs runs for 6
Holding penalty on Carter
2-5-E25   Barber runs for −1

3-6-E26   False start, center Shaun O'Hara
3-11-E31 (shotgun) Manning passes to Burress for 31
    and the winning touchdown

Giants 30, Eagles 24

Going for the ninth sack with a sellout blitz, the Eagles left Plaxico in the solitary custody of cornerback Sheldon Brown, seven inches shorter. Manning had just enough time and touch to throw a rainbow into the left corner of the end zone. Toomer, the regal presence on the team, who caught twelve passes for 137 yards and two touchdowns, didn't see Plaxico's winning catch. "Cutting across the middle on that last play," Amani said, "I thought, 'I'm open! I'm open! I'm open!' Then my legs told me, 'No, you're not,' and I just keeled over. As the celebration was going on, I looked at our sideline and said, 'Could somebody please come get me?'" Four bags of fluid were emptied into Toomer's veins before he was even bendable enough to take off his uniform. In fact, he couldn't remove it. That was done for him.

Barber held his left arm as if it were broken; it wasn't. Between Shockey and Snee, they totaled two working limbs, finding it convenient, therefore, to use each other for crutches. "I never felt better," Shockey said. Everybody in the room was bruised, exhausted, and rejuvenated. "That one was fun," Coughlin said, "but the most important game is the next game."

In the first game, against the Colts, the Giants played well enough to win, and didn't; in the second game, against the Eagles, they played poorly enough to lose, and didn't. Against Philadelphia, Manning passed for 371 yards and three touchdowns; McNabb threw for 350 yards and two touchdowns. Both Philly and New York were now 1 and 1.

"Are you shocked that you won?" a Philadelphia writer asked left offensive tackle Luke Petitgout. "Am I shocked?" Luke said, balancing his chin on his fist like Rodin's *Thinker*. "You're in the wrong locker room, buddy. If you're looking for shock, you'll find it next door."

"Not in a million years," veteran middle linebacker Jeremiah Trotter was muttering next door. "Not in a million years." "We let them hang around," McNabb said with a shrug. "That's on us. It's our own fault."

When the field was otherwise empty, Accorsi walked out on it alone to take a last sentimental tour of the battlefield and bid what he hoped was a final competitive farewell to Philadelphia, where he had been a sportswriter once, where Hershey's old team (but never his) resided. "I always hated the Eagles, I don't know why, since I was ten," Ernie said. "Maybe I tended to root against teams that everyone around me was rooting for. I rooted against Notre Dame that way."

Accorsi was a Rams fan first. "I liked their helmets," he said. When the Rams dropped by Hershey in 1952, Ernie and his cousin Gary Ponzoli trailed the holy-rolling fullback "Deacon" Dan Towler all over town. Towler promised them each a team picture but couldn't talk the PR director (Pete Rozelle) out of more than one. So they had to share it. "We passed it back and forth, month to month," Ernie said, "until we discovered girls." Next he became a Colts fan, "and I sort of liked the Giants, too," he said. "But I had a reason to dislike the Eagles in Hershey. They were so raucous, in that little town. They just took it over, [lineman] Bucko Kilroy and that crowd. I have nothing against [owner Jeffrey] Lurie and [president Joe] Banner—they're nice people. And Andy Reid is a hell of a coach. Before the game, I shook his hand and said, 'If this is the last one in Philly, it's been great competing against you.' He says, 'Are you going back to Hershey? You can come to our games all the time.' 'No,' I say, 'I'll be going to Giants games, thank you.' I hope this is my last trip here. I hope they miss the play-offs. I hope we make them."

It didn't occur to him that they both might make the play-offs and meet again at this same spot in January.

5

THE BALTIMORE COLTS:

DRAFTING JOHN ELWAY

THE BALTIMORE COLTS belonged to a charming rogue named Carroll Rosenbloom, who inherited a dungarees factory from his father and turned it into a hot moneymaking property—by torching the place, his sister alleged. In the late 1950s, with the help of Johnny Unitas, Rosenbloom led the National Football League into the new age. Around that time, with the help of Meyer Lansky, he bet on Fulgencio Batista against Fidel Castro and gave the points. In the early 1970s, with the help of Robert Irsay, he swapped the Colts straight up for the Los Angeles Rams, avoiding those nettlesome capital gains taxes that normally applied when property acquired for $25,000 was unloaded for many millions. In the late 1970s, Rosenbloom either was murdered off Golden Beach near Miami or became the best swimmer in the history of the NFL ever to drown accidentally.

Rosenbloom's general manager in 1970 was another colorful scoundrel, Don Klosterman, a dashing former quarterback at Loyola University in Los Angeles, and a debonair man about many towns across California, Texas, and New York. Though Klosterman was drafted in the third round by the Cleveland Browns, he had a good deal more fun playing for the Calgary Stampeders of the Canadian Football League, after which a nearly fatal skiing accident left him with a pronounced limp. As Accorsi finally touched down in his first front office, Klosterman had just taken over the GM post from Harry Hulmes, an old shoe who probably had the finest won-lost record (32–7–3) of anyone ever pushed out of the job. But, unlike Klosterman, Harry never had an actress on his arm, and Rosenbloom decided, "I want a GM who dazzles people." Klosterman went by "Duke," the "Duke of Marina Del Rey," or the "Duke of Dining Out." In addition, he was a hell of a football scout.

"I was scared of Duke, he was jazzy and slick," Ernie said. "I'd never seen anything like him. As I was pulling away from Penn State, Paterno gave me a pep talk. Here I am, moving out of this tower of morality into this den of thieves, and Joe tells me, 'You're swimming with the real sharks now, Ernie. If you try to play their game, you'll be eaten alive. Just be the way you are. Vince Lombardi and Art Rooney prove that you don't have to join 'em to beat 'em. And don't ever forget, these people are just as afraid of us as we are of them'—isn't that a great line? 'They can't handle honesty and integrity, either. That's not the game they play. Play your own game, Ernie. You can be successful playing your own game.'"

The first new colleague who walked up to Accorsi in the Colts' office, sticking out his hand, was player personnel director Upton Bell, son of the 1950s NFL commissioner Bert Bell. "He looked harried, he was a bit disheveled," Ernie said. He was wearing Columbo's raincoat. "His left arm was wrapped around a stack of newspapers. 'I'm Upton Bell,' he says. 'Welcome to the Colts. Nobody in this league has any balls.' And then he walks out."

The second time Accorsi bumped into Uppie, Ernie had his son Mike with him. "That little boy there," Bell said without smiling, "either has a quick release right now or he doesn't. He can either hit major league pitching right now or he never will. His feet have to be quick enough to pass-block. Right now! Okay? Or it's too late for him." And he raced off again.

Another member of the staff, a fellow $14,000 employee, was a large and bespectacled ex-lineman from Bucknell (he looked like a snow-man), George Young. Young's eyesight was so feeble that, in the era of night games played under dim lights with white footballs, he was known for once pouncing on and "recovering" a white helmet that had flown off someone's head. George made the equally unusual jump to the NFL from high school football coach and history teacher after Baltimore head coach Don Shula hired him on a temp basis to grade an overflow of college films. More than impressed, Shula was astounded by the quality both of George's draft book and of his penmanship—Palmer method. That year, Ernie's first, Young would make another uncommon leap, from Bell's assistant to offensive line coach for the Colts in Super Bowl V. But, like Accorsi, George was really a GM-in-waiting. Both of them in turn would come to hold that title with the New York Giants.

"Did you go to readin' and writin' school?" George asked Ernie slyly when they met.

"'I went to Wake Forest,' I told him, 'okay?'"

But it didn't take even a full day for the ice to melt. That night, they bumped into each other at a diner and talked for several hours.

"More than anybody," Accorsi said, "he picked up where George Welsh left off. Young taught me. My office was in the back of that wooden firetrap, and his office was on the third floor—the attic. At the close of each day, I could hear his two hundred and ninety pounds shuffling down the stairs. He'd drop into a chair in front of my desk and just start lecturing. That was my graduate school." "Do we always have to throw long and run short?" Young would say in his high-pitched, exasperated-sounding voice. "Is there something wrong with throwing short and running long?" Football was a simple game to both Georges, Welsh and Young. "Young made me read an Alonzo Stagg book," Ernie said, "*Stagg's University,* about the University of Chicago. Knute Rockne once said, 'Stagg has tried everything that's ever been tried and ever will be tried in a football game, and the rest of us just keep recycling it.'" Out of the blue, Young might shout down from the attic, "Stagg put in the shotgun formation, for crying out loud!"

Ernie had his public relations work cut out for him, trying to make Rosenbloom and Klosterman seem like just folks to Baltimoreans. "These fuckin' people, they hate me," Klosterman told him. "Why do they hate me?" "Because you're a silk suit," Ernie answered in a perfectly concise sentence. Bell said, "What I loved most of all about Ernie, from the very first moment I saw him, was the fact that he always gave you his opinion with the bark on, whether you liked it or not. He wasn't afraid of Rosenbloom, either. Ernie figured out right away that the trick with Carroll was to try to absorb from him a little bit at a time—his brilliance—and then get the fuck away from him as fast as you can. Carroll was kind of a genius, but he trafficked in weaknesses instead of strengths. Once he knew somebody's weakness, he knew exactly how to deal with them. How to control them. Rosenbloom was always sizing up your weaknesses. Ernie was always sizing up your strengths."

To Accorsi, the football part was the authentic pleasure of the job, and his information had been correct. Though his title said public relations, he was included in the football. Just five people scouted for the Colts: Bell, Young, Accorsi, Dick Szymanski, and Fred Schubach. Szymanski—Sizzy—had been the second in a long gray line of centers for Johnny U, who, though his knees practically bent both ways, was still trudging along for Baltimore in his fifteenth NFL season; Schubach was a second-generation equipment manager. "Uppie and I went together to a West Virginia game," Accorsi said. " 'Okay,' he tells me, 'I'm here to look at Dale Farley, a linebacker. I'm not going to say a word. You watch him, too, and anyone else who catches your eye, and write out a report when we get back. We'll go over it together.' " Bell looked at football as "a game of explosions" in which the basic skill was "the ability to make a quick decision." Through the eyes of Uppie and the others, Ernie started to see. "The Duke told me early on, 'Do not evaluate a quarterback the way you evaluate the other twenty-one positions. They're playing a different sport. With a quarterback, it's the things you can't put down on paper that make all the difference.' "

After history's second *Monday Night Football* game, ABC broadcasters Howard Cosell, Don Meredith, and Keith Jackson attended an elegant cocktail party at Klosterman's apartment, and Ernie was thrilled to be included. "Even though the Duke did kind of turn me into a waiter," he said. As Bell recalled, "I don't think Ernie ever said to the Duke, or to me, or to anyone, that he wanted to be a general manager. He didn't advertise himself that way. Do you know the book *What Makes Sammy Run?*, Budd Schulberg's book? Ernie wasn't Sammy Glick. Ernie was his own completely original character, like nobody else. He just *was* a GM. Later, when I became the GM for New England, I asked permission to talk to Ernie about being my assistant—twice. Rosenbloom said no both times. I'm going to say I was probably the first personnel guy to mount little nameplates of rosters and prospects all over the walls—not just my office walls, all of the walls upstairs. And it seemed that every time I came to work, there was Ernie looking up and down those charts."

"Hello, I'm John Unitas," the Colts quarterback said to Accorsi, as if an introduction were required. "I don't need a program to know who you are," Ernie thought. They became lifelong friends, fellow conspirators. Two years later, as Unitas stood at a Colts locker for the final time, Accorsi came around to collect John's last game jersey for the Pro Football Hall of Fame. Pulling the number 19 over his head, Unitas handed it to Ernie and said, "Here, I don't want you to give it to them." "What?" "I'll get them another one. One that I wore. They won't know the difference. I want you to have this one."

"My first year with the Colts," Accorsi said, "Klosterman made two important trades, both with Pittsburgh. First he traded running back Preston Pearson and defensive back Ocie Austin for linebacker Ray May. I always thought this deal cost Mike Curtis the Hall of Fame, because Curtis was moved to middle linebacker from left linebacker, where he had been making Pro Bowls. We had the Stork [Ted Hendricks] on the other side. Then, in an exchange of receivers, Klosterman gave up Willie Richardson for Roy Jefferson. I'll tell you what, we wouldn't have won the Super Bowl that year without Jefferson. Duke was great at the big picture. He just stood up in the office one day and said, 'We don't have a big-time receiver here. Let's go get Jefferson.'"

Coming off a spitting incident with the Pittsburgh writers, the unsanitary Jefferson had a reputation for belligerence that wasn't helped by the fact that he showed up in Baltimore wearing a German

World War II helmet. Like most African Americans, Roy was not deeply or philosophically attached to the Third Reich. He just liked the way the hat rode on his head. That first morning, as assistant coach Dick Bielski sought to time Jefferson in the forty-yard dash, Roy told Bielski to go fuck himself. This was a dangerous thing to say to Bielski, an old Philadelphia Eagle still in the NFL record book for catching a half-yard touchdown pass from a half-pint quarterback, Eddie LeBaron. But Colts tight end John Mackey interceded before any bones were broken. "Room Jefferson with me," Mackey whispered to Ernie. "I'll show him how we do things around here." Thereafter, through the years, Accorsi would deliver many a problematic newcomer into the care of an old pro.

"Roy was great for us," Ernie said, "but he never stopped being a little peculiar. In the clubhouse one day, he was war-dancing around the lockers naked, patting his hand to his mouth and chanting like an Apache Indian. Unitas just sat there with a wry smile on his face. John actually liked him. 'What do you see in this guy?' I whispered. 'He blocks,' Unitas answered [typically]. 'I don't care how he dresses, I don't care what he sings, as long as the son of a bitch blocks.'" Jefferson also caught three passes, including an acrobatic twenty-three-yarder, that were necessary to the Colts' 16–13 victory over Dallas in the Super Bowl.

In 1972, Rosenbloom arranged for Robert Irsay to buy the Rams, then traded him straight up for the Colts. Klosterman accompanied Carroll to L.A., as Irsay replaced the Duke with Joe Thomas, an early-day Colts assistant coach who had brokered the curious Rosenbloom-Irsay shell game that led inexorably to the franchise being moved from Baltimore to Indianapolis. Joe was another evil genius. Being the only bachelor on the Baltimore coaching staff in 1954, Thomas had been asked to stay over on the West Coast at the season's conclusion to scout college prospects through Christmas and New Year's. Come the first round of the draft, he talked the team out of Auburn quarterback Bobby Freeman or Georgia Tech linebacker Larry Morris and into Wisconsin fullback Alan "the Horse" Ameche. In the matter of a quarterback, Thomas pushed for George Shaw of Oregon or Ralph Guglielmi of Notre Dame. It was on Ameche and Shaw that the Colts' foundation was built.

Later, employed by the expansion team about to be born in Minnesota, Thomas asked Paul Brown for permission to hang around the Cleveland Browns just to see how the mundane details of a football franchise could be handled with grace. A sucker for anybody who genuflected in front of him this way, Brown let the fox inside the henhouse, and Joe absconded with placekicker Fred Cox—Lou "the Toe" Groza's secret understudy—and every other buried body on the premises. Wherever Thomas went, he was uncannily prescient and universally despised. While scouting for the Dolphins in Miami, he engaged in a high-decibel screaming match with owner Joe Robbie, who was infatuated with the Heisman Trophy–winning quarterback from the University of Florida, Steve Spurrier. Thomas preferred Purdue's Bob Griese. In the first round, Spurrier went third to San Francisco, Griese fourth to the Dolphins. "Joe picked Bert Jones for us, too," Ernie said, but as instructive as it was to be around this gifted judge of livestock, Thomas represented a challenge to a PR man. Though Charlie Finley and Alvin Dark were pretty good on the baseball side, Irsay and Thomas might have been the all-time headline waiting to happen.

In an especially drunken moment, Irsay fired head coach Howard Schnellenberger and, without consulting Thomas, named Joe his successor. "The players went crazy," Ernie said. "Joe told them, 'Hold it! Hold it! Hold it! Everybody calm down. I never wanted this to happen!' 'The hell you didn't,' Curtis said, 'you've been fueling this fire all season long.' 'You shut up!' Thomas said. 'Fuck you, I'm not shutting up,' Curtis said." A more erudite player, center Bill Curry, told Thomas flatly, "You're no football coach, Joe."

Thomas went on to prove that in the last eleven games of the season, nine of them losses. The signature moment came when halfback Don McCauley was dispatched from the bench into the huddle to tell quarterback Jones, "Thomas says to run that thing we run where we pitch the ball." As Ernie said with a sigh, "Joe didn't even know the names of the plays. But then Ted Marchibroda came in as head coach and the ship was pretty quickly righted."

For young executives in the NFL, a common path to advancement was to serve a kind of fellowship in the league's New York office. Commissioner Pete Rozelle brought them in for polishing, and then usually sent them straight back. "There were six of us when I was there," Ernie said. "Only one stayed." But all the while he was at finishing school, Accorsi never got off the phone with Thomas. "Joe would call me up to say, 'Goddamn it, we're winning the division and I'm not receiving any credit. Teddy's getting all of the credit.' I said, 'Joe, Casey Stengel got all of the credit with the New York Yankees, but George Weiss is right there in the Hall of Fame with him. Relax. You're going to be named executive of the year.' 'Yeah, but that little son of a bitch . . . and when's the last time anybody wrote anything nice about me?' I said, 'Do you know what your problem is, Joe? You've got Harry Truman's balls and Lyndon Johnson's skin.'"

Disliking the neutrality of the league office ("I'd be at the game of the week—Redskins-Cowboys—and it didn't mean a thing to me"), Accorsi was glad to return to the competitive life in Baltimore, where in 1982, after a term as assistant GM behind the well-meaning but overmatched Szymanski, Ernie ascended to the job of his dreams. "I started learning the money side," he said. "We had a linebacker named Stan White, undersized but smart, pretty good—he could see the ball and intercept it—but he was just six foot even. Stan had been offered twenty thousand and was holding out for twenty-five. That's how long ago this was. I'm having a conversation with his wife, Patty, who tells me, 'You don't know what it's like trying to raise two kids on twenty thousand dollars a year.' I say, 'You're a hundred percent right, Patty, but I do know what it's like trying to raise three kids on fifteen thousand dollars a year.'"

The money in sports would multiply like sorcerer's brooms, but the insular life of the pro athlete never changed. Years later, Giants defensive end Michael Strahan would look Accorsi hard in the eye and say without laughing, "Ernie, I don't mean to be disrespectful to the organization, but your offer of an eleven-million-dollar signing bonus doesn't really excite me." When Accorsi passed that tidbit on to Wellington Mara, the Giants' owner said, "If he had to *pay* the eleven million dollars, I'll bet it would excite him." "And just think," Ernie said, "after Mickey Mantle won the Triple Crown in fifty-six, George Weiss mailed him a contract with no raise."

Joe Thomas ended up in San Francisco, where, losing his touch, he gave away a deplorable slice of the 49ers' future for the broken-down remains of O. J. Simpson. "When Eddie DeBartolo called me at Stanford," Bill Walsh said, "and asked if I wanted to coach the 49ers, the first thing I had to know was, 'Will Joe Thomas be the GM?' I guess I asked it in such a way that he got what I was saying. 'No, not if you don't want him to be,' he said. 'Do you have somebody else in mind?'" As a matter of fact, Bill did—Accorsi.

"Bill and I talked for about four hours," Ernie said, "and when I came out of that room, my head was spinning. This guy was amazingly smart. It only began with football. But I had three kids—ten, nine, and five—and I didn't want to bring them up in California. Not that I thought the Bay Area was going to contaminate them or anything. I just figured they might wind up going to school out there and eventually living on the West Coast. I didn't want to spend my old age on an airplane, because I knew I'd end up in the East. Ironically enough, one of my sons now lives in San Jose."

Walsh said, "I think the truth was just that Ernie had started out to be a general manager in Baltimore, and he happens to be a guy who finishes what he starts." When Walsh was unable to attract any of the comers on his list—"I couldn't sell George Young, either"—Bill became his own GM in San Francisco. "A GM has to look to next month and next year and five years from now when everybody else is looking to Sunday," he said. "Everybody else is focused on one thing. The GM has to see everything. There probably are as many different kinds of general managers as there are owners, but all of the good GMs have a panoramic vision. When I went to San Francisco, I was confident about the on-the-field part. The other stuff scared the hell out of me." Not so long ago, Accorsi told him, "You were one of the best GMs of all time, Bill. Of course, you had one of the best coaches working for you— yourself."

Ernie inherited his first head coach, Frank Kush, who had hammered out a reputation for physical toughness ("when Kush comes to shove") at Arizona State, where a Sun Devils punter once sued the university for $1 million, alleging Kush socked him. In the coaching fraternity, Frank was not what you would call beloved, and one of the leaders among those who had no use for him was Jack Elway of San Jose State, whose son John played quarterback for Stanford.

"Kush wasn't nearly the maniac he was made out to be," Ernie said. "He was a better guy than he seemed. And he wasn't really all that tough, I didn't think. We draft this kid Holden Smith, a receiver from Cal, in the eleventh round. But he doesn't sign. He goes and plays baseball. A year later, he calls us back, and this time he signs with us, even though he doesn't have to. He's a free agent. Well, it turns out, Holden's a lot better than we thought—in fact, he has all of the talent in the world. Right away, he catches a couple of touchdown passes in the first exhibition game against the Vikings and I'm thinking we may have caught lightning in a bottle. But he's an independent thinker, typical Berkeley guy, and the first time Kush and he clash, Frank cuts him. In the dining hall, Smith loads up a tray of food, walks over to Kush's table, and drops it on his head. Now Frank and I are walking outside, and the food is still dripping down his face, and into his ears, and he asks me if I wouldn't mind switching rooms with him that night. He was afraid Holden might come get him in his sleep. I thought, 'This is the tough guy?' 'No trade,' I said."

Ernie and the Colts owned the top pick in the 1983 draft, and the obvious choice was John Elway. "I went to scout the East-West game," Accorsi said. "Elway was the quarterback of the West team, and his father was the coach. I had pretty much been sold on one pass John completed against Ohio State, where he threw across the field for a touchdown—

unbelievable. Now, Freddie Schubach and I are watching him at practice. Kush is supposed to be there, too, but we don't know where he is. Elway takes the snap, rolls to his right. The receiver is running down the sideline until he looks to be out of range. Elway goes, whoosh, flat-footed. Throws this missile seventy-five yards diagonally across the field. I said to Schubach, 'I have to get back to Baltimore, but if Frank shows, tell him we're picking this guy, no arguments. I've never seen a throw like that in my life.'"

Elway publicly swore he would never play for Baltimore (just as Jack Elway privately swore that his son would never play for Kush). Threatening to jilt football for baseball, John made a flourish out of signing a minor league contract with George Steinbrenner and the New York Yankees. "Do you remember Bob Nieman?" Accorsi asked. Sure, he was a left fielder with the Orioles in the fifties, number 4. "Nieman was the Yankees bird dog who scouted Elway. Bob's dead now, but if Steinbrenner finds out he slipped me his report, George will probably dig him up and fire him. I just wanted to know how serious this baseball threat was. Truth be told, Nieman didn't believe there was any way in the world that Elway would ever hit Triple-A pitching, let alone major leaguers. But that wasn't the worst of it. The line in Nieman's report that really jumped out at you was 'Elway has just an average arm.' Baseball and football arms are two different things, evidently. Anyway, that told me the baseball threat was baloney. I knew what I faced now."

With one exception, Baltimore's sportswriters were urging the team not to risk throwing away its number one pick on Elway. Only Al Goldstein of the morning *Sun* pushed for the Stanford quarterback, under the headline "Dare to Be Great." "So I come into work," Ernie said, "it's dark, and the first thing I see is 'Dare to Be Great.' That did it. Goldie screwed up my life. Nah, I was going to pick Elway, no matter what anybody said." When Accorsi reached his office, he found Irsay at the general manager's desk, working the phones personally. "He's taken over the entire situation, wheelin' and dealin', and I'm sitting on the couch in my own office. All I can think of is how Pittsburgh let Unitas get away forever. The funny thing is, Unitas thought I should take Dan Marino. There were a lot of whispers around Marino at the time, all of which turned out to be nothing. 'You're just saying Marino because he's a western Pennsylvanian,' I told Unitas. 'I'm just saying Marino,' John said, 'because he's the best passer of the lot.' It's not that I didn't love Marino, too, but I thought Elway was that much better. Well, look at the record. He was."

Patriots GM Chuckie Sullivan was on the phone with Irsay. " 'Just a second, Chuckie,' Irsay says, putting his hand over the phone and turning to me. 'How about [All-Pro tackle] John Hannah?' 'And what?' I said. 'Hang up on him!'

"Irsay tells me, 'Go get the coach.' So I leave him babbling away with Sullivan and I go to Kush's office. 'Frank, he's talking about trading the pick for John Hannah. We have to stick together now. I may have to quit. We both may have to quit.' 'I'm with you, boss,' he says.

"But as we're walking into my office, Irsay calls out, 'Coach! How would you like to have John Hannah?' 'Love to, boss!' Frank says. That's how long it took for him to throw in his jock strap. I look at Kush like, if my eyes were machine gun bullets, he'd have thirty-seven holes in his body. So I say to Irsay, 'Would you please tell Sullivan you'll get back to him.' I didn't want anyone listening in as I quit.

" 'If you trade him,' I say to Irsay, 'there are going to be two press conferences. You're going to announce the trade, and I'm going to announce my resignation.' The only thing I had going for me was he knew that people in the city and the media liked me. I had some capital in the bank. And he was already being lambasted as it was. Anyway, I didn't know why, but he blinked. After one more call, I took back my office. The last caller was [San Diego owner] Gene Klein, God rest his soul, the son of a bitch. 'Tell him to go to hell!' I told Irsay, and Bob finally surrendered. 'All right, do what you want to do,' he said. Exactly one second after seven A.M., the start of the draft, I pick Elway. Someone in the room screams, 'It's Jay Berwanger all over again!' "

Berwanger of the University of Chicago, the first Heisman Trophy winner, was chosen number one by Philadelphia in the inaugural NFL draft of 1936. The Eagles promptly traded his rights to Chicago. Unable to coax enough money out of George Halas, Berwanger accepted a job as a foam rubber salesman instead and never played in the pros. "In the next instant," Ernie said, "Elway has that famous press conference with his mop hair, demoralized all to pieces by being the number one pick— like we were all supposed to do everything to make him happy and to hell with the Baltimore Colts. Who's looking out for the Baltimore Colts? That night, Howard Cosell and Unitas went on *Nightline* to debate the pick. John never mentioned Marino. He just wondered who is this kid who is too good to play quarterback for the Baltimore Colts?"

Returning from the press conference to his office, Accorsi was stopped in the hallway by a secretary with an index finger pressed to her lips. "Irsay and his moneyman, Michael Chernoff, are talking," Ernie said. "Chernoff is saying, 'He doesn't have the right, you should have stopped him. Elway is going to cost us five million dollars. We can't afford five million dollars.' 'Mike, Mike,' Irsay says, 'let Ernie have his moment. We can do what we want later.'"

Accorsi said, "Here's where I made my big mistake. That Friday night, Elway called me up. 'Look,' he says, 'I'd rather play football. Let's wait until everything calms down, and then we'll talk about it.' He wouldn't have had any choice but to play for us. But, stupidly, I tell Irsay about the call, and that same night he deals Elway to Denver for quarterback Mark Herrmann, tackle Chris Hinton, a number one in the next draft, and a pair of freakin' preseason games. Because we weren't drawing in the preseason, he traded Elway for two $250,000 paydays! I found out about the deal while watching a basketball game on TV. A streamer came across the screen. So I called Kush. 'Are you watching the NBA?' 'I never watch the NBA,' he said. 'Well maybe you ought to put it on, Frank, because they've just traded your quarterback.'"

The moment for quitting had passed. The moment for insurrection was near. "The final week of the eighty-three season," Ernie said, "I called Pete Rozelle and asked if I could come to New York and see him the Monday after the game. Sitting in his office, I told him the franchise was in deep trouble, that Irsay was going to try to move the team, that I had studied the constitution and bylaws, and that there were provisions that covered suspending him for his actions and saving this franchise for Baltimore. This was much more than a general manager trying to do what was right for his franchise. This was a man fighting for his boyhood dream, the Baltimore Colts. But there wasn't much Pete could do, and I knew it. I just had to play that hand."

Accorsi went back to Baltimore and resigned. "Can we talk about this?" Irsay asked. "Are you serious?" Accorsi replied. "You have to give me a reason," the owner said. Two words were enough for that: John Elway. But, just to be perverse, Ernie said, "Michael Chernoff." Two months later, Accorsi was in Cleveland serving Art Modell first as assistant to the president and then as executive vice president for football operations. Both job titles were synonyms for general manager. The duties were the same, but Art liked to think of himself as his own GM.

About ten o'clock on a lonely March night at a Cleveland Marriott, the phone rang. It was an old video cameraman for the Colts, Art Eich. "They're moving the club," he told Accorsi. "I'm standing guard on my equipment . . . they're not stealing this equipment, it's mine. But they're taking everything else." Ernie telephoned a friend whose apartment overlooked the training facility in Owings Mills, Maryland. "'Do me a favor,' I said. 'Take a look out your window.'" Blinking through the fog and the snow was a convoy of tractor-trailers. "From having done that stint in the league office," Accorsi said, "I had Rozelle's private home number that he answered no matter what. The phone rings. I say, 'Pete, this is Ernie, I'm really sorry to call you so late.' 'That's okay, Ernie, what's up?' 'Have you heard anything about Baltimore?' 'No.' 'They're moving tonight.' 'They are?' 'Right now.' Pete was stunned and silent. He didn't know. He absolutely didn't know. I thought to myself, 'Well, I told you all this three months ago.' But I didn't say it."

An eminent domain bill had been proposed in the state senate that afternoon, and Irsay and Chernoff were fleeing to Indianapolis while the fleeing was good. "Instead of Route 70," Accorsi said, "the normal way to drive to Indy, they took 81, the quickest way to a state line. They used Virginia instead of Maryland movers, too. They didn't miss a trick."

To this day, Accorsi remains convinced that "if Elway had been signed, everything would have been different. There would have been an excitement around the city of Baltimore. It would have translated into season ticket sales. It might even have changed the political climate around a new stadium." If Accorsi and Elway had spoken a second time on the telephone, Ernie would have told John that someone else had hired Kush, that Ernie certainly wasn't married to Frank.

"The Baltimore Colts," Accorsi said, "didn't have to die."

6

THE CLEVELAND BROWNS:

STEALING BERNIE KOSAR

THINKING QUARTERBACK AND coach—"I'm always thinking quarterback and coach"—Ernie began his new life in Cleveland convinced that with head coach Sam Rutigliano and quarterback Paul McDonald, the Browns were 0 for 2. "I'd seen plenty of McDonald in college. Southern Cal. They won a national championship. He was a soft, nice, methodical player—great guy. But he had a big windup. A left-hander with a big windup. That's okay if you're Warren Spahn, but NFL defensive backs are way too fast for that. So, we're in the preseason. We're going terrible, but it's only preseason—we're at Anaheim, playing the Rams. The game is over, and as Art would do, he held a committee meeting. He'd go around the room. When he gets to me, I say simply, 'We got no chance with this quarterback.'

" 'Don't tell me that!' Art yells.

"Rutigliano had just talked him out of Brian Sipe and into McDonald. They gave McDonald all of the money and let Sipe go to the USFL. Brian had put together some good years in Cleveland. He was kind of a folk hero there. 'Okay, I won't say it,' I said, 'but we'll never win with this quarterback.' Well, we start one and seven, McDonald is terrible, and the seventh loss is to Cincinnati—Paul Brown, Modell's nemesis—and, on an impulse, Art fires Sam. 'You couldn't wait until the end of the season?' I said. Rutigliano blames me, of course. Art says, 'I want you to go to Penn State and see if Paterno is interested in the job.' 'Art, he's married to Penn State. Even if the NFL could dynamite him out of that place, which it can't, he'd never choose Cleveland. Green Bay, maybe, because of Lombardi and history, or the New York Giants. Can we be reasonable here? Let's talk about Marty Schottenheimer.'"

"I was the defensive coordinator," Schottenheimer said. "When I got the call from Art to come to his home, my first thought was that he was going to fire me. But he mentioned that Ernie was there with him, and I knew Ernie believed I could be a head coach in this league. He had told me so. And I sort of had an inkling about what was coming." When Modell informed Schottenheimer that Sam was out and offered him the head job on an interim basis, Marty was ready.

"'I appreciate it,' I said, 'but I have no interest in taking the job on an interim basis. An interim coach has no clout, no authority. The players will say to themselves, 'I don't have to be accountable to this guy.' Art and Ernie excused themselves. They left me sitting there alone for quite a while, and I guessed that Ernie was trying to talk him into me. 'Okay,' Art said when they returned, 'we'll give you a contract for the rest of this year and two years more.' That's how my head coaching career began." Ernie said, "All I kept telling Art was, 'He ain't bluffin'.' By the end of that season, Marty and I had started to mesh."

The Browns won four more games, raising their record to 5–11. "It's around Thanksgiving," Accorsi said, "and here comes another committee meeting. I just repeat, 'We'd better get a quarterback around here.' I'm starting to convince Art, who turns to Marty and asks, 'What do you think?' 'Well,' he says, 'I think we can win with Paul if we surround him with the proper supporting cast.' I say, 'Who, for example? The AFC Pro Bowl team?'"

In the next instant, Doug Flutie of Boston College completed the all-time Hail Mary pass to beat the University of Miami, and Ernie's telephone rang. Of course it was Modell. "I want that kid!" he shouted. It's funny, but Ernie wanted the younger kid on the other side of the field, who passed for 447 yards in the loss. Earlier, on his way to a Browns game in Buffalo, Accorsi had stopped off at Penn State to have a firsthand look at Flutie, the five-foot-nine wonder. As a sophomore and junior, Doug had passed for 520 and 380 yards against the Nittany Lions. Now he added his own 447-yard day to total 1,347—more than three-quarters of a mile against Paterno alone. "After the game," Ernie said, "it took me about fifteen minutes to go down the press box elevator, because there was such a long line, and the public address announcer needed just about that long to recite all of the records Flutie had broken. But BC lost. Every time the game was on the line, he got blitzed up the middle. As incredible a college player as Flutie was, he wasn't my kind of pro quarterback. I told Art, 'Bernie Kosar is the guy. He's just a sophomore but he might be worth waiting for. Maybe we could make a stopgap trade in the meantime.' Of course, I didn't know yet that there was a way to get Kosar sooner."

"Look," Kosar said, "I realize that there are more important things in life than football. But when I played, nothing was more important to me. If a big game was coming up, nothing—not my father, who I love, not my family, not curing cancer, not world peace—meant more to me than that game. I'm sorry."

He relished being the quarterback of the Hurricanes, who by stopping a two-point conversion when a kick would have meant a tie pulled off a grand upset against Nebraska in 1983 to bag a national championship. Eligible to play two more years of college football, Kosar hoped to collect another trophy, from the favorite's position this time. But his dad wanted him to hurry up and turn pro. "If you knew my father," he said, "he's the type of guy who always has to have his own way—with me. I'm never right, and he's never wrong."

The Kosars lived near Youngstown, Ohio, where, Bernie said, "I was the first guy in my family not to work for U.S. Steel." The mills were closing, the industry was dying, unemployment was out of control, "and my dad," he said, "didn't have a very good work situation. I kept hearing 'You need to go pro, you need to go pro.' That drumbeat didn't leave me a lot of choices. I said, 'Dad, I really, really love playing football at Miami. We could win another championship.' But he used the old father guilt on me, and I was finished. The team we had coming back was absolutely loaded. It turned out they lost to Penn State in the Fiesta Bowl, with Vinny Testaverde at quarterback."

Against all percentages, Kosar's father found a loophole completely unknown to the ribbon clerks of the NFL. Provided he had already earned his degree, a sophomore could be eligible to play in the league. How often had that situation come up? And there was a second section to the Kosar puzzle. This was the part assembled by Accorsi. "I had always taken extra credits," Bernie said, "even in the summer. And instead of electing scuba diving, like a lot of football players at Miami, I took real courses—finance and economics. I was so far ahead that, if I wanted to, I could graduate in July."

Buffalo held the first pick in the draft and, because the USFL was still in competition, the Bills were already in the process of signing defensive end Bruce Smith. Houston owned the second choice. As Ernie said, "The word was going around that Bernie, his father, and his agent, a Youngstown dentist named John Geletka, had found a way for him to come out early. And, believe it or not, his preference would be to play for the team he had always rooted for, the Browns. So I'm poring over the NFL constitution and the bylaws, and I get a call from the dentist. We started talking regularly. I shouldn't have spoken to him at all. Modell said, 'If the league ever subpoenas our phone records, you're going to have to have all of your teeth pulled.' I called Joel Bussert, my old colleague in the league office—I'll never forget this conversation—and I said, 'Let me paint you a scenario . . .' 'Drop this entire thing!' he said. 'You're going to cause a hell of a lot of trouble!' I said, 'I don't have a quarterback! I don't care how much trouble I cause!' That year the combine [centralized workouts for auditioning draft choices] was in Arizona, the last time it was outside, the most un-Arizona weather you ever saw. Damp and rainy and Paul Brown gets that respiratory thing that he never fully recovered from. I go up to the Buffalo GM, Terry Bledsoe, to confirm that the Bills are really after Bruce Smith. 'If you can't sign Smith,' I said, 'what would you take for your pick?' 'We're going to sign him,' he told me. 'Who is it you're angling for?' 'Doug Flutie.' 'Come on, you're up to something.' 'No, my owner likes Flutie.' "

Because of hatred (Paul Brown), Modell would never deal with Cincinnati. Because of love (Art Rooney), he would never deal with Pittsburgh. In the division, that left only the Oilers. "Buffalo is definitely taking Smith," Ernie informed Houston GM Ladd Herzeg. "Would you trade your second pick?" "Sure," Herzeg said, "for the right price." "So," Ernie said, "we had eight million conversations. I'd say, 'Tell me who you want,' and he'd say Chip Banks or Hanford Dixon. He'd keep bringing up players and I'd keep saying yes. But the price went up and up and up until eventually he wanted a couple of Pro Bowlers, the Vatican, the Kremlin, and the Library of Congress. By the time the league meetings rolled around, he and everybody else had figured out that I wanted Kosar. Herzeg and Mike Lynn, the Minnesota GM, were walking around the headquarters hotel arm in arm, laughing at me. The Oilers already had a quarterback, Warren Moon, so Herzeg was trying to find someone who'd give him more for Kosar than I would, and he ended up trading his pick to the Vikings. In the meantime, Kosar and Geletka showed their research to the league and it was now accepted that Bernie could come out. But here was the thing—he had to write a letter within eight days of the draft applying to be included. After that, it was buyer beware, because he couldn't graduate by draft day in April—he needed summer school. Therefore, if he graduated later, the draft choice would take effect. If he didn't, it was wasted."

From scouring the bylaws, Accorsi figured out another wrinkle, which was communicated to Kosar through the dentist. If Bernie *didn't* send in that letter before the draft, he wouldn't be eligible. If he sent it in *after* the draft and then graduated, mightn't he be fair game for the supplemental draft? Buffalo topped that list as well. "When I called Bussert," Ernie said, "he doubled-checked what I was proposing now and came to the conclusion that I was right. I called Bledsoe and offered Buffalo our number one the following year, plus a player, for their first pick in the supplemental draft. Terry didn't want any of our players. He ended up making the deal for the number one in 1986, a third-rounder in 1985, and a sixth-rounder in 1986."

When the various mathematical possibilities were whispered to Kosar, Bernie got it immediately. He was not a scuba-diving major. "Of course I still had the pressure of graduating," he said. "Hell, I'm only twenty years old. I would be the youngest quarterback ever to start in the NFL, the youngest one ever to start a play-off game, too. There was another hitch then. The Minnesota Vikings."

On April 8, opening day of the baseball season—"it was snowing like hell," Ernie said—Terry Bledsoe felt chest pains. "They take him to the hospital and find out he needs open-heart surgery right away. I call him in his room and say, 'I hope you feel better, but have you sent in the twix yet?' In those days you had to finalize trades on the TWX wire. 'Terry, I love you like a brother, and I hope you don't die, but could you please call your office before the surgery and make sure they've sent this deal in?' He did. The trade went through. No more than twenty minutes later, Herzeg calls from Houston. 'Ernie, I thought I owed you the courtesy and the respect to tell you that I just traded Bernie Kosar to the Minnesota Vikings.' I said, 'No, you didn't. You just traded the second pick in the regular draft to the Minnesota Vikings. I think that out of all the respect due to you, I should inform you that I just traded with Buffalo for their first pick in the supplemental draft. Bernie Kosar won't be in the regular draft. He'll be in the supplemental.' That's when all hell broke loose."

Commissioner Pete Rozelle froze the many Kosar transactions and summoned representatives of the Browns, Vikings, Bills, and Oilers to New York City. Tampering charges were flying around what everyone called "the old conference room." Lawsuits were being filed and counterfiled. "And on top of a hundred lawyers," Ernie said, "Herzeg had retained the agent Howard Slusher. He was Agent Orange in those days. He was like Scott Boras is today, only worse. Slusher's the guy who held out most of the Steeler line. But I thought from the moment I saw him— after deciding not to have my own heart attack—that Herzeg had miscalculated badly by bringing Slusher into this. Rozelle probably didn't want Slusher to win anything either.

"'What do you think?' Art whispers. 'Either we just lost it,' I say, 'or we just won it.' Bussert was there, too, but his larynx had been removed. Poor Joel was afraid to say anything. By this time, he was only talking to me from pay phones. 'This guy Bussert and Accorsi are best friends,' Slusher says to the assembly, 'and a secret road map for this nefarious transaction was passed from Bussert to Accorsi. It was a tampering plot all along. They were sending signals in the night.' I finally stood up and said, 'Here's the bottom line of this whole situation. We knew the rules and you didn't. That's *your* problem.' And a little balding attorney for Buffalo says, 'If there was a road map, and you're walking down that road, it isn't going to be a very pleasant journey for you, because there are land mines all along the way.' Rozelle doesn't say a word until he issues his finding in a press release."

National Football League Commissioner Pete Rozelle today approved both trades involving University of Miami quarterback Bernie Kosar.

Rozelle said that under current NFL rules Kosar, through academic achievement, has an option to be selected in the regular draft next Tuesday or in the supplemental draft this summer, should he choose to play in the League this year.

In ruling on a dispute that included four clubs, Rozelle said that the trade will stand in which the Minnesota Vikings obtained the second spot in the April 30 draft from the Houston Oilers, as well as a separate trade in which the Cleveland Browns obtained the first choice from the Buffalo Bills in any supplemental draft involving Kosar in 1985. Buffalo has already committed the first spot in the regular draft by signing Virginia Tech defensive end Bruce Smith. The Bills also held the first choice in any supplemental draft under the same priority order as the regular draft, a procedure followed in the League since 1977. One or more supplemental drafts have been held every year since 1969.

Rozelle said that Kosar, who played the past two seasons at Miami, must notify the League in writing by midnight, April 25, of his intent to graduate in order to be included in the 1985 regular draft. If he fails to give such notification and subsequently graduates before September 1, Kosar will be eligible for the supplemental draft. In either case he must actually have graduated before he can sign an NFL contract. If Kosar opts to do neither, his eligibility to play again for Miami is in the hands of the NCAA and the university.

"After weighing all facts in this matter, including a hearing attended by the four clubs and a thorough discussion with the Kosar interests, I have determined to apply the rule as written, and as applied in the past," Rozelle said.

"In the circumstances of this case, I did not feel it was appropriate for the NFL Commissioner to make a definitive determination of Kosar's collegiate eligibility status, as Minnesota and Houston had requested. The NCAA has informed us that it has not declared Kosar ineligible and would not further consider his status unless Kosar attempts to resume college football participation. We received no clear evidence that would justify a determination that Kosar has lost his eligibility."

In an attachment to Rozelle's decree, the Browns and Vikings were granted three days apiece to be alone with Kosar, to recruit him like a high school star. This was unprecedented in the NFL. "Our recruiting trip," Ernie said, "consisted of Art and I going to Youngstown and having dinner with him and his dad. That's all we did. Minnesota staged an extravaganza, complete with 'Kosar the Viking' campaign buttons. I still have one." Legendary coach Bud Grant, with one of those buttons pinned to his chest, was dispatched to Youngstown in a private jet. "I liked Bud Grant," Bernie said. "I was a little awed by him, to tell you the truth. And Mark Tressman, my mentor at Miami—the quarterback coach—now had a job with the Vikings. That didn't hurt their cause, either. Plus— and you may not believe this, but—I've never been a guy who likes to ruffle feathers. I don't get off on being different. Part of me wanted to conform and just go to Minnesota."

But the other part loved the Browns, and even loved Cleveland. "I signed a five-year, $6 million contract with Ernie," Kosar said, "one of the biggest at the time. The best thing he did was set it up so that a hundred thousand dollars a year would go directly to my father. It wasn't just business to Ernie. It wasn't just football. He saw the human side. This way, Dad wouldn't have to get the money from me, though of course ultimately that's where it was coming from. Ernie could see the closeness of my family, and he could see the tensions, too. He understood."

He also seemed to know exactly what Kosar could give the Browns on the field. "I'd like to tell you I was the greatest athlete in the world," Bernie said, "but I wasn't. I was tall, skinny. I certainly wasn't the fastest dude around. Minnesota kept talking about things like running, jumping, bench-pressing, getting bigger, getting stronger, and all that. But Ernie just said, 'When you're as slow as you are, Bernie, you better have something else going for you, and you do.' He saw this thing that couldn't be measured today on a computer screen. Among all these guys, I knew he was the true believer. Ernie could see what I had, and what's more, he helped me see it."

Schottenheimer said, "The whole strategy, all of that maneuvering, Ernie had discussed with me—but, hell, I didn't understand it." When the kid came in, and he could really play, Marty understood that. The coach said, "As a community, Cleveland had been taking a pounding. The town was the butt of national jokes. 'The mistake on the lake,' people called it. To have a young person like this who didn't *have* to come to Cleveland but sincerely *wanted* to come to Cleveland, who had no ulterior business motives—well, it did something wonderful for the town. I'm not contending it did everything, but it helped—a lot. And when we started to have a little success, you could actually feel Cleveland's sense of self getting stronger."

"The Browns had won just one division championship in fifteen years," Kosar said, "the 'cardiac kids' of Brian Sipe. The city was bankrupt. The Cuyahoga River was on fire." And with a twenty-year-old rookie quarterback who had a funny, sideways kind of style, the Browns won the division championship at 8–8 and went on to post marks of 12–4, 10–5, 10–6, and 9–6–1 as the 1980s ran out. "Bernie wanted to wear number seventeen," Accorsi said, "for Sipe. I said, 'No way, you're wearing number nineteen. Johnny Unitas gave it to me and I'm giving it to you.'"

In Kosar's sophomore season, the Browns were losing a divisional play-off to the New York Jets, 20–10, with 4:14 to go in the fourth quarter. To his teammates in the huddle, Kosar said, "If every one of you does his job from here on in, I'm going to win this game." Ozzie Newsome, the veteran tight end and future Hall of Famer—not to mention future GM with the Baltimore Ravens—said, "I got chills up and down my spine when he said that." With Kosar setting postseason records for pass attempts (sixty-four) and yards (489), Cleveland won in double overtime, 23–20. For that Jets game—for all of their play-off games—the Browns practiced in a drier, warmer climate at Vero Beach in Florida, Dodger Town. "Men, hold up your room keys," Schottenheimer had said after the final workout there. They all did. "Keep them, men. Don't turn them in. We're coming right back." In the Cleveland locker room after the great victory, the players shook those keys like bells.

The Browns highlights and lowlights in the Kosar era were, of course, the same. In January 1987 and 1988, Cleveland made it to the AFC Championship Game twice, and to within a breath of the Super Bowl both times. "The toughest one was the first one," Schottenheimer said, "at home." A forty-eight-yard touchdown pass from Kosar to Brian Brennan gave Cleveland a 20–13 lead over the Denver Broncos with

5:34 left in the fourth quarter. Muffing the kickoff—all but losing the ball and the game right there—the Broncos started first and ten at their own two-yard line. Ninety-eight yards to go, just to tie. The Denver quarterback was Accorsi's ghost of Christmas past, John Elway. In the Broncos' huddle, guard Keith Bishop, a Texan, started the drive off with just the note that the situation called for. "We got these guys right where we want 'em," he drawled. Elway, who afterward said he might have felt tighter at the twenty than at the two, told the boys, "We have a long way to go, so let's get going. Do whatever it takes, and something good will happen."

BRONCOS

1-10-D2   Elway passes to Sammy Winder for 5

2-5-D7   Winder runs for 3

Denver takes its first time-out

3-2-D10   Winder runs for 2

1-10-D12 Winder runs for 3

2-7-D15   Elway runs for 11

1-10-D26 Elway passes to Steve Sewell for 22 yards

1-10-D48 Elway passes to Steve Watson for 12

1-10-C40 Elway passes incomplete

2-10-C40 Elway sacked for –8

Denver takes its second time-out

"Let's try for half of it on third and half of it on fourth," Coach Dan Reeves told Elway, who wasn't listening.

3-18-C48 Elway passes to Mark Jackson for 20

"Dave Puzzuoli has just sacked Elway," Schottenheimer said, "and now it's third and eighteen. Elway's in a shotgun at about his own forty-five. He puts Steve Watson in motion, and as Watson is coming across, the center snaps the ball early and it nicks Watson on the hip. Now this, to me, is the classic difference between winning and losing a football game. Here's that serendipity we all sign up for and leave ourselves open to. A split inch farther back and that ball hits Watson flush on the hip and is rolling around on the ground. Third and eighteen." But Elway makes this terrific little athletic move to catch the carom off Watson's hip and, maintaining his poise and purpose, he moves around with the ball until he finds Jackson open. "There it is," Marty said. "There's the play. That's the play."

1-10-C28 Elway passes incomplete
2-10-C28 Elway passes to Sewell for 14
1-10-C14 Elway passes incomplete
2-10-C14 Elway runs for 9
3-1-C5   Elway passes to Jackson for 5 and the
   touchdown (:31); Rich Karlis kicks the extra point
                   Broncos 20, Browns 20 (:31)

In overtime, Karlis kicks a thirty-three-yard field goal to win for the Broncos, 23–20.

"If anyone could do it, it was us," Karlis said. "When you have Elway," Bishop said, "anything is possible." "Anytime you have John Elway," Reeves said, "you have a chance." That had been Accorsi's exact position four years earlier.

"We used to sit around Modell's office after the games," Schottenheimer said, "Ernie and I and all of our families. My son Brian was about eleven or twelve. It was a bit uncomfortable, but Art always wanted to know instantly what happened." Kosar passed for 258 yards, Elway for 244, but 120 of Elway's yards had come on Denver's final two drives, when he scrambled for twenty more. John Elway was what happened.

"All of a sudden," Ernie said, "I thought, 'Oh, my God, my mother! Did she survive this?' A ninety-eight-yard drive and a seventy-seven-year-old woman! This may be worse than crossing on the *Saturnia*—in steerage! I ran to my office to call her." All these many football seasons later, Mary Nardi Accorsi had begun to understand the sport that enchanted her son. When the Browns were on TV, she'd sit in front of the set, praying. Mary was three years old in 1913 when the *Saturnia* docked in America. She was carried off the boat in the arms of a man named Galiano Marani, whose grandson, Ed Ionni, is Ernie's best friend today. Hershey must really be Brigadoon. "Mom, are you okay?" her son asked when he finally got her on the phone. "I'm fine, Ernie," she said, "but you're going to have to do something about that coach."

Returning to the inquest, Accorsi told Schottenheimer, "You just got second-guessed." "I expected that." "By my mother!"

At the second AFC championship game, this time in Denver, the other terrible shoe fell. Rather, it was dropped by one of Accorsi's all-time proudest draft choices, an eleventh selection (the second Browns pick in the tenth round) from East Carolina, running back Earnest Byner. Perfectly turning the tables, the Browns were the ones driving to the tying touchdown with 3:51 left in the fourth quarter. Kosar, who was outgunning Elway, 356 yards to 281, took possession at the Cleveland twenty-five, first and ten.

BROWNS

1-10-C25 Byner runs for 16

1-10-C41 Byner runs for 2

2-8-C43　Kosar passes to Brennan for 14

1-10-D43 Kosar passes to Brennan for 19

1-10-D24 Encroachment, Denver

1-5-D19　Byner runs for 6

1-10-D13 Kosar passes incomplete

2-10-D13 Offside, Denver

2-5-D8　　Byner runs for 5—he is officially credited for the full 5 yards, but is actually hit near the goal line by Jeremiah Castille and fumbles backward to Castille at the 3, and the Broncos conclude the scoring by surrendering a strategic safety

Denver 38, Cleveland 33

"Jeremiah Castille," Ernie said. "His son is playing for Alabama now. I hear his name and I get chills. Our wide receiver, Webster Slaughter, failed to clear Castille out. Earnest looked like he was getting ready to spike the ball in the end zone and I think Castille may have swatted it out of his hand at the goal line. I couldn't even see. It was so far away and dark. Paper was flying all over the place. All I could make out were the Broncos players jumping up and down." In a curiously grumpy mood afterward, the cornerback Castille refused to discuss the play with the Denver media. "I'll tell you about it at the Super Bowl," he said, and left.

Byner, who scored two second-half touchdowns on a thirty-two-yard pass from Kosar and a four-yard run, was actually asked in the locker room why he wasn't crying. "I played my heart out today," he said. "I don't really have any emotions left for crying. Maybe later. Twice now Bernie has brought us to the doorstep of the Super Bowl, and we just can't seem to walk in. I wasn't getting ready to spike the ball. Castille didn't hit it, either. I was splitting two defenders and it just . . . popped out. I don't know why. I gave everything I had today, and all year. I hope that helps when people start coming down on me. I mean, I know it's not going to help them. But I hope it helps me—get through it." Ernie didn't blame Byner, but ultimately traded him to Washington. "I thought he was Ralph Branca," he said, meaning the Dodgers pitcher who gave up Giant Bobby Thomson's pennant-winning home run. "I was wrong about that. Looking back, I think trading Byner away was the worst deal I ever made. He was a good player, and a good guy."

Accorsi's and Schottenheimer's working relationship and close friendship survived these most bitter disappointments, which was unusual. Coaches and GMs—coaches and personnel men generally— are normally in a triangular death dance with the owners. "There isn't enough talent here," the coach will complain. "He won't play my young players," the personnel man will reply. Or, in the alternative, "He hurried my young players." "I'm going to tell you something about Ernie Accorsi," Schottenheimer said. "The greatest thing about him is that he never gives a damn who gets the credit for success. They could put that on his tombstone. He just doesn't care. It was never about Ernie in Cleveland. And you could trust him. That quality alone almost made him unique in the business."

In between the two killer losses, Schottenheimer and Accorsi went together to St. Andrews in Scotland to play the Old Course. "Talk about bonding," Schottenheimer said. Ernie birdied the first hole—"You're leading the British Open," Marty told him. "No one's ever been better!"— and Schottenheimer birdied the last. "You know how the townspeople all stand around the fence there at eighteen?" Marty said. "The birth-place of golf. The coach and the GM are walking together through the Valley of Sin to the last green. The wind is blowing like a son of a bitch. Does it get any better than that?"

No. As Modell's and Schottenheimer's tolerance for each other ran out, Marty was gone by the end of 1988. Accorsi replaced him momen-tarily with a crusty old defensive genius named Bud Carson, on the the-ory that Carson might know how to win that last game against Elway. "I thought I was hiring Earl Weaver," Ernie said, "but I was really hiring Eddie Stanky." In 1977, Stanky managed the Texas Rangers to a victory in the season's opening game and then resigned. "Bud was ready to quit even before we started," Ernie said. Accorsi and Modell had already settled on Carson when Ernie sat down with a leftover candidate, young Bill Belichick.

"The interview took place in the Hilton lobby restaurant," Ernie said, "and I missed practice that day, he was so good. I didn't want to leave. It was like listening to John F. Kennedy when he was running for president. You said to yourself, 'This guy has been preparing to be presi-dent since he was ten years old.' That's the feeling I got with Belichick. 'Let me tell you something,' I said when we were through, 'you were down by thirty points in the last quarter and you cut it to one as time ran out. And you had the ball.' Two years later, Ernie replaced Carson with Belichick. "First I had to unhire Mike White," he said, "who won a Rose Bowl at Illinois." Acting like his own GM again, Modell had phoned Accorsi to say brightly, "Well, we got a coach! Mike White! He's at my

house now! I'm sending him over to you!" But Ernie talked Art out of
White and into Belichick.

"People now say Belichick failed in Cleveland before he succeeded
in New England," Ernie said, "but he didn't fail in Cleveland. He went
to the play-offs in ninety-four, beat the Patriots and Bill Parcells." The
Browns lost to Pittsburgh then, but they were outmanned by the Steelers. "Halfway through the following season," Ernie said, "the fans were
rooting against Bill in his own stadium because Art had announced he
was moving the team to Baltimore." Accorsi had already departed, in
1992, Belichick's second season, "just because it was time," Ernie said. "I
believe in runs, and I'd had my run there. I wanted to get back east." In
2000, during a phone conversation with Accorsi, Belichick all of a sudden blurted out, "I really screwed up that thing up in Cleveland, Ernie."
" 'You didn't screw up anything,' I told him. 'You took over a head coaching job for the first time in your life, and the next thing you knew, your
general manager was saying goodbye. I'm proud of the job you did
there.'" Thinking back on their phone conversation, Ernie said, "Almost nothing in life touches me more than humility. People who say
Belichick doesn't have it don't know him. I love Bill Belichick."

Because of a series of injuries, Bernie Kosar didn't make ten years in
the league. "After that elbow in eighty-eight," Ernie said, "he hurt his
hand in eighty-nine and played with a splint. He got beat up pretty bad
in ninety and ninety-one—we just weren't a very good team around him.
Smoky Burgess could hit a line-drive double today, if he's still alive
[Burgess, the great pinch-hitting catcher, died in 1991 at sixty-four] but
guys who *aren't* naturals don't last as long. Bernie put us in the Super
Bowl twice. He got us the lead twice. The defense couldn't hold it. I've
heard people say that Kosar didn't have a great arm—the hell he didn't!
He could throw long with anybody, and he had a hair-trigger release."
Bernie also had that thing no one could measure on a computer screen,
that thing Accorsi saw and helped him see.

"Didn't he wear the number nineteen well?" said Ernie, who now
had both John's and Bernie's jerseys framed in his home.

7

THE NEW YORK GIANTS:
SIGNING KERRY COLLINS

ACCORSI WENT TO WORK as a special advisor to Maryland governor William Donald Schaefer, trying to replace the Colts with an NFL expansion team. In six weeks, they sold out a hundred skyboxes in an imaginary new stadium. In eight weeks, all of the seventy-five hundred club seats were gone. But the league anointed Charlotte and Jacksonville instead.

"Leaving the Browns that way," Ernie said, "violated one of my theories: it's okay to be down five–nothing in the third inning, but don't take risks in the seventh inning of your career. It might be too late to recover." In any case, he felt obligated to come home, to be near his eighty-two-year-old mother in Hershey. "And if Baltimore was going to be awarded a new franchise, I wanted to position myself at least to have a shot at becoming its GM." The instant that hope fell through, Orioles owner Peter Angelos called. Ernie's luck was still pretty good.

Just as Accorsi had once imagined, he was momentarily in the baseball business. His title was "executive director of business affairs." His pleasure was to sit between Orioles GM Rollie Hemond and Hall of Famer Frank Robinson at the games. "Frank Robby would call out the pitches one after the other," Ernie said. "'Are you stealing the signs?' I asked him. 'No,' he said. 'I'm reading the outfielders.'"

But Accorsi wasn't wandering in the wilderness very long when Joel

Bussert called from the league office to feel him out about returning to pro football. The conversation was as nebulous as Ernie's baseball duties, but he could read between the lines. "Before you go any further, Joe," Ernie said, "did George Young put you up to calling me?"

"Um, yes," said Bussert, proving again that he was not cut out to be a secret agent. By now, Young had been the Giants' GM for fifteen years. "He'd like to hire you as his assistant," Joel said, "but if you don't want the job, he doesn't want to put you in the embarrassing position of turning him down." "I said, 'Tell George to call me.'

"So, the phone rings two seconds later and here's typical George: 'I don't want to ruin your life.' Those are his first words, even before hello. He starts filling me in on the entire situation. 'Look, I can't put you in this chair. I can't promise you the general managership after me. They may not like you. But I think they will.'" A dollar figure was mentioned. "Is that okay?" George said. "Yeah, that's good, George," Ernie replied, "but ask your secretary to send me the real estate section of the *Bronx Home News*—not the nice part, the part where they have the abandoned warehouses. I'll go get a sleeping bag and . . ." They fell right back into their old rhythms. When the deal was done, Young sighed and said, "Good. Maybe I'll live a little longer now." He would live seven more years. "One final condition," Ernie said. "Harry stays."

Harry Hulmes, the old shoe who was euchred out of the Baltimore GM job by Don Klosterman, had landed in Young's anteroom in his seventies. Harry was a good scout in every sense of the phrase; too good, Young would say only half kiddingly. Hulmes' reports maximized players' virtues and minimized their drawbacks. He was that way about everything in life. "Harry is such a nice guy," Ernie said, "that he even sees the good in the agents. He actually sides with the agents! Harry would come into George's office and say softly, 'George, I think Drew Rosenhaus has a point here.' Through my office wall, I could hear George bellowing, 'Harry! Harry! Harry! Call him back and tell him to go to hell!' 'I can't do that,' Harry said. 'Harry, I'm dialing the number and you're going to tell Rosenhaus to go to hell!'" But Harry stayed.

The four years that Ernie assisted George felt like a partnership to both of them. Young made most of the personnel decisions. Accorsi negotiated most of the contracts. When Young stepped down after the 1997 season, to become vice president of football operations in the NFL office, Ernie was named the new Giants' GM. "This is the right man," Young said at the press conference, "for the right job at the right time."

They still saw each other. They still talked football. "When George started working in the league office," Ernie said, "he moved to Sixty-sixth and Third in Manhattan—I got him the apartment. Mine was on Sixty-ninth. Labor Day weekend of 2000, we go to see Penn State and USC at the Meadowlands, and he's fine. We're talking strategy on the car ride home. The FDR is packed. 'Shouldn't we get off here?' he says. He was absolutely fine. We park the car, we're walking up to his apartment, and he says, 'Ernie, can I just say . . . where am I?' 'You're home, George.' As soon as he went inside, right on the spot, I called [Giants trainer] Ronnie Barnes. 'Something is wrong with George,' I said." The diagnosis was Creutzfeldt-Jakob disease, a rare U.S. relative of the UK's mad cow disease. Rapid, progressive dementia. Always fatal. Young died in a hospice that December 8, not knowing where he was.

Just about the only thing Ernie liked about Giants quarterback Dave Brown was the fact that George had liked him. But this wasn't nearly enough. "He'd look pretty for a while," Ernie said. "There've been all kinds of those guys. They look beautiful. But when you're playing against them, you don't fear them when the game's on the line." Taking over for Phil Simms in 1994, Brown was the New York starter for three and a half seasons. Accorsi said, "Mike Ditka had ripped him just before Ditka took the head coaching job in New Orleans. So, after we beat the Saints in ninety-seven, fourteen to nine—it felt like two to one, and Brown was awful—Dave ran across the field and shook his fist in Ditka's direction. 'Take that!' 'He didn't do shit,' Mike told me later. 'He was the only reason we were in the game!' I cut Brown in my first twenty-four hours as GM. So our quarterback was Danny Kanell, who had gone in after a Brown injury in ninety-seven and kind of *managed* the team to a division title. Danny didn't do badly, but he didn't have a strong arm. I liked him, but he wasn't going to get us to a championship. I signed Kent Graham, whom I wasn't in love with, either, but Kent was good enough to back up Kanell."

Then along came the troubled former Penn Stater Kerry Collins.

At college, Collins won the Davey O'Brien and Maxwell awards, signifying not only the top quarterback but also the most outstanding player. He set Penn State records for completions, completion percentage, passing yardage, and total offense. After leading the Nittany Lions to an undefeated, Rose Bowl–winning season in 1994, Collins was the fifth player taken in the first round of the NFL draft, by the Carolina Panthers. But it went bad for him there.

A drunk-driving arrest led to a stay in a rehab clinic in Topeka, Kansas, but the more defining incident occurred at a team party when— under the influence, Collins acknowledged—he aimed racial epithets at African American and Hispanic teammates Muhsin Muhammad and Norberto Davidds-Garrido. Kerry later swore this wasn't racism. Rather, it was a misguided attempt at team bonding that only made sense in a haze of alcohol. Davidds-Garrido, an offensive lineman, knocked Collins right on his ass. The quarterback was eventually waived.

"From there he went to New Orleans," Ernie said. "That was a mess. No discipline. No coaching." Finally, he was a free agent, looking for a job. "I've always believed," Accorsi said, "that if a kid was ever a good kid, he can be a good kid again. If he was never a good kid, don't waste your time." Paterno and everybody else at Penn State vouched for Collins, although they knew he drank there, too. "Kerry was a Lebanon, Pennsylvania, guy," Ernie said, "twelve miles from Hershey, so I had a certain bead on him. I went all of the way back to his junior high, checking on him." Over a disagreement with the coach, Kerry's father had pulled him out of one high school. "Then I studied tape after tape after tape. He threw a lot of interceptions. He was sloppy. But he played hard. He played his heart out. I looked at our old reports on him. All of our scouts had high grades on Kerry. *I* had high grades on him. So, on a Saturday morning in the wintertime, he and I went to breakfast at the Sheraton Meadowlands Hotel. I looked him straight in the eye. He looked me straight in the eye. 'If you didn't come from Lebanon,' I said, 'if you didn't go to Penn State, if you hadn't played for Paterno, we wouldn't be having this conversation.'

"He said, 'Ernie, I dreamed about playing in the National Football League all my life. The Eagles, the Giants, the Redskins, the Bears. But I found myself playing for the Carolina Panthers, wearing this funny-looking uniform, and I didn't even feel like I was in the NFL. That started my problems.' 'If we take a chance on you,' I told him, 'you're going to have to sign up for counseling immediately. Miss an appointment and you're gone. One slip-up and you're gone.' 'I won't let you down,' he said."

When Collins walked into the Giants' clubhouse for the first time and began emptying his duffel into a locker, a black cornerback silently got up and moved out of the locker next to him. But in a moment or two, still without a word being spoken, black fullback Charlie Way left his own station and moved into the abandoned digs. Accorsi said, "You know how, at the end of their careers, players will come back to their old team, to be a 'Giant for a day' so they can retire a Giant? The cornerback asked to do that. We told him no."

Collins had a live arm but a high release that had always bothered Ernie. "I'm not talking about beauty and esthetics here—I don't care about that," he said. "What it does—this hitch—is it gives the defensive backs a chance to react. [Coach Jim] Fassel did a great job with Collins, trying to iron that out. They never got rid of it completely, but it was a lot better." However, Kerry's biggest drawback wasn't mechanical.

"Physically he was as tough as they came," Ernie said, "but emotionally there was a fragility there. I wonder if that doesn't follow from rehab. Rehab can put a player's pieces back together, but can it make him whole again? I don't think so. He hasn't been rebuilt; he's just been repaired. And a lot of his new strength is artificial. It's words. For the rest of his life, he has to walk around on eggshells. If Kerry felt he was going to have the time back there to throw, he'd cut your heart out. But if he felt that he wasn't going to get the protection—whether he got it or not—he was skittish. It wasn't that he was gutless—he had plenty of guts. It's just that he was . . . well, *fragile*'s the only word I can think of. I figured him for moments of absolute splendor and then for four interceptions."

In the eleventh game of the 1999 season, Collins went in for Graham. With Kerry at the controls, the Giants mostly lost down that home stretch, including the last three games in a row. But the moment of absolute splendor was just ahead. Throwing twenty-two touchdown passes in 2000, recording personal bests in every category, Collins led New York to a 12–4 regular season record and a division title. When Philadelphia was beaten in the first play-off game, 20–10, only the Minnesota Vikings blocked the Giants' way to the Super Bowl.

"I'm thinking," Accorsi said, "we're going to have to score forty points to have a chance. All week long, in my dreams, the Vikings scored eight thousand points. All I dreamt of were Randy Moss, Chris Carter, and Robert Smith running up and down the field. The day before the game, John Fox, who was our defensive coordinator then, said, 'Why have you been avoiding me all week? Every time I look at you, you look the other way.' 'I don't like to think about our defense right now,' I told him. 'We're going to be fine,' he said. 'We may shut them out.' And we did. Our corner, Jason Sehorn, took Moss out of the game early, demoralizing their entire team. Moss quit and the whole team quit. It was amazing."

No more amazing, though, than Collins. "I don't think anyone will ever have a better game at Giants Stadium than Kerry had that day," Ernie said, "January fourteenth, 2001." Just four plays into the game, Collins threw a forty-six-yard touchdown pass to Ike Hilliard, ultimately completing twenty-eight of thirty-nine passes for 381 yards and five touchdowns. The Vikings were destroyed, 41–0. New York was in Super Bowl XXXV, against the Baltimore Ravens.

Ernie said, "You know how sometimes you say to yourself, 'I just wish my father could have been here tonight to see this?'" That's what the

GM was thinking when he got home from the game and saw the message light blinking on his machine. "Do you know who it was?" he said. "Beano." Carroll "Beano" Cook was a sports gadfly and football oracle from Pittsburgh, an occasional columnist, sometime broadcaster, Monongahelan Winston Churchill, and the number one advocate of Mary Tyler Moore, chocolate chip cookies, and the University of Notre Dame. Beano was the best friend of almost everyone he knew in sports, which was almost everyone. Hardly needing to identify himself—he had the voice of a plumbing fixture gargling Drano—Beano left Ernie a seven-word message that showed once again how intuitive he was: "If the Gipper knew, your dad knows." *Click.*

"In the days leading up to the Super Bowl," Ernie said, "I became more and more worried about Kerry. You could see that he wasn't taking the bit in his mouth. I knew what was coming." "That Super Bowl was over in a series," according to Tony Siragusa, the Ravens' hugest defensive tackle. "I watched Collins standing at the line, getting ready to call out the signals, and he wasn't looking up the field or at his receivers or at the defensive backs covering his receivers. He was looking at us, the guys who were coming to get him. I thought, 'Man, this game is over.'" The Ravens were better anyway—many times better defensively. They won going away, 34–7. Collins threw four interceptions.

With occasional brilliance, followed by inevitable disappointment, Collins saw the Giants through to the quarterback-rich draft of 2004, when in the fourth pick of the first round Ernie took Philip Rivers of North Carolina State and traded him to San Diego along with three draft choices (including the Giants' number one in 2005) for top selection Eli Manning. It was the Elway power play all over again, in reverse. Because this time Accorsi was on the other side. "There was no question," Ernie said, "we knew we were going to pick a quarterback. We were coming off a four-and-twelve season—Fassel had fired himself—and we told every coach whom we interviewed, 'Don't even think you're going to come in and change our mind.' When it comes to young quarterbacks, coaches have a natural tendency to think, 'By the time this guy

gets good, I might be fired. We can get by with so-and-so.' Nope. This
was going to be a franchise pick, and if everything fell into place, it was
going to be Manning." Ben Roethlisberger of Miami of Ohio was a Li'l
Abner who made plays. Rivers of North Carolina State was a brilliant
kid—that's how he got by. But Manning was the guy.

Almost the only thing Ernie knew about A. J. Smith, the Chargers'
GM, was that Smith and head coach Marty Schottenheimer barely
spoke. "I called A.J. in March," Accorsi said, "to get the ball rolling. We
touched base again in April. Finally, on the Thursday before the draft,
we really started to talk. Eli wasn't nearly as adamant about San Diego, I
didn't feel, as Elway had been about Baltimore. But historically the
Chargers hadn't been the biggest winners, and the fact that Archie had
languished his entire career for a down team in New Orleans had to be
foremost in Eli's mind. Friday, I thought the deal was dead. But I was
tipped by a writer that A.J. was going to pick Eli and call me. So, San
Diego takes Eli, Oakland takes tackle Robert Gallery, Arizona takes
receiver Larry Fitzgerald, and we're on the clock. Fifteen minutes. I'm
waiting, I'm waiting. At the seven minute mark, A.J. finally calls."

Just before that, the Browns called. Cleveland owned the sixth selection. "They offered me a second to change places," Ernie said, "and I
almost did it. But I stopped and thought, 'You know what? If I drop
down to pick up a second, and now Cleveland makes the Manning trade,
I'll kill myself.' That's when A.J. called. I knew I'd have to give up the
next year's number one, but they wanted [defensive end] Osi Umenyiora,
too. 'Deal-killer,' I said, and he knew I wasn't bluffing. We were on the
clock. So we made a package of draft choices and I picked Rivers for
them in exchange for Eli. The Browns were really mad. I reneged, they
said. But there's no such thing as reneging until the computer thing is
in. I never really said yes, I just almost said yes. So now the deal went
through and I was exhilarated. We had a quarterback. I knew what that
meant. I'd had them—the best—and I'd not had them. And I'd played
against the great ones, so I knew. I realized that I could turn out to be
wrong on this kid, there was no question about it—maybe I'm going to

be wrong. And I knew we might not know for sure until years after I leave. But I could live with it. We had a quarterback."

The following morning, Collins barged into Accorsi's office, demanding, "I want to go, I want to leave, I want out of here! I want to know what you're going to do with me!"

"I said, 'Well, you're under contract, Kerry, you're the quarterback—for the moment.'

" 'I want out of here!'

" 'Okay, I'll think about it.'

" 'No, I want out of here *today*.'

" 'Kerry, I'm sitting on this side of the desk, you're sitting on that side. I'll do this when I decide to do it.' "

A couple of days later, Accorsi released Collins, acquiring veteran Kurt Warner to squire Manning for half a season. Kerry went off to Oakland, the NFL's traditional late career stop.

The list of potential Fassel replacements was pared down to four finalists, whom Accorsi and Giants president John Mara interviewed at length: Tom Coughlin, a former Giants assistant to Bill Parcells who could have had the job after Parcells left in 1990 but didn't want it then; Lovey Smith; Romeo Crennel; and Charlie Weis. "Lovey was really sharp, impressive," Ernie said, "but we had less history with him than the others." Coughlin, Crennel, and Weis had all been Giants assistants, and now Crennel and Weis were serving Belichick. "For about two hours before a Patriots game," Ernie said, "I talked to Bill about Romeo and Charlie, and then I scouted the game and watched everything they did. I was trying to figure out how much of the defense was really run by Romeo. I knew Charlie was running the offense. Weis started out fourth on the list but finished second. Similar to that first time I interviewed Belichick, I told Charlie, 'You were down thirty-five points and you closed it to two with the ball.' I also told him, 'You know, the best thing that ever happened to Jack Kennedy was losing the vice presidential nomination to Estes Kefauver in fifty-six.' I'm not sure he got that."

A backfield mate of Larry Csonka's and Floyd Little's at Syracuse,

Coughlin played for legendary coach Ben Schwartzwalder and set records both as a pass receiver and as a student. He was the quarterback coach at Boston College, where one of his charges was Doug Flutie, and later the head coach at BC for three seasons. "I saw his second game, against Michigan," Ernie said. "They played the Wolverines tough for a long while. Near the end of his time there, Coughlin beat George Welsh's Virginia team in a bowl game. Virginia had four or five top choices; he didn't have that much, Glenn Foley at quarterback. But Welsh told me the week before, 'We can't figure out their passing game. There's a timing mechanism to it. We've studied it for three weeks, but I'm not sure we can stop it.' Well, BC completed every friggin' pass and killed them, 31–13."

A year and a half before the Jacksonville Jaguars played their inaugural NFL game in 1995, Coughlin signed on as the new franchise's charter head coach. After just one losing year, the Jaguars made it to postseason play four straight times, the only expansion team ever to do that. Twice Jacksonville reached the AFC Championship Game. "A number of coaches," Accorsi said, "including Schottenheimer, told me Coughlin was a bear to coach against. Marty said, 'You're probing all the time, you're changing all the time. You can't set a game plan for him. If something doesn't work, he's quick to try something else.' So when John Mara and I sat down with Coughlin at the Newark airport, he was the favorite."

They had streams of questions to put to him, but, pulling out a legal yellow pad, Coughlin asked if he could make an opening statement. Twenty-five minutes later, he was still filibustering. "It annoyed me, turned me off," Ernie said. "'When is this misery going to end?' I thought. I was just about ready to scream 'Enough already!' when he finally stopped. Answering our questions, though, he was good. He fit the part: Jesuit-trained, smart, devout, winner, integrity, clean. I told John Mara later, 'He double-bogeyed the first hole but he still shot sixty-eight.' Tom had done an incredible job with no players at BC. He had made Jacksonville competitive right away. All that said, you're bothered by the three losing seasons [7–9, 6–10, 6–10] at the end in Florida. But the more we studied it, the more we thought it was mostly a personnel problem, and he wasn't going to be in charge of our personnel. He had screwed up the salary cap, too, not signing the right guys, giving too much money to the wrong ones. But he wasn't going to have control of that here, either."

Wellington Mara had been a naval officer, and the Giants' organization was run by chain of command. The Maras didn't fire coaches, or anyone else, blithely. At the same time, Wellington used to say, "Though I'm loyal to you, I'm more loyal to the structure. You'll get yourself fired if you're not." Leaving the Coughlin interview, Accorsi told Mara, "If we can't win with this guy, I'm taking up tennis."

In the midst of the 11–5 2005 season, with Coughlin and Manning settling into place, Ernie was coming up on sixty-five and planning to call it a career. As a matter of fact, he threw himself a farewell party in Baltimore and started to look for a town house in Hershey to serve with his New York apartment as co-headquarters for his retirement. But Wellington's death in October, followed twenty-one days later by the death of Preston Robert Tisch, patriarch of the family that owned the other half of the Giants, made leaving then unseemly. Ernie especially didn't want to abandon John Mara. So there would be one final season for Accorsi, a sentimental last journey through all of the years.

By the way, on the final day of 2005 in Oakland, the Giants had to beat the Raiders, quarterbacked by Kerry Collins, to win the NFC East Division Championship. "I kept telling defensive coordinator Tim Lewis," Ernie said, " 'You better blitz him,' 'You better blitz him,' 'You better blitz him.' It almost cost us the game, my big mouth. We blitzed the hell out of him, but the Raiders picked it up, and Kerry was great. He really wanted this one. We survived, thirty to twenty-one, but he was absolutely great. He threw for, like, three hundred thirty yards [331] and three touchdowns." Ernie sounded proud of him. "I was," he said. "I was glad we survived, but I was also glad for Kerry, that he had that moment."

Of splendor.

8

SHOCK

SEATTLE'S QWEST FIELD, known for its din as the land of false starts, had been the Giants' saddest stop in 2005, when they dominated in yardage, first downs, and takeaways but lost in overtime to the eventual NFC champions, 24–21. Near the end of the fourth quarter and twice in sudden death, Jay Feely missed field goal attempts of forty, fifty-four, and forty-five yards. "I love Jay," Accorsi said, "but I'm still pretty wounded by that." The loss reordered all of the home field advantages at the close of the season. In other words, it changed everything.

Tight end Jeremy Shockey had been particularly busy that day, catching ten Eli Manning passes for 127 yards, including a clutch two-point conversion to tie the game near the end of regulation. So it's possible that Shockey had come back to the great Northwest more bent on revenge than anyone else. But not only was there no revenge, there was hardly any football game. On five touchdown passes by Matt Hasselbeck, older brother of Giants backup quarterback Tim Hasselbeck (both of them sons of former Giant tight end Don Hasselbeck), the Seahawks built a 35–0 and then a 42–3 lead, coasting from there to a misleading 42–30 victory. Shockey caught four passes for fifty-eight yards, only one of those before halftime, when the score was 35–3. This year, he was the star of the postgame show.

Not in response to a query, but rather by way of a declaration, Shockey waited until almost everyone had showered before he suddenly announced, "We got outplayed and outcoached," accent on the latter. "Write that one down."

"We played hard," he said, but in case he wasn't heard the first time, he reiterated with fresh emphasis, "We got outplayed and *outcoached.* There are no excuses, no 'twelfth man' or crowd noise to blame. We just lost. Why do I say outcoached? You watched the game. They used defenses we weren't expecting. They did things we haven't seen. The job of the coaches is to put us in the best possible position to succeed."

Apprised of Shockey's outburst, Seattle's Hasselbeck felt unfairly shorted. "How *could* they prepare?" the Seahawks quarterback wondered. "That was the first time we used some of those formations in a game. We ran routes we've never shown before." Other Giants offered blurbs on the team's performance, but "outcoached" was the one that led the review.

"They had fourteen points before we were even lathered up," Tom Coughlin said with unusual flair.

"It's embarrassing," said Tiki Barber. "That's the easiest word."

"Right now," Antonio Pierce said, "we're a horrible team."

"Too much bad football," Manning said, in the simplest expression of all.

The last two players to leave the New York locker room were Shockey and Luke Petitgout. When Petitgout was asked if it mattered that the Giants had scored those twenty-seven late points, he responded with a ringing "No!" "I think it does," said Shockey, contrary to the end, sounding ready to reopen fire. But Luke said, "Shock, come on. The bus is leaving."

Tight ends are in a tough position. They are expected to be as fleet as wide receivers, who are much lighter, at the same time that they are required to block defensive ends, who are much larger. Tight ends get called for holding quite often, but what choice do they have? They are always a little injured, more than a little frustrated. And in Shockey, a regular at the Pro Bowl, every quality was exaggerated. Mike Pope, the Giants' assistant coach in charge of tight ends, told the *New York Times,* "Impulse can be a hard thing to control. This is a very spirited racehorse." Center Shaun O'Hara said, "He's our emotional leader, sometimes for good, sometimes for bad. But you know you're going to get the same thing from him every time, and I love him for it. I wouldn't want anyone else out there."

Ernie saw Shockey for the first time in 2001, when Miami opened its season at Penn State. "I hated him and I loved him," Accorsi said. "They killed Penn State that day [33–7], and Jeremy pranced all over the end zone after scoring touchdowns. I thought, 'I hate this guy.' But what a player."

Did he have his tattoos yet?

"I couldn't tell. I was in the stands."

Come on, Shockey's radiating tattoos were visible from at least the upper deck, if not the blimp.

"We had a psychologist here then," Ernie said. "We don't anymore. He told us flat out, 'You can't draft Shockey.' He had all of these theories about why not. He even came up with some kind of legal thing that I didn't think was true. It became personal for some reason. 'I'm not going to let you draft him,' he said. 'What?' So I went to John Mara. 'Do you mind if I ask the Tisch family [holders of the other 50 percent of the Giants] to borrow their airplane? I need to go to Ada, Oklahoma, to find out the truth about Jeremy Shockey.' Right about that same time, I get a call from the agent Drew Rosenhaus. He and I had a big fight over his constant demands to renegotiate the contract of Jessie Armstead, a linebacker from Miami. Now, Shockey was choosing an agent and Rosenhaus was taking a hell of a chance. He had Jeremy on the line. 'Other agents,' he said, 'are telling Jeremy you won't draft him if I represent him. Will you please tell him that's a crock?' I said, 'Jeremy, Drew and I had problems over one player, but that has nothing to do with you. If we decide to draft you, we'll draft you, whoever your representative is.'"

As usual that year, the University of Miami players snubbed the NFL combine in favor of their own private preview before a mass assembly of GMs and coaches. A half dozen potential first-rounders were on display: offensive tackle Bryant McKinnie, cornerback Phillip Buchanon, safety Ed Reed, cornerback Mike Rumph, running back Clinton Portis, and

Shockey. "Mike Pope was having an orgasm over Shockey's workout," Ernie said. "I told him, 'Mike, come over here. All of the other teams are watching. If you don't quit French-kissing this guy, we're not going to have any shot at him at all. Back off, will you?'"

"Of course I knew who Ernie was," Shockey said. "Everybody in the business knew Ernie Accorsi. I noticed he was the only one who didn't have a team cap on. He was wearing a black golf sweater. When it came my turn to run the forty, he ran, too, to get himself in the best position to see. That was pretty funny, but all of the other GMs moved out of his way. I thought, 'Uh-oh, I better be good now.' It was raining slightly. I was sprinting in a mist. Man, was I moving!" He must have looked like a revolving lawn sprinkler.

When Accorsi reached the Teterboro airport, bound for Oklahoma, the beautiful Tisch airliner was not there. Instead, a trade-out had been arranged. His ride was a rumpled little plane with a young pilot and a trainee for a co-pilot. But they made it to Ada all right. "Landing there," Ernie said, "was like a scene out of a Western movie. A tiny brick building. A pole with one of those wind sleeves on top. A guy with a baseball cap on backwards sitting on the fender of his pickup truck. That was Jeremy. Walking up to him, all I could think of was Mickey Mantle, Commerce, Oklahoma, 1949. Shockey asked, 'What do you want to see first?' I said, 'The police station.'"

They sat in an interrogation room with two cops. "It was a crusty old building," Ernie said. "There was everything except one of those lantern bubble lights on the desk. I began, 'There's a rumor that Jeremy was arrested the night of his high school prom or graduation, gun in the trunk, marijuana in the car, blah, blah, blah.' 'Nope,' one of the cops said deliberately, after rustling through a stack of records, 'nothin' like that, nothin' at all.' 'I ain't never done nothin' wrong!' Jeremy exclaimed [still two shy of the local record for multiple negatives]. I told him, 'Well, there's a lot of money involved here. I'm just checking you out. You want to be a multimillionaire, don't you?' 'Yeah,' he said, and smiled. We hit it off right away."

Straddling a bench in the Giants' training room, Shockey chuckled at the memory and said, 'The truth is, we did get pulled over but I wasn't the one driving. Of course, we were all drinking. And they did find a gun, but it was a paintball gun. I don't know what all they found in that car, a bunch of stuff. We were held for firearm possession and for being under the influence, but we were never charged. We went to jail, but they didn't keep us overnight. It was a place where all the drunks were taken. Concrete floors. We had a good time messing with all the drunk people there for a while. We fit right in. Everything eventually got dropped, though. I ultimately had to pay two hundred dollars to have the arrest expunged. I really didn't do anything wrong."

Their next stop was Ada High School, where as a senior Shockey returned four punts for touchdowns. A transcript was pulled for single mother Lucinda Shockey's famous son, Jeremy Charles Shockey, whose address of record was Rural Route 4, Box 388. The document showed that in his freshman year, Shockey made five C's, in English, algebra, science, history, and Introduction to Composition. The next year, he had three D's, in English, algebra, and French. But something must have happened then. In his third year Shockey posted A's and B's across the board, and in the second semester of his senior year, he received just one B, in English, otherwise all A's. The ACT testing scores were another story, but by Accorsi's reckoning, Jeremy didn't just pass, he passed with distinction.

"I picked our next stop," Shockey said, "Bob's Barbecue. I'll tell you something for a fact, I desperately wanted to be a New York Giant. To me it was the marquee franchise in the NFL. The red, white, and blue. I even more desperately didn't want to be a Cincinnati Bengal. That's where I was hearing I might go. While we were eating the barbecue, Ernie and I talked about everything, and he just seemed so honest that I finally told him the truth about the paintball gun. We talked about sports, all sports. As much as anybody I've ever met, Ernie has an amazing love of sports."

"He tells me," Ernie said, "'You're never going to eat barbecue as good as this the rest of your life.' Jeremy ate a double portion, I had a single—and I couldn't eat again for three days! It was phenomenal!

Oklahoma Sooner memorabilia was plastered all over the joint. 'Why didn't you go to OU?' I asked him. 'When I got out of high school,' he said, 'they didn't want me. Nobody wanted me. I weighed about a buck seventy-five. I hoped to go to Arizona, but I ended up playing junior college ball instead, putting on a few pounds. Then everybody wanted me. But there weren't many schools in the country—there still aren't—that threw to the tight end. Miami did, so I became a Hurricane.'

"We had just a great day," Ernie said. "He drove me everywhere around town. I didn't meet his mom. She was in Dallas. But we talked about her. I liked the way he talked about her. I liked him." Shockey mentioned that former Jet Mark Gastineau was from Ardmore, just fifty miles away, but said, "We've produced more country singers than football players." "Jerry Walker, the old Orioles bonus baby, was from Ada," Ernie told Shockey. "Did you ever hear of him?" Walker threw his arm out in the 1950s when manager Paul Richards let an eighteen-year-old kid pitch a sixteen-inning shutout. "He was the youngest pitcher ever to start the All-Star Game," Accorsi told Shockey, "the youngest one ever to win it, too." Leaning back in the training room, Jeremy said, "I always enjoy hearing someone who loves something go on and on about it. I wonder if there's anything in sports that Ernie doesn't know."

The first man drafted in Shockey's year was Fresno State quarterback David Carr, who went to Houston. Tennessee was picking fourteenth, the Giants fifteenth. As the auction moved along, Rosenhaus called Accorsi to tip him that the Titans might be trading their choice to someone who coveted Shockey. "I figured it was to Oakland," Ernie said. "Big, redheaded tight end, you know. Hadn't Al Davis been searching for another Dave Casper for about twenty-five years? I was criticized for this later, but I gave Tennessee a fourth-round pick to move up just that one rung. You know, to be sure of Jeremy. I don't have any idea who that fourth pick ended up being, and I don't want to know."

"It meant a lot to me that Ernie traded up," Shockey said. "When we were sitting around at Bob's Barbecue, just talking, he told me that a football team is a jigsaw puzzle with a lot of oddly shaped pieces. 'We need a tight end,' he said, 'and I think you just might be the perfect fit. You know, this game is all about mismatches. You're too fast for a linebacker to guard. You're too big for a safety to guard. Who are they going to put on you?' I thought of nothing else but that all through the morning of the draft."

McKinnie ended up going fifth to the Vikings, Shockey fourteenth to the Giants, Buchanon seventeenth to the Raiders, Reed twenty-fourth to the Ravens, Rumph twenty-seventh to the 49ers, and Portis in the second round to the Broncos. "Pretty good Hurricane class, huh?" Jeremy said, "but I felt like the big winner. After I ran for Ernie that time in Miami, we talked a little bit about the five other guys. He agreed with me about four of them, but about the fifth one, he wasn't so sure. And you know what? He was right."

"Jeremy says things I wish he wouldn't," Ernie said, like the word *outcoached*, "and he does things I wish he wouldn't," like throwing his arms up in dismay when Manning missed him with passes. Eli didn't respond in kind when Shockey dropped them. Perhaps he should have. Unitas would have bounced the next pass off the back of his helmet, and the one after that off the front. "But he's just a good-hearted kid from Ada, Oklahoma," Ernie said, and both Shockey and Accorsi agreed that New York City was a challenging place for a good-hearted kid from Ada.

"Yeah," Jeremy said, "I come from a town so small that you could pick up the newspaper, read it, and actually believe what's in it. It's not like I'd never been out of Oklahoma before I came to New York, but I just never dreamed of the media being like this." "Miami," Ernie said, "is a pro town primarily. Almost anything that came out of Jeremy's mouth wouldn't be the biggest story that day. But here, he's perfect for the social and rumor pages, and 'Page Six' of the *New York Post*. In the beginning, I think he got caught up a little, not realizing where he was. But all of the Shockey mannerisms, all of the things that nobody's crazy about, stem from the tremendous pride he has. Jeremy wants to dominate every game he plays in. When he doesn't, he goes almost crazy with frustration. Starting with the fact that he plays the game of football so unbelievably hard, even in practice, he's just a naturally self-destructive character, and of course he's going to clash with Coughlin."

They'd had a lot of small, stupid arguments, like the time Jeremy was fined $100 for being two minutes late to a meeting. He told Ernie, "I wasn't late; Coughlin messed with the clock." "'Jeremy,' I said, 'pay the hundred dollars.' 'I shouldn't have to pay it. See if you can get me out of it.' 'There'll be times, if it's really important, when I'll intervene on your behalf. But this ain't one of them.' 'Well, goddamn it, I wasn't late!' 'I know what you're making, okay? Do you want me to lend you the hundred bucks?' 'No, I'll pay his fine. But I'm not happy with him.'"

Coughlin's object had never been to make Shockey or any of the other players happy with him. "I came into the league as a head coach in ninety-four, okay?" Tom said, sitting in his office. "In Jacksonville I had the most motley group of people you ever saw in your life. Now, how am I going to mold these players together? Well, one way. Be hard on them. Be tough. Nine-on-seven drills every morning. Make them go to training camp four or five days early. The union's bitching: 'That son of a bitch!' But I'll tell you something, I only had maybe one guy who didn't come the day I asked, and he was still early.

"They're coming off the field every day, every day, they're screaming, 'Aaagh!' So they hated one guy, me. But you know what? They were the toughest bunch of football players you ever saw. The next year we go to the AFC Championship Game with this bunch of guys . . . I don't even know how to describe them."

The French Foreign Legion?

"That's pretty good. The French Foreign Legion. That's it. Unbelievable. That's who you get in expansion. Mercenaries. So I got cast in a certain way. But the simple fact of the matter is, my thing—and people never look at it this way—is that I have a hard time with myself if I treat one person one way and I'm different with someone else. There are certain fundamentals that I believe in, and that's just the way it is. Coaching is making players do what they don't want to do so that they can become what they want to become."

Team leader Michael Strahan, the Giants' fourteen-year defensive end, the only NFL pass rusher ever to record a twenty-two-and-a-half-sack season, said, "The thing is, Tom doesn't make it very easy for you to like him. The first meeting I ever had with him, I walked out of there saying to myself, 'You know what? I'm playing one year with this guy and then I'm leaving.' I hated him. He kind of went at me in that first meeting, and I didn't know him from Adam. 'Why is he coming at me like this?'"

But Strahan didn't leave after a year. In fact, now he was into a third. "Because," he said, "the more I sat down with Tom one-on-one, the more I came to realize that he's a better guy than he gets credit for. He wants to win. I respect that. He really wants to win. He'll do whatever it takes. At the same time, more than almost anybody I've ever been around, he misses the human element. I think a coach has to show a human side, and that's what Coughlin doesn't do. He doesn't do it enough, anyway. Even professional players need to feel their coach cares about them. Talking to Tiki, that's Tiki's whole thing. Tiki said, 'It's like, Coach couldn't give a shit about me,' and I think that led to Tiki saying, 'Screw me? No, screw you. I'm outta here.'"

About a month before it broke in the news, Ernie mentioned that Barber's tenth pro year would almost certainly be his last. Yet Tiki was playing better than ever. "It's amazing, isn't it?" Accorsi said. "Tiki's amazing." Coughlin had long since cured Barber of his well-known case of fumble-itis. Maybe Tiki resented Tom for that, too.

It's a negotiating ploy, right? Threatening to retire at the top of his game?

"I don't think so," Ernie said. "I'm not even going to try to talk him out of it. Maybe my successor will. But, to tell you the truth, I don't believe it has anything to do with Coughlin or with anyone except Tiki. This has been the plan all along. He wants to be a television journalist, the next Matt Lauer. Tiki won't be reading the baseball scores at eleven o'clock at night, I can promise you that. He'll be interviewing kings and prime ministers in the morning."

Tiki and his identical twin, Ronde, a defensive back for Tampa Bay, played their college ball together at the University of Virginia, for George Welsh. "When Coughlin took over as the Giants' head coach," Welsh said, "I asked Tiki, 'What's he like?' 'He's like you,' he said. I took that to mean tough, maybe even too tough."

Strahan said, "Tom doesn't know it, but his main philosophy—'Treat everybody the same'—is wrong. He's scared to death someone will say, 'Look, that guy over there is getting special treatment.' Hell, special treatment is what makes a football team work. I've had conversations with Tom about this, trying to tell him that each player is not the same. You can't treat Tiki the same way you treat Brandon Jacobs. You can't treat me the same way you're going to treat a rookie, Kiwanuka. I told him, 'Coach, you just can't treat everybody the same. You don't treat your kids the same. You shouldn't treat your players the same. Hell, we're all special.'

"Listen to this. Tom once said this to me: 'I tell somebody to do something and they hate me. You tell them to do the same thing, and they go off and do it.' I said, 'Of course, Coach. You've got to know the guys. You've got to care about them, try to understand their different personalities.' But he looked at me like I was speaking a foreign language."

Interestingly, the tension between Coughlin and the New York media flowed from the same source. "I don't do any of that sidebar stuff," Tom said. "I don't have special writers or broadcasters who call me on the side for additional information, and you know, they hate me for that. Some of the media stars expect you to play this 'if you do things for me, I'll do things for you' game. The first year I was here, one of them wanted to do a family story. My family. I did it. They killed me. Another thing: we've got this little practice area, and there's a box for the media. I've always had that. Part of it's for safety. Part of it is just so I'll know where they are, so we can do our work without everybody being underfoot. Well, they hate me for that, too, because they had total free rein under Jim Fassel."

On the rare occasions when Yankees manager Joe Torre came under media fire, Tom thought he could detect a self-interested restraint on the part of the beat men and an unspoken threat from Torre. "Just reading between the lines," Coughlin said, "it sounded to me like if the writers happened to go too far, Joe just might stop playing ball with them. With me, on the other hand, they know there's no possible repercussions because I don't play ball anyway. 'Coughlin doesn't give you anything,' they tell each other, 'so there's nothing to take back.'" Out of left field, Torre telephoned Coughlin once just because Tom looked so miserable to Joe on television. Torre didn't even know Coughlin, but seeing him on the sideline, he was worried about him.

Football coaches have always been stereotyped by their sideline demeanors. Tethered to his frozen headset in Minnesota, Bud Grant used to be the "iceman." Standing as erect as a Scoutmaster at the Dallas bench, Tom Landry was the "plastic man." Tearing up yardage markers and coldcocking opposing brigands who intercepted passes off clean-cut Buckeyes like Art Schlister, Woody Hayes was the madman of Columbus, Ohio. In fact, all three could be terrifically charming people away from the field. "They've done that to me here, too," Coughlin said. "I'm that crazy person running up and down the sidelines. But I'm not going to apologize for being passionate. If they stamp you, you're stamped. But if they think I'm going to stand there like a statue, I can't do that. I'm not Tom Landry. And I don't look that good in a fedora." Finally, Coughlin allowed himself a small joke.

"Football's a complicated game," he continued in a slower meter. "The media try to make it a soap opera because they understand soap operas better than they do football. Most of them don't study the game. They don't really see it. I don't think most of them even really like it. They listen to other people who don't know, either, and formulate their opinions based on that. There's no depth to it. They latch on to everything that doesn't matter and forget about the game. That's not the game. *The game. The game.*"

Pat Hanlon, the Giants' PR man, who may be the most thoughtful one in the industry, probably knew Coughlin the best, as it usually fell to Hanlon to steer Tom through the media shoals. "This is a business," Pat said, "where the head coaches are always telling you how hard they work, how many hours they put in at the projector, how many nights they sleep in their offices. I've been with several head coaches who wore that on their sleeves as a badge of honor. How awfully, awfully hard they work. How terribly, terribly tough it is. They just can't stop reminding you.

"Well, this guy has never once even hinted that the hours are diffi-cult, or that the work is impossible. *Woe is me. I have to be here at five in the morning and I don't leave until eleven at night, if I leave at all.* None of that. Never. And I'll tell you something, Coughlin works twice as hard as any of the others I've known. And on an intellectual level he's miles ahead of all of them. He's the brightest person, by far. I just wish he could—or *we* could—communicate to the public how much Tom loves the game of football, how much it really matters to him. That might help. He told me, 'The day I retire will probably be two days before I kick. If I didn't have football, I don't know how I'd keep living.'"

In every football town, a few of the players and a few of the reporters whisper to each other about the head coach. That's traditional. "Right, they're kindred spirits," Hanlon said. "They both feel he doesn't give them the attention they deserve, at least not in the way they want it to be given. Griping players and their media soul mates are an institution. But wouldn't it be nice if everybody would shut up for just a minute and take a closer look at this guy?"

"By the way," Ernie said, "on my return trip from Ada to Teterboro, the trainee is flying the little plane and the young pilot is talking her through it. They have all the manuals open and spread out across the dash. We're not on instruments, it's clear. I'm nervous as hell. This is no joke. We're zooming and sliding, and all of a sudden we blow right past the Meadowlands and Teterboro. I say, 'Uh, excuse me a second, but wasn't that the airport back there? Far be it for me to interfere, but we're not going to England, are we?' 'Hey, you're right!' They were from Buffalo, both of them. We made it down okay."

Accorsi didn't kiss the ground, but he thought about it. Anyway, he had his tight end.

9

THE DRAFT

O N HIS WAY TO winning the Heisman Trophy in 1972, a gas station robbery turned up in Johnny Rodgers' past. This slight embarrassment, combined with his five-nine, 165-pound dimensions, dropped the sensational Nebraska running back to the bottom of the first round of the NFL draft. In a famous colloquy repeated in draft rooms every April, Lloyd Wells, head scout of the Kansas City Chiefs, still argued for selecting Rodgers. "If we pick this guy," coach Hank Stram argued back, "we'll have to build a jail cell." "Build it in the end zone," Wells said.

"After going to ten straight championship games with Otto Graham at quarterback," said Accorsi, "the Cleveland Browns had their first losing season in 1956 with George Ratterman and Babe Parilli sharing Otto's old job. At the next draft, Paul Brown was desperate for a quarterback and the Browns were picking sixth. The guy they wanted was Len Dawson. As the first few picks were rattled off, Mike Brown told me, 'My dad was, like, he couldn't breathe.' Now came the fourth choice. Now came the fifth. The Pittsburgh Steelers took Dawson. With a thud Brown dropped his head on the table. He was despondent. 'Dad, what are we going to do now?' Mike whispered. The clock was ticking. In a resigned voice, without lifting his head, Paul said, 'I guess we're stuck with Jim Brown.'"

Looking at the board in the Giants' draft room, Accorsi said, "We start to get ready for a draft by gathering all of the scouts together—the heroes of the whole process—and talking about every player in the country who's even remotely a prospect. We grade them, both overall and by position, and stagger the names all over these walls. We'll get together often during the year, finally in a marathon meeting that lasts two or three weeks. By the time April rolls around, every top player has had five, six, seven looks. We start plugging them in by rounds, our own lists of thirty-two." Nodding toward a small photograph of Wellington Mara, Ernie said, "We put Well here because he always sat right here. From the first meeting in February, he'd have all of his materials out. He would take notes. Just take notes.

"On draft day itself, the feeling is incredibly tense. I sit here, Tom Coughlin sits here, [player personnel director] Jerry Reese sits here, scouts fan out around the room, assistant coaches huddle in the back. Reese presides. He's incredibly well organized. We'll talk about Jerry some more. You have to listen to each other. There have been too many incidents in my career where the only guy in the room who likes or dislikes a player is right, so you better hear them all. Take Tom Brady, for instance [a sixth-round pick from Michigan, the second man selected by the Patriots in that round, the 199th player chosen overall]. After Brady started winning Super Bowls with New England, I went back and looked at all of our Brady reports. Everybody killed him except one guy, Whitey Walsh. If you read Whitey's report on Brady, it's a prediction of exactly how it turned out. He was the only guy who saw it. Sometimes you have to listen to the one guy."

There were banks of phones. "But I've learned to leave the room to field trade offers on draft day," Ernie said. "You get a thousand pitches for last-minute deals, because everybody is trying to screw you. 'I've got five extra sixth-round picks. Do you want two of them for your third-rounder?' I say no to almost everything. I'm not going to sell my scouts down the river. But I stopped using this phone when Jim Fassel was still coaching here, because he would kibitz. 'What's the offer?' 'The Jets want to give us so-and-so and a fifth for our second.' 'Take it! Take it!' he'd yell. Half the time he didn't even know what kind of players those picks represented."

One of the most memorable moments in the annals of Giants drafting occurred in 2004, as the first round was bleeding into the second. "Reading the board and sort of doing the math," Ernie said, "it looked to me like we might land on Chris Snee." He was a 314-pound guard from Boston College, but there was an interesting complication. Snee was already the father of Coughlin's grandson Dylan but not yet the husband of Tom's daughter, Katie. Tennessee took Antwan Odom, defensive end from Alabama; San Francisco took Shawntae Spencer, cornerback from Pitt; Cleveland took Sean Jones, safety from Georgia. "Tom," Ernie told Coughlin, "it's looking like Snee. It's your call. I'm giving you the whole say. We can bypass him if you want." "Let's wait until we get there," Coughlin said. New Orleans took Courtney Watson, linebacker from Notre Dame; Kansas City took Kris Wilson, tight end from Pitt; Carolina took Keary Colbert, wide receiver from USC. "Tom, it's Snee. I think it's Snee. Make a decision." New England took Marquise Hill, defensive end from LSU . . .

"Finally," Ernie said, "Tom called home and spelled it out for his wife, Judy. 'We can take him or leave him,' he said," something husbands often wish they could say to wives about men who are only prospective sons-in-law. "Tom hung up," Ernie said, "and told me, 'Okay, let's take him.'" So, in the second choice of the second round, on the recommendation of the coach's wife, the Giants took Chris Snee of Boston College, who became an immediate starter. As it turned out, the ending was happy all around. Chris and Katie married, and they quickly gave Dylan a baby brother, Cooper Christopher.

Though Ernie knew he wouldn't be participating in any more college drafts, which was almost his favorite part of the job, he made a few final scouting trips anyway, sentimental Saturday journeys, starting in the Giants' post-Seattle bye week. Over Accorsi's three and a half decades as a bird dog, the only major football campuses he hadn't scoured for talent were Baylor, Oregon, Oregon State, and Purdue. "Purdue's a total mystery," he said, "I don't know how I ever missed Purdue."

His habit and pleasure was to stroll university grounds on crisp Friday afternoons searching for "the original heart of the campus before billionaire alumni and high-rise architects turned these beautiful little gardens into industrial parks." As long as he was there, he would satisfy his addiction for collegiate sweatshirts ("I can't live long enough to wear all of the ones I already have"), and he usually attended the pep rally.

The first stop, as always, was Penn State, for a game against Northwestern at Beaver Stadium. Ernie stayed in an economy hotel in the center of University Park, where the drapes could have been the same ones he remembered from the 1960s. Before meeting his old boss, Jim Tarman, for dinner, Ernie milled with the students through the streets of the college town and remembered everything. He joined the Tarmans—Louise had Beano Cook's vote for best wife in the history of collegiate athletics—at Centre Hills Country Club, hard by a golf course and in sight of Mount Nittany. Joe Paterno was too busy to join them, plotting the game and shaking off a practice-field collision that broke three ribs, though he didn't know it yet. "I can't even blow my nose," Joe said the next day, "my chest hurts so bad." A bigger collision was ahead, but nothing ever stopped Paterno. "Why would Ernie Accorsi retire?" he asked me. Why would anyone retire, he meant.

Saturday was a dingy day—gray thunderclouds sat on the stadium. But the flapping white towels and the other school cheers worked as brighteners. "The NFL doesn't have this," Ernie said, setting up his pens and notebooks in the front row of the press box. "It has a lot of great things, but it doesn't have this." A gigantic offensive tackle, Levi Brown, seemed to interest Accorsi most. Ernie also scribbled a few notes on defensive tackle Jay Alford, who wore a strange number for a lineman, 13. As usual, the Nittany Lions employed a linebacker worth evaluating, an Aliquippa, Pennsylvania, honor roll student with the football-sounding name Paul Posluszny. He must have been pretty good because Accorsi's look at him was the Giants' seventh. "Posluszny had a little problem with his right knee," Ernie said, "and I think it may have cost him some outside speed. But he's got instinctive quickness in the box. He's got nice footwork, doesn't he?"

Notre Dame was another mandatory port of call.

"I flew into South Bend on a commuter plane," Ernie said when he arrived. "Flying over the Golden Dome, all of a sudden the pilot actually dipped the wing to give us the full effect. A woman across the aisle from me was almost overcome with emotion. Not for herself, I figured. I doubt she was a football fan. I bet it was for a husband or a father. But she told us that this was her first look at Notre Dame, and it was some moment. Like landing in Lourdes." As a matter of fact, Ernie wanted to stop first at the grotto, to kneel where Paul Hornung had knelt in a classic *Life* magazine photograph, and to light a candle. All of the vigil stands were ablaze, so a couple of candles had to be discreetly blown out and relit. Then he went looking for the Irish coach, Charlie Weis, runner-up for the Giants job.

"Didn't you tell Mr. Mara I went to Mass every day?" Weis said, still a little sore. "No, I didn't tell him that," Ernie said, "because you don't. He thinks you're Jewish, Charlie." Like most football coaches, Weis was the hero of all his stories. His old boss, Bill Parcells, took Charlie's most brilliant ideas and passed them off as his own. (All former assistants tell these same exact stories.) Good-naturedly, Weis needled Accorsi for spurning him in favor of Coughlin. "You're rooting your heart out against Tom, aren't you?" Ernie said. "What d'ya mean?" Charlie said. "I'm a Giants fan!" "Save that back-door slider you throw for somebody else," Ernie said. But, in a becoming moment, Weis murmured, "Just because you want a job doesn't mean you're ready for it."

The Irish opponent the next day was North Carolina, whose coach had already been fired. So this amounted to a bye week for Notre Dame, too. At the players' final run-through in the field house, Charlie had to dig unusually deep to find something about which to sound pissed. Calling quarterback Brady Quinn and the rest of his charges together at midfield, Weis said, "If NBC homes in on any of you after the game and you're not mouthing the words to the alma mater—and they better be the right words, too—you and I are going to have a big, big problem." But after dismissing the team, Charlie giggled at Accorsi and brought him in on the evening's plot to spring "Happy Birthday" on Charlie's wife at the pep rally. "I'm going to get everyone to sing to her," he said. "She's going to kill me, but it's going to be great." Taking his cue from a profanity-laden profile of Weis on *60 Minutes,* the leprechaun mascot introduced Charlie to the assembly as "the best bleeping coach in America."

For memory collecting, Accorsi rated only two colleges ahead of Penn State and Notre Dame: the Naval Academy and West Point. Though Phil McConkeys, never mind Roger Staubachs, were becoming rarer and rarer at Navy, Ernie still liked to walk the cobblestones of Annapolis, to throw pennies like a plebe at Tecumseh, and to answer the questions in the midshipmen's Reef Points booklet: How's the cow? "She walks, she talks, she's full of chalk. The lacteal fluid extracted from the female of the bovine species is highly prolific to the nth degree." Even more, he loved West Point. Of all the side benefits that have flowed from being the GM of the Giants, by several touchdowns the most wonderful was an invitation Ernie received, as if he were MacArthur, to address the senior class of cadets.

"I have walked the streets of Saint-Lô, through the trees of the Ardennes, been to the Remagan bridge, the beaches of Anzio, stood on Monte Cassino, and been to the grave of George Patton in Luxembourg," Accorsi said in the middle of his talk. "If I have one unfulfilled dream in football, it is that I never had the chance to hire Patton as my head coach. Do you think he might have won the Super Bowl?

"When we select players, we are selecting people. In the final analysis, it's not the biggest and fastest player that prevails. It's the best competitor. The best man . . . [An old Marine] once told me, 'I learned two things from the Marine Corps. Officers eat last, and the troops fight for each other.' They don't fight for their commanders. They don't fight for their division. They fight for their buddies. When I select a football player for the Giants, I can't help thinking of that. 'Will this guy be a good teammate? Will this be the kind of man that my players will fight for?' Because that's how you win . . .

"Every fall, usually when the leaves are at the peak of their splendor, I scout an Army game at Michie Stadium. I don't expect to find Dan

Marino out there, but I don't come here for that. I come here because I want to hear the corps sing 'On Brave Old Army Team,' the grandest of all college fight songs. I don't sit in the press box. I sit in the lower stands across from the home side because I am only here for one reason—the corps. It is always my favorite trip of the season. It is my honor to be with you at this sacred place . . .

"Beat Navy!"

When the Giants' bye week ended, it seemed that a lot more than fourteen days had passed since the Seattle debacle, especially for Accorsi, refreshed from scouting. But the players hadn't exactly been on vacation, and extra time to think was, historically, never a benefit to the Giants. A lifetime supply of seventeen post-bye-week games yielded a grand total of three victories, none in the last five years. And journalistically it had been a restless fortnight in New York, where the phonograph needle was stuck on the word *outcoached*.

The Washington Redskins were in town, encouraged by two straight victories built on five-hundred-yard offensive explosions detonated by Coughlin's old Jacksonville quarterback, lefty Mark Brunell. "Our game plan was not to think too much, just go," Michael Strahan said. "Our game plan was to stop depending on our individual talent," Tiki Barber said, "and become a team." "Our game plan," said center Shaun O'Hara, "was to stop playing with a sense of entitlement and start playing with a sense of urgency." Also, O'Hara said, "to stuff the ball down their throats."

Tiki took his lead from, of all people, Coughlin, paraphrasing one of Tom's midweek addresses. "I was going to ask you for a players-only meeting," he told the coach, "but you did it for me." Stop depending on individual talent. Become a team. Coughlin also instructed John Hufnagel to instruct Eli Manning to hand the ball to Barber, which he did twenty-three times, and Tiki logged 123 yards rushing.

Washington gained only 164 total. In a defensive statement featuring sacks from Strahan, Osi Umenyiora, and Fred Robbins, each one followed by a fake basketball jump shot that must have been unsightly even to former Jet exhibitionist Mark Gastineau, the Giants killed all suspense in the first drive of the third quarter and went on to win, 19–3.

GIANTS

1-10-G31　Barber runs for 9
2-1-G40　Barber runs for 5
1-10-G45　Manning passes incomplete
2-10-G45　Manning passes to Brandon Jacobs for 9
3-1-R46　Jacobs runs for 2
1-10-R44　Barber runs for 7
2-3-R37　Barber runs for 2
3-1-R35　Jacobs runs for 4
1-10-R31　Manning passes to Plaxico Burress for 5
2-5-R26　Jacobs runs for 6
1-10-R20　Manning called for intentional grounding
2-20-R30　Manning passes to Burress for 4
3-16-R26　(shotgun) Manning passes to Amani
　Toomer for 21
1-G-R5　Barber runs for 3
2-G-R2　Manning passes to Burress for 2 and the
　touchdown; Jay Feely's extra point is good
Giants 16, Redskins 3

Afterward, Coughlin wasn't able to laugh off all of the "insurrection in the locker room" stories (a couple of months later, they would resurface as "mutiny" stories), though laughter would have been a good option. "There wasn't anything that had to be quieted down," he said in a Commander Queeg–like reply to a leading question. "You take one statement [Shockey's] and run with it, which you all did—and enjoyed it—for two weeks. There wasn't any problem in the locker room." *And enjoyed it* was the part of his speech soaked in strychnine.

Newly acquired free agent LaVar Arrington, who figured to be the Washington game's central character, put in a mellow performance, making one tackle, batting down one pass, being just a serviceable cog in the combined defense. Once he was the Redskins' second overall pick in the draft, from Penn State. In March 2006, Arrington left the team after six seasons by mutual delight, weak-kneed but rich. In the New York tabloids, LaVar was known as "the $49 million man," a reference to what Ernie had agreed to pay him over seven years. It didn't take even a month of mediocre Sundays for this headline to appear: "LaVar Arrington. Why Did We Bring Him Here?" "You're supposed to act like those things don't bother you," LaVar said, "but they do."

Before his grudge match with Washington, Arrington mischievously hinted that he had pinched his old playbook, seven hundred pages thick, and brought it with him to New York. Redskins cornerback Shawn Springs and, more surprisingly, linebacker coach Dale Lindsey countered that LaVar had never seemed to grasp what was in that book anyway. "They literally insulted my intelligence," Arrington said huffily. "I had heard that expression my whole life." After the Giants' victory, LaVar could have razzed them both if he wanted to, but decided against it. "On the field," he said, "I did do a little trash-talking, but in a good spirit, because I know so many of them. Trash-talking used to be a big part of my game, even at Penn State."

Days after Washington was beaten, LaVar was sitting in the players' lounge with the television muted. He was kind of muted himself. "You know, I was always the star," he said, fiddling with his dreadlocks. That was certainly true. From the peewee leagues on, Arrington stood out above everyone else. As a senior running back and linebacker at North Hills High School in Pittsburgh, he was *Parade* magazine's trumpeted selection as the best prep player in the nation. At Penn State, Arrington won the Chuck Bednarik Award for being—if its namesake means anything—the most wanton defensive player in all of college football. LaVar also took home the Dick Butkus trophy as the premier linebacker. The NFL drafted him ahead of the likes of Jamal Lewis, Brian Urlacher, Bubba Franks, Plaxico Burress, Shaun Alexander, Thomas Jones, and Chad Pennington. Quickly LaVar staffed three Pro Bowls.

"But, you know," he said, drawing the words out carefully, "I've never lived up to the hype. Go back to draft day, 2000. The second pick overall. I've never lived up to what I was supposed to be. How could I? You know, since I was a little boy, I've never been allowed just to make a tackle. It's not enough for LaVar Arrington just to make a tackle. It has to be an extraordinary tackle. It has to be a tackle that takes *everyone's* breath away. He has to leap over the line in a single bound. He has to knock the quarterback unconscious, or something of the sort. So, he tries to do it that way, and you know what happens? He misses the sound tackle he might have made because he has to do it in the most dramatic fashion. And a game is lost. That's been my life in football."

For the first time in his life, LaVar was attempting to play within himself, within a system, and the coaches were generally satisfied. He heard no major complaints during film critiques. "He was poised and professional today," Coughlin said after the Redskins game. "He wanted to play well. He was physical and involved." But the media weren't happy. LaVar's performances looked dull to them. Here was another guy who seemed like he didn't care all that much.

"I would never ask anyone to take exactly what I say and run with it," Arrington said. "I mean it. I would never say, 'Write this about me or I'll never talk to you again,' because that's not fair. That's not life. They have to include their take, their part. I understand. I get it. But can't I have a little part, too? There's a picture being painted here, and it's supposed to be a picture of me. Can't I hold the brush for just a second? Please let me put a little paint on the damn canvas, so that this stroke here, that stroke there, are *my* strokes. They may not completely coincide with what's being written or what's being said, but there'll at least be touches of what I consider to be the truth. Most often, isn't the story already written by the time they come to you? Let's be straight here. Don't they just need a quote or two to fit into the second paragraph and the fifth? But I go on talking to them, and I'll tell you why. Because I figure that even if the publisher and the editor say this is the story they want, at the end of the day maybe I can raise the individual reporter's consciousness level just a little. Just one brushstroke. For what it's worth, that means something to me. I'll still get ripped, but I'll have had a small impact."

If LaVar were Dorian Gray, what would the picture in his attic look like?

"Like a veteran in his seventh year," he said, "who's finally learning how to play football and may not be allowed to do it much longer."

Sometimes, he said, looking around the New York locker room, he felt homesick for the Nittany Lions. "As always, there I was, trying to stand out; and there Joe Paterno was, trying to keep anything from standing out." The plainest white-and-blue uniforms. Bare legs. No names on the jerseys. If he could, Joe probably would take the numbers off as well. "Yeah, I bet he would," Arrington said. "I'll tell you, though, I learned so many lessons from that man. Of course I didn't know I was learning them at the time. How to win, how to lose, how to draw, how to love, how to hate. Do things the Penn State way, they told you, and your life will be a lot smoother. You want to hear something hysterical? I'm just starting to do things the Penn State way."

A few other players, including Manning, came into the room then and turned on the TV. So Arrington got up and, slapping his flip-flops against the floor on the downbeat, moseyed back to his locker. "No, I've never lived up to the hype," he finished as he had started. "Maybe that's why I can relate to Eli. He hasn't lived up to his hype yet, either. God, who could?"

Back in the front office, Accorsi said, "I want to show you something. My heart skipped a beat when I saw this." Ernie led the way to a couple of musty file cabinets tucked into an alcove around the corner from the draft room. "They're Wellington Mara's," he said. They were full of old college football magazines. Like *Football Quarterly,* autumn 1949, 25 cents. Charlie Justice of North Carolina was on the cover in a leather helmet. *Football Annual,* 1948, Chuck Bednarik snapping the ball between his legs for Penn. "This is Wellington's," Ernie said. "This is how he scouted in the old days. Look at the names he has underlined, only the right ones. Ernie Stautner, Ed Songin, Art Spinney. Almost every underlined name is someone who wasn't the biggest college star but ended up a solid player in the league."

There was a time when NFL teams didn't have so many resources, so many scouts. Oh, hell, let's just take Jim Brown.

10

RONNIE

I'M EXHAUSTED, I'M HURTING, I've got ice bags all over me, I love this game," said the old Giants tight end Mark Bavaro a few years ago, speaking pretty much for everyone.

Early Monday morning, even after night games, the players drag themselves back to the stadium and into the training room like casualties of war in a *M*A*S*H* episode. The relatively uninjured lift weights. The others line up for their various treatments or to schedule MRIs. They appear even huger up close, and yet more human. Many of them are the size of British telephone booths with heads like microwave ovens or nineteen-inch color television sets. To explain this race of super-people whose program weights are underestimated at 302, 303, 306, 308, 310, 315, 317, 318, 319, 327, and 335 pounds, "strength" coaches point to modern training apparatuses like the Nautilus machines already clanking and humming before 7:00 A.M. But not even someone with the imagination of Jules Verne could stand beside an NFL offensive lineman and believe this is a product of normal exercise and natural nutrition.

In an area adjacent to the Giants' locker room, stainless-steel heat tubs were boiling and blue-padded examination tables were bustling. Win or lose, pro football players never sleep too long or too well on Sunday nights. "No, no, they can't," said Ronnie Barnes, the Giants' head trainer. "Adrenaline doesn't just stop flowing on a dime, you know. It's amazing, but no matter how early in the morning we arrive here on Mondays, there are always players waiting for us."

"Us" included assistant Johnny Johnson, a Giants trainer for more

than half a century, who back in the 1950s taped the ankles of old number 42, the Mississippi quarterback Charlie Conerly. Upon hearing that,
another Ole Miss quarterback, Eli Manning, politely asked Johnson if,
just one time, he wouldn't mind taping Eli's ankles the same way. "I considered that to be a real good sign," said the old trainer with the world's
most creased and kindest face.

"Johnny will be ninety this year," Barnes said. "He still loves it. He
still cares. I think if his wife had not died he would have retired, but I'm
glad he's still here. He's our continuity. That's a word I've always associated with the Giants. It's kind of typical of this organization to care
about continuity."

Pro football players start to recover from the games the second they
emerge out of the steam cloud of the locker room into the damp cata-
combs of the stadium where their families are standing in wait wearing
their Sunday best. The youngest children are so innocent of injuries and
losses that their fathers just have to smile again, to laugh, and even to
sing. "I don't think that's phony, either," Barnes said. "It's a way for them
to kind of put all of the bad stuff out of their mind, temporarily. But
when they walk into this building the next morning, the pain comes
back, and the memories, too. The penalties they were called for, the
passes they could have caught, the runs that didn't go quite like they'd
hoped they would. Mental well-being is a very big concern of this job.
Plain, simple encouragement. On a regular basis, we have to pick them
up and get them going again. We do it in a lot of different ways. If they
want to talk about the game and talk about themselves, we do that. If
they want to talk about absolutely anything other than football, we can
do that, too. We do that frequently."

Many NFL teams, as Ernie had said, tried employing psychologists
or psychiatrists for a while. But most of the shrinks turned out to be
creeps. "They're outsiders; they're not insiders," Barnes said, "and they
don't work very well in this setting. The players have a sense that they're
snooping. Reading minds, collecting information, and not necessarily
for the players' benefit, either. For management. You have to develop a

trust with these guys to treat them. If you have their confidence, you can help them in a good many ways. Ernie sometimes asks me about conversations I have with the players, but he knows I'm only going to tell him so much. What he's really asking is: what kind of person do I think this player is? Of course, the cover doesn't always show you what's inside, what a player is struggling with. It may be two brothers in the penitentiary, or a mother who's recovering from a crack addiction. These are human beings, and though they're not adolescents, they're still learning how to be adults. From the cradle until here, they've been taken care of. Someone made sure they got to class. Now they have a real job. They're employees. And sometimes their supervisors don't say very kind things. The 'renewal contract' is the one that teaches the players this is a business, and they actually express that. 'I know it's a business, but . . .' What happened to that game they used to play?"

They are, as anyone can see, the most tattooed body of men this side of D block or the merchant marine. Written across one muscular back, in perfect block letters, was the philosophy "Everything happens for a reason." These elaborate etchings (Shockey's right arm might have been co-designed by John James Audubon and George M. Cohan) don't necessarily say anything about class or culture. When Dartmouth graduate Reggie Williams was serving both as a linebacker and as a city councilman in Cincinnati, he sported a musical tattoo on one bulging forearm. "It's a crescendo," Williams told me once. "Don't you have to have a certain rhythm in your life?"

Giants players often confide in Barnes, even about their contracts. They ask him how they're doing, too. He isn't always sure what to say. But they probably already know that answer. "I'm a medical guy," Barnes said, "so for me to tell Ernie 'I don't think this guy is going to be very good' wouldn't be appropriate. I wouldn't do it. Maybe the hardest part of this whole job is how much you know. You know what the coach thinks about a guy, what the general manager thinks about him, what the other players think about him. And then you have the one-to-one relationship with him. All these things are spinning around in the back of your head when a player is looking you in the eye and asking you, 'How do you think I'm doing?' 'What do you think my chances of coming back here next year are?' 'Do you think I'll get a contract extension?'

"I've stopped saying to myself, 'You shouldn't tie yourself emotionally to every single player,' because you really have no choice. They all get injured and you can't help but feel something. When they do have to leave, whether they retire, get cut, or leave by injury, every one of these guys takes a little piece of you with him and takes something away from you forever."

Barnes was born in Rocky Mount, North Carolina, and grew up loving all of the games that he was too slight to play. Because his father was a Baptist minister, Ronnie didn't see much professional football. Sundays were spent in church. By kickoff time, one o'clock, his father was just hitting his sermonic stride. Reverend Barnes could talk. Not so much a fire-and-brimstoner, he was more of a teacher. "His congregation appreciated that," Ronnie said.

Nineteen sixties integration, something North Carolina called "Freedom of Choice," delivered Barnes and ten or eleven other black children all the way across town into the midst of some twelve hundred white classmates at Charles L. Coon (swear to God) Junior High School. Barnes tried out for the basketball team but ended up the equipment manager, a first-aider, an adhesive taper, and a medic, one with a valuable sense of when to call the real doctor. Finishing high school in 1970, he majored in sports medicine at East Carolina University and pursued anatomy, physiology, kinesiology, and all of the body sciences to a master's degree at Michigan State. Ronnie studied compassion, however, under Wellington Mara.

A football owner who wouldn't ride in a limousine, Mara died on October 25, 2005, at eighty-nine, but remained a presence on the team. He was the conscience of the New York Giants. Everyone in the front office was still striving to meet his standard. At every turn, they asked themselves, "What would Wellington say? What would he do?" Barnes, maybe more than any of the others, had the answer. "He knew right from wrong," Ronnie said, "and he insisted on doing right."

Most of Mara's senior adult life, he was in relatively good health. But he had an octogenarian's typical list of maladies and took blood-thinning medication. "Coumadin," Barnes said. "Mr. Mara didn't like going to doctors, so I sort of became his physician. He'd drop down here to have his blood pressure checked or to have me look at something." Ronnie was the one who found the inflammation in Mara's lymph node. He was the first person to feel a stab of dread.

"I was scared," Barnes said. "He was planning to see a general surgeon, but I talked him into going to Memorial Sloan-Kettering. It's the best New York has to offer and probably the world. After his surgery, I spent the night with Mr. Mara in his hospital room. There was a couch there. That summer while we were in training camp, he recuperated at home. For the first two or three weeks back from camp, I didn't go to practice. He'd come down here. There were some skin issues, and I was helping him with those, and then we did some rehabilitation. He was convinced that if he could just get his arm back up he'd be all right. He was a hell of a competitor."

But he was growing weaker by the visit. "At first he started to hold on to the walls," Ronnie said, "then he would hold on to me, and finally on a Saturday morning I got a call saying, 'Dad doesn't want to come in today for rehab; he can't get out of bed.' 'He's got to go to the hospital,' I said. They called me back to tell me, 'He doesn't want to go; he wants to stay here.' But they put me on the phone with him, and I talked him into it. That's when I started staying with him every night on the couch."

For many days, Barnes left his players to the care of the assistants, concentrating on Wellington. At one point, Ronnie felt derelict enough in his duties to call Coach Coughlin and apologize for running out on the team. "'I've abandoned you,' I said, getting a little emotional. There was a pause on the line. Tom told me in a low, cracking voice, 'You're doing God's work.'" The cover doesn't always show you what's inside. "My first year," Coughlin said, "there was one guy in the locker room every Sunday. He stood up against the wall, never said a word. He was just there. The players saw him. Wellington.

"I get hired, we get off to a pretty good start, but then we begin losing ball games. Little notes of encouragement start coming from Wellington. He'd stick his head in my office and say, 'I agreed with what you did there, we're thinking the same way,' little things like that. As much as this business puts you on an island and makes you feel like you're all alone, you were never alone if you worked for Wellington Mara."

Ronnie said, "In the hospital Mr. Mara and I talked about everything, about his family and how much he loved them, everything but football. One night he lost his rosary in the bedding. Just couldn't find it. We had this handoff routine we had silently worked on. If he got up in the middle of the night to go to the bathroom, he'd hold out his hand with the rosary and I'd take it. As soon as he was back in bed and had his pillows situated, he'd reach out again and I'd wind the beads around his fingers, and off he'd go to sleep." Cardinal Edward Egan replaced the lost rosary, and Mara graciously pretended that the substitute was just as good as the starter. There were bunches of rosaries tangled up in a drawer. "But we were both so glad when a nurse found the real one," said Barnes, the Southern Baptist.

New York was having a nice season, but Mara seldom asked about the Giants. "He had so much faith in John Mara," Barnes said. "He wouldn't say, 'I trust John to run the team. He always used both names, 'John Mara,' in what I took to be a sign of respect. 'Ask John Mara.' 'John Mara can handle it.' Mostly we talked about everything but the Giants.

"He asked about the night baseball games that he would start to watch on TV but in the middle of which he would inevitably fall asleep. 'How did the Yankees do, Ronnie?'" For some reason Mara became seriously wrapped up in the fortunes of the Cleveland Indians. In a panic, Barnes called Accorsi to ask, "Quick, what do I need to know about the Cleveland Indians?" They were hot. Ernie filled him in on the broadest details, and every day after that Accorsi sent Barnes the updated standings and statistics by BlackBerry, as well as the scuttlebutt surrounding the pennant race. Ronnie said, "My job was to straighten out the bed, elevate his legs, take his temperature and blood pressure, guard his rosary, and keep him abreast of the Cleveland Indians."

Eventually they talked about things much deeper than baseball. Barnes said, "There was an evening . . . you know, you lose your dignity when you're in the hospital. You're wearing hospital gowns, nurses are coming in and out. There was a particular moment when he said to me, 'Ronnie, I'm terribly embarrassed,' and I said, 'Mr. Mara, I'm here so you won't be embarrassed.' These are tough things for me to talk about because I lived them, but as much as I'm avoiding telling you some of the details, I remember every detail. I never thought that I could . . . I don't have children, never had children, and I've been told that once you've had children, the slightest noise in the night wakes you up. Now I understand. I wasn't sitting vigil with my eyes wide open. I had made my little bed and fallen asleep. Yet in the smallest voice he'd call out 'Ronnie?' and I'd be awake. Every hour almost on the hour he'd open his eyes and talk for a few minutes, and I wasn't tired the next day, either.

"Two or three days before Wellington died, in the middle of the night, he asked me for some water. So I got some cold water with ice. He drank the whole glass. I said, 'Would you like another?' 'Yes, I'd like another.' And then another. So having held on to this cold glass for so long—it was freezing—he began to shake. I went and got a bath towel, ran some hot water over it, and wrapped it around his hands to warm him. He looked straight at me. I think he was afraid. You know, Mr. Mara never said as much to you in spoken words as he did with just his eyes."

On their thirtieth day together in the hospital, Mara woke up and said, "Ronnie, I need you to tell me about my case." "I tried to think of something compassionate to say," Barnes said. "I didn't want to say, 'Mr. Mara, you're dying.' But it came out pretty straight. 'There's an awful lot of fluid around your lungs,' I told him, 'and it's apparent that the cancer has spread. Mr. Mara, the situation is quite grave. And I think at this point, given your great faith, you should put your hands in the hands of the Lord, and he'll take care of the rest. He'll lead you home.' Where

that came from, I don't know. Probably somewhere in my Baptist background, maybe from my father. He said, 'Ronnie, I want to go home.'
This was four o'clock in the morning. 'I'll have you home,' I whispered,
'before sundown tomorrow.' A few days later, he died at home."

Forty-eight hours after the funeral, granddaughter Kate Mara led
the forty grandchildren, eleven sons and daughters, and 78,630 Giant
Stadium spectators in a rendition of "The Star-Spangled Banner" that
should have thrown a chill into the Washington Redskins because it was
apparent in every note that this wasn't a normal Sunday. Coming off a
three-point loss to Dallas and a one-point victory over Denver, the Giants
beat the Redskins, 36–0, in what amounted to a perfect game. In the
locker room afterward, Eli presented the ball to John Mara.

"You can't know anything about the New York Giants," Barnes said,
sitting behind his desk, "unless you know something about Wellington
Mara." On a bookshelf behind the trainer sat a framed photograph of
the two of them. "He gave it to me two Christmases ago, but I didn't read
the inscription then. I don't know why. I just didn't notice it until after
he was gone. I remember the day exactly. I had this X-ray of someone's
swollen knee or shoulder or ankle and I was trying to show it to the
coaches. Well, you know coaches. They don't want to see it, because if
they see it, they'll have to consider it. As soon as you start to hold up an
X-ray to the light, coaches scatter. 'I don't want to look at that,' they say.
They absolutely don't want to see it."

Back in his own office, still holding the X-ray, Barnes thought of
Wellington Mara. "I imagined him storming in here and saying, 'Ronnie, I don't want you to play so-and-so until he's a hundred percent
healthy, and I want you to call his wife right this minute. And I want you
to call his mom and dad, too. No, never mind, I'll call his parents.'"
Barnes looked away from the X-ray and up at the picture on his shelf,
reading the inscription for the first time: "With appreciation and affec-
tion. Your patient, Well."

Then Ronnie called Ernie and told him that the player in question
was definitely out of Sunday's game.

11

THE CAP

ATLANTA, THE GIANTS' next stop, represented a statistical haunted house. In their four games to date, the Falcons had allowed only one touchdown. On the offensive side, their 234.3-yard rushing average was on pace to break a seventy-year-old NFL record. Of course, the main hobgoblin was scrambling quarterback Michael Vick, who, sure enough, weaved twenty-two yards through the middle of the Giants' line to score the only touchdown in a 7–3 first half. On Atlanta's opening play of the third quarter, compact running back Warrick Dunn went ninety yards for a touchdown, farther than any Falcon had ever gone from scrimmage, causing Shaun O'Hara to say for the Giants, "So there we were, in our old, familiar back-to-the-wall position."

After a false start penalty on first down at the sixteen-yard line, that was about right.

GIANTS
1-15-G11 Eli Manning passes incomplete
2-15-G11 Tiki Barber runs for 29 yards

"Here's where the momentum changed," Barber said later, and Luke Petitgout, his destroyer escort, concurred. Luke said, "It's funny to look back on a running play that doesn't even get you out of your own territory, a play that leads to a punt, but that was the play that changed the whole fabric of the game." Falcons cornerback DeAngelo

Hall said, "Even earlier, it seemed to me that they were outhitting us. But we were leading, so I tried to tell myself, 'You must be mistaken.' But I didn't believe myself. I'm a terrible liar. Then Tiki ripped off that long run to make a first down. From that moment on, I had a bad feeling."

1-10-G40 Manning passes incomplete
2-10-G40 Barber runs for 16
1-10-F44 Brandon Jacobs runs for −1
2-11-F45 Manning passes incomplete
3-11-F45 (shotgun) Manning passes to Tim Carter for 15
1-10-F30 Barber runs for three
2-7-F27   Defensive pass interference
1-2-F2   Jacobs runs for 2 and a touchdown; Jay Feely's
          kick is good
                    Atlanta 14, New York 10

Following a three-and-out Falcons series, an effective punt backed New York up once again.

GIANTS
1-10-G9   Manning passes to Barber for 16
1-10-G25 Barber runs for 9
2-1-G34   Jacobs runs for 5
1-10-G39 Manning passes to Jeremy Shockey for 19
1-10-F42 Jacobs runs for 8
2-2-F34   offsetting penalties
2-2-F34   Jacobs runs for 3
1-10-F31 (shotgun) Manning passes incomplete
2-10-F31 (shotgun) Manning passes to Shockey for 16
1-10-F15 Barber runs for 15 and an apparent touchdown,
          but the play is challenged and reversed; Barber stepped
          out at the 2

1-G-F2 Manning passes to Shockey for 2 and the
   touchdown; Feely's kick is good
New York 17, Atlanta 14

"This is just wrong, man," Jacobs muttered to Barber on the sideline. Brandon was probably the only one in the park mindful that, as much of a workhorse as Tiki had been for the Giants, he had yet to score a touchdown in 2006. "You shouldn't think that way," Barber told him. "I don't."

After a good Feely field goal and a bad Atlanta punt, New York was on the move again.

GIANTS

1-10-G45 Barber runs for 0
2-10-G45 Manning throws to Jim Finn for 6
3-4-F49   (shotgun) Manning passes to Shockey for 10
1-10-F39 Barber runs for 17
1-10-F22 Barber runs for 2
2-8-F20   Jacobs runs for 12
1-G-F8   Barber runs for 0
2-G-F8   Barber runs for 4
3-G-F4   Manning passes to Shockey for 4 and the
   touchdown; Feely's kick is good
New York 27, Atlanta 14

That was the final score. Barber carried twenty-six times for 185 yards, but the most telling numbers in the game, certainly the most satisfying ones to Tom Coughlin, were seven and four. The first was how many times Vick was sacked. The second was how many times he was pillaged, and subsequently fumbled. "Guys like Coughlin," Ernie said, "don't like to trick you as much as they like to punch you in the mouth. They want to beat the hell out of you. This game spoke to the fibers of what he believes. Smash-mouth. Physical. Vick took a tremendous beating, and we ran the ball down their throat with two backs, one of them

[Jacobs] weighing 260 pounds." Brandon accounted for fifty-three inside yards.

"What we do best," Barber said, something he had been saying for most of his career, "is run the ball. You may like two deep passes and a touchdown, but I like grind-it-out, NFC East–style football. First we wore them down, and then we wore them out. For me, this means more than coming back against Philadelphia. That was partly due to the Eagles' mistakes. This time we came back because of our own will. To my way of thinking, this was a lot, lot more satisfying."

"I hate to date myself," Michael Strahan said, "but the way Tiki hides behind an offensive lineman and then all of a sudden breaks out from the back of him into the clear reminds me of Emmitt Smith. That's what Smith did for the Cowboys throughout the nineties." Proving a victory can make a GM slightly light-headed, Accorsi looked at Barber in the locker room and thought he saw Jim Brown. "Maybe that was the last time we watched a running back get better, better, and better," Ernie said, "coming down the home stretch of his career." Brown scored three touchdowns in the Pro Bowl before he retired in costume on the London set of *The Dirty Dozen*. Ernie said, "Tiki has never played stronger, I don't think, than he's playing right now, and he's about to walk away."

At halftime, Coughlin came to Barber with a plea. "We need a boost," Tom said. "We're flat as hell." Maybe that's a key to Tiki because he seemed to grow taller after being consulted. In fact, he appreciated the compliment so much that he passed it on. To several waves of questioners, Barber said, "Don't forget to give the coaching staff some credit. Atlanta has a good defense, but we had a better plan. I'd say, if you boil it down to one thing today, everything went according to the coaches' plan."

Linebacker Brandon Short and defensive end Osi Umenyiora had two sacks apiece on Vick. "You have to be disciplined against him," Short said. "I'm talking about rush lanes and assignments, classroom stuff. You have to stick to your own job and resist the temptation to help somebody else do theirs. It's only human nature to want to make the play yourself. Everybody wants to do that. But you can't, not against guys like Vick. If he has success up the middle, the defensive men containing the outside have to stick to containing the outside. Otherwise, against a team this quick, you're lost. Except for two plays, we were a damned disciplined defense today."

Eli completed the fewest passes he had all year, seventeen; Vick completed the most, fourteen. The fact that Shockey, aching foot and all, caught six of Manning's throws for fifty-five yards and two touchdowns brought a new slogan to the Giants' locker room: "The renegade is back!" Jeremy felt good but was trying hard not to make any news. "My mother heard Troy Aikman say on television that I cry too much when I don't get the ball," he said. "Well, who doesn't want the ball?" One of the reporters asked Shockey, "What did you do to get open on that last touchdown?" He replied unhelpfully, "I got open," whispering aside, "I don't have to give all of my secrets away, do I?"

This was the bye week for the Indianapolis Colts and, on a busman's holiday, Peyton Manning journeyed to the Georgia Dome to observe Eli. "He came to see me last year," Peyton said in the vestibule, "so I owed him one."

What did Peyton notice?

"Ball control," he said. "How long did the Giants hold the ball there for that one stretch?"

Twenty-one of the first twenty-six minutes of the second half.

"There you go," Peyton said. "That's pretty impressive."

"It was Tiki," Eli said. "As soon as Tiki gets rolling, the play-action stuff starts to work. He was the one who was impressive. The game plan was impressive, too." The Giants were 3 and 2.

"Nice going, Field Marshal," Accorsi said to Coughlin, who looked at him quizzically. "Tom had a real good day," Ernie said. "George Young used to call all head coaches 'U-boat commanders,' because they're such natural generals, and they want to have complete control.

" 'Where are your people from?' I asked Coughlin once. He says, 'My father is from County Kerry.' 'So, are you a hundred percent Irish?' 'No, my mother was German.' 'That explains a lot.' Traveling in Ireland last summer, I brought back a rock from County Kerry and presented it to Tom. I said, 'Keep this rock for the season, for luck.' I hope one of us doesn't kill the other with it."

Back in the office, it was time again for reviewing the salary cap situation, a never-ending concern that has to be revisited every few weeks. One of the worksheets read: "Possible roster cuts and corresponding cap savings—Tiki Barber, $4,000,000; Luke Petitgout, $3,210,000; Michael Strahan, $2,271,710; Amani Toomer, $1,750,000; Carlos Emmons, $1,000,000; Fred Robbins, $996,664; Tim Carter, $915,000; R. W. McQuarters, $900,000; Jeff Feagles, $820,000; Bob Whitfield, $753,332; Jason Bell, $610,000; Jim Finn, $560,000; Tim Hasselback, $501,666; Ryan Kuehl, $435,000; Chad Morton, $425,000; Jamaar Taylor, $410,000; Sam Madison, $400,000; Will Demps, $365,000; Ryan Grant, $285,000; LaVar Arrington $100,000."

Other sheets bore titles like "Candidates for Contract Extensions" and "Which Players Should We Allocate to NFL Europe in 2007?"

"In every other sport," Ernie said, "you want the developing players to have somewhere to play during the off-season. In baseball, they're sent to winter leagues in places like Venezuela and Puerto Rico. There are a million lower basketball leagues where a young kid can get off the end of the bench. But in football we generally prefer that they stay with us and work out with the coaches, so that we can develop them ourselves. Europe makes sense for some—it gives a guy a chance to play, a quarterback in particular. While Jared Lorenzen, the hefty lefty, our two-hundred-ninety-seven-pound backup quarterback, would seem a perfect guy to send to Europe, we don't dare send Jared over there because of all the sauerbraten. He'd come back weighing three hundred and fifty pounds. Lorenzen's not going to go over there and eat egg whites, you know." Such were the heavy decisions a GM had to make.

Because this was Accorsi's final season, he had resolved not to trade any draft choices in 2006, to preserve the full allotment of picks for his successor (who, incidentally, he hoped would be player personnel director Jerry Reese). "I'm trying to stay away from any decisions that influence the future more than the present," Ernie said, "because it just isn't fair. For example, Strahan is signed for two more years after this one. 'But,' his agent, Tony Agnew, asked me, 'what about the future?' I told him, 'I don't feel I have the right to make that decision. I'm not going to obligate my successor to do something that maybe he won't want to do.'"

Scott Pioli of the Patriots, considered by some a candidate for Accorsi's job, came back at Ernie several times during the last college draft. "Pioli kept asking me, 'Look, we have some extra choices. I'll give you some choices this year for some choices next year.' I said, 'Scott, I'm surprised you want me to put holes in next year's draft for you.' He didn't laugh at first."

There were a number of GM decisions Ernie purposely wanted to leave dangling. "Like, our field goal kicker, Jay Feely," he said. "I love the guy. He's a great guy. His contract is up after this year. He'll be a free agent then. My recommendation? I wouldn't extend him right now. I know a kicker is hard to find, but sooner or later, and probably sooner, Jay's going to have to win a game. He missed the winning kick three times in Seattle last year, and we lost in overtime. I mean, that really changed our season. We still won the division, but if we had gone to the play-offs as the number one seed—which we would have—there might have been a better aura around us, not to mention an easier path through the play-offs. I'm still feeling a little raw about that. Let's see how Jay does. Let's find out if he has recovered from Seattle."

Looking down the cold list, Accorsi's eyes stopped at receiver Tim Carter, who was probably a lame duck, too. Accorsi had always been Carter's sponsor, and Ernie wouldn't be there in 2007 to protect him anymore. "The coaches call Tim a heartbreaker," he said, "because on one side he has so much talent and on the other he's had so many injuries. You know football coaches—not just here, all football coaches. They blame the players for the injuries. And it's absolutely true that some players won't play hurt. But look at this guy's injuries: broken hip, broken collarbone, torn Achilles tendon, most of them occurring while he was doing something courageous. Kurt Warner, who quarterbacked that aerial circus in St. Louis, told me Carter was the fastest receiver he ever threw a ball to. It's not just Tim's brilliance, either, that makes me stand up for him. It's his makeup. When Carter became a free agent, he could have just walked away. He knew most of the organization was down on him. But he told me, 'You drafted me in the second round, I owe you for that. I want to prove myself *here*.' I tell the coaches, 'Do you want to know what heartbreak is? I'll tell you what heartbreak is. Heartbreak is Sunday night when you leave the stadium and go home and watch that kid catching touchdown passes all across your TV screen.' They might learn about that heartbreak next year."

There is one salary cap fact that everyone in the NFL grasps. As Accorsi said, "To be over it invites a million-dollar-a-day fine." "At the beginning of the cap," former Packers GM Ron Wolf said, "we weren't sure what the league was going to do if you were over. Take money from you? Strip you of players? And if it was players, would they go by alphabetical order or what? Nobody seemed to know. So, just to be on the safe side, in Green Bay we always made sure that we had a lot of players whose names began with letters that came before *F* [for Favre]." "When I became the Giants' GM," Ernie said, "the first thing I was handed was the cap. It was a mess. We were eleven million over, and I had like two weeks to get it down. There are tricks to it, of course. If I sign Strahan and give him a ten-million-dollar signing clause for a five-year contract, I can prorate that at two million a year. But if I trade him, I get hit with the whole ten. So that's the penalty that baseball doesn't have."

Coughlin left Jacksonville in what NFL teams call "cap hell." It wasn't his job, but Tom controlled the football operation, so he basically brought the players in who caused the cap trouble. The GM didn't say no. He has to say no. "Go ask Kevin Abrams for a simple explanation of the cap," Ernie said, "and then come back here and explain it to me."

Abrams said, "I only knew George Young a little bit, but he probably fell under the category of those who grew up in one NFL system, and when a new one came along in 1993, they just didn't want to embrace it. He may have re-signed a few too many of our players to deals that weren't commensurate with what they were going to be able to do for us. And when you have a cap, all of a sudden some of those wrong decisions can end up biting you in the ass. There was always a cash consequence to it, but now there's a functionality consequence as well. So we got in a little trouble with that.

"If you're over the cap, the league will call you in and say, 'You've got until midnight.' I've never been through this, never been in that situation. Of course, you go out of your way not to be in that situation. But the theory is, if you're over the cap, they'll give you X amount of time to get your ducks in a row. Then on the last day they'll say, 'If you can't get under it by midnight, we're just going to start lopping players off your options.' The players will become free agents, and you can try to re-sign them, but so can everyone else. I presume they'd start at your highest-paid guys, not the lowest, because that's going to make the biggest difference. This year the cap is a hundred and two million for your fifty-three-man roster and your practice squad and whatever injuries you might incur during training camp. Next year it's a hundred and nine million. And it's a firm cap, though not as firm as hockey's, which is absolutely firm. Ours can be considered over a number of years. The most simplistic way to say it would be that if you spend a hundred and five million this year, then that three-million overage is going to count against your cap next year and the years going forward, so whatever you spend over this year, it means you're going to have a cap deficit in future years, depending on how many years down the road you decide to allocate money that you're spending now. Sooner or later, you'll have less to spend than the rest of the league. Of course everyone's kiting to some extent. It's like credit card spending. But you don't want to push too much of the money off into the future, because if it doesn't get you this year, it's going to get you eventually.

"As for the million a day, it depends on what you've done that's in violation of the rules. For something very minor, it could be a five-thousand-dollar slap on the wrist. If it's something really egregious, they could take draft picks away and fine you even more than the million. But once you get into it, the cap isn't really all that complicated, though I have to admit we've had a number of young people in the office who have thrown up their hands and said, 'Let me out of here.' I've always wanted to have a second person who could read contracts and proof-read and double-check my interpretation of the cap rules. So whenever anyone expresses the slightest interest, I get them all the guidebooks and maybe even schedule them for a labor seminar so they can listen to all the issues and get into things like insurance and arbitration and grievances and all that. But, invariably, the next thing I know, all of the books and charts are back on my desk. 'I don't want to talk about it any-more,' they say. I guess it is a little dull, but it's a part of the game.

"Take a team like Washington. They had a big off-season this year. I think they gave five players ten-million-dollar signing bonuses, and they already had a lot of players on their books for significant amounts of money. They're under the hundred-and-two-million salary cap, but I've got to believe they spent closer to a hundred thirty-five million this year. Because they've done that, they're going to have years coming up where the spending limit is a hundred nine million or a hundred sixteen, and a good bit of their money won't be there. If you think you're close to winning, or—for whatever reason—your sense of urgency is a little greater one year than it is another, you can do a lot of tricks with the money. But it's going to catch up to you eventually. It's going to happen. You'll end up in cap hell."

"Any questions?" Ernie said.

Though he was always more comfortable with a stopwatch in his hand than a calculator, Accorsi eased his way into the money part during those prehistoric days in Baltimore and Cleveland. "What I did, first of all," he said, "was know this: as long as you say no, you're safe. Number two, and I started this—a lot of others copied it—get a ladder in your mind. I put the players on rungs in my head, and if I had you tenth or eleventh, that's how you were going to be paid. The biggest problem I ever had with the ladder was in Cleveland, when both Kevin Mack and Earnest Byner were gaining a thousand yards apiece. I didn't want them coming up for renewals the same year and turning into an entry like Don Drysdale and Sandy Koufax. So I staggered them with two-year contracts. One jumped ahead one year, the other jumped ahead the next. 'Look, Mack is making more than you now,' I'd tell Earnest, 'but you're going to be making more than Mack soon.' It was the only way I could think to do it, and for some reason they let me. Maybe it was just a simpler time. Mack was actually better, but just a little. I loved both of those kids. That was a tough balancing act, but I got through it. The ladder kept me alive."

To review, the two things to remember: the fine of $1 million a day, and as long as you say no, you're safe.

12

PARCELLS

HAD CELL PHONES BEEN as omnipresent in January 1996 as they are today, Tom Coughlin's predecessor, Jim Fassel, never would have been the head coach of the New York Giants. Bill Parcells, whose eight-year run between 1983 and 1990 delivered two Super Bowl championships to the Giants, would have been brought back from New England for a second go-round in New York if only the Maras and the Tisches had been able to reach George Young in time. They missed him by approximately two minutes.

"There was no question that Dan Reeves was out," Ernie said. "'I think I should go,' he told everybody in a meeting, and none of us disagreed. 'But you're going to pay me, right?'

"Bob Tisch said, 'You're quitting. We're not firing you.'

"'Well, I think I still should get paid.'

"After they went back and forth like that for a while, Reeves said, 'Pam and I need to go home and pray over this.'"

Rumblings were coming from New England that Parcells was of a mind to return to New York. Of course, Parcells was a man who changed his mind rather often. Accorsi said, "Bill was telling everybody, including Will McDonough of the *Boston Globe*—they were close friends—that by some technicality in his contract he was free to leave the Patriots and return to the Giants if he wanted to. I happened to know the option was [New England owner] Bob Kraft's, not his. The Giants would have had to pay a very steep and severe compensation, two number ones and more, whatever it was. They started to look into it but hadn't yet figured out what the compensation would be. They were still trying to decide whether to offer him the job. He had already told the Maras he wanted it."

Did Wellington have an especially warm feeling for Parcells?

"He didn't feel warm about him," Ernie said, "but he wanted him back."

On hiring a general manager or a head coach, both halves of the ownership—Mara and Tisch—had to vote unanimously, 2–0. "George had to get both owners to agree," Ernie said. "At first, Joel Goldberg, who was the psychologist, talked Bob Tisch out of Parcells. And Young was trying to sell Fassel to Wellington. Jim had been an assistant here and George sort of liked him, though we had drawn up a list of potential Reeves replacements the year before—Lindy Infante, Joe Bugel—and Fassel wasn't even on it. George had decided Fassel was the man who could help him prove you could win with Dave Brown as quarterback, a hopeless cause if there ever was one."

Young had developed an undisguised dislike of Parcells, which was odd because, as Accorsi said, "they saw the game the same way, and everybody respected Bill as a coach. One day George quietly calls me into his office, asks Janice to get his moneyman on the line, and shuts the door. George's accountant was a former quarterback of his at City College High School in Baltimore. 'Bob,' Young says on the phone, 'do I have enough money to retire?' Well, I almost fall off the chair. George had his First Holy Communion money in an envelope, okay? He was making a million dollars a year for about six years. So he hangs up and says, 'Look, I'm going down to Wellington right now and tell him that if they hire Parcells, I quit. I'm sure you'll be my replacement.' I thought to myself, 'Yeah, I'll have the title of GM, but if Parcells is the head coach, will I really have the job?'" Maybe that's how Young felt as well.

Before George could issue his ultimatum, Wellington informed him that Tisch had put the kibosh on Parcells. "George said to Wellington, 'In that case, Fassel is really the only guy out there.' He wanted permission to offer the job to Jim right away. Reluctantly, Well said, 'Okay, go ahead.' Fassel was waiting nearby, at the Sheraton Meadowlands. As

John Mara says, 'That's the only time in George's life, including when he was twelve years old, that he ran a four-point-three forty.' But he isn't gone even two minutes when Bob Tisch calls to say he has changed his mind. 'If you want to hire Parcells,' he says, 'go ahead.' So John quickly calls our switchboard up front. 'Did George Young leave the building yet?' 'Yes, he just ran out.' They phone the hotel as quickly as they can, trying to cut him off. But they can't find him.

"Eventually they call Fassel's room, asking for George, and he comes on the line. Either John or Wellington, I can't remember which one—both of them, essentially—asks George, 'Have you offered the job to Fassel yet?' George says, 'Yes, I have.' 'Has he accepted it?' 'Yes.' 'Okay.' The Maras being the Maras, once the offer had been extended on their behalf, they weren't about to take it back."

By the way, this wouldn't be the last time it was whispered around the Giants' front office that Parcells was interested in returning to New York.

That 3-and-3 start for which Accorsi had only hoped remarkably became 4 and 2 when the Giants beat Parcells and his Cowboys, 36–22, on a Monday night in Dallas. "I'm ashamed to put out a team that plays like that," Parcells said immediately afterward. "They outplayed us. They out-everythinged us. They outcoached us. I apologize to all of the people who came out to watch that." In one of the papers, his monologue was punched up slightly to read more dramatically at the finish, "I apologize to the people of America." In either case, he was sorry.

Not three minutes into the game, Eli Manning threw a fifty-yard touchdown pass to Plaxico Burress, but the second Giant score and the events that followed were more lasting.

"Watch me this week," I heard LaVar Arrington whisper to Ernie in the lunch line a few days earlier. "This is the week I'm going to make you glad you brought me here."

With four minutes to go in the first quarter, Jeff Feagles punted the Cowboys all the way back to their own one-yard line, where on second down Arrington found a crack in the Dallas line and flashed through it to tackle thirty-four-year-old quarterback Drew Bledsoe for LaVar's first sack of the season and the only safety of his pro career. One series later, at about midfield, Bledsoe handed the football to running back Julius Jones, who took a step and a half, slid to a stop, and flipped the ball back to Drew. The flea-flicker fooled the Giants so thoroughly that Bledsoe had his choice of two open receivers, Terrell Owens on one side or Terry Glenn on the other. But as Bledsoe released the pass, Arrington's right arm got in the way, deflecting it incomplete. LaVar was having the game he promised.

Then, halfway through the second quarter, on the first down of a ten-play, eighty-yard Dallas drive, Arrington was clipped by a phantom blocker nowhere near the ball. The play was a simple dive off-tackle by Jones for three yards. "I thought somebody hit me from behind," LaVar said. "I was fuming. But then I looked around and nobody was there. I reached for my left leg. I said, 'Okay, if it's your knee again, you're fin-ished.'" But it wasn't his knee, it was his Achilles tendon, which had rup-tured. He went off the field on a cart and home that night on crutches. Arrington's season was over, obviously; his Giants career, too, it turned out; maybe his whole football life.

With New York leading, 12–7, the most fateful series of Bledsoe's fourteen NFL seasons closed the first half. Thanks to a Barber fumble, once commonplace but now a rare event, Dallas was at the Giants' fifteen-yard line and poised to take the lead. Tiki was knocked completely uncon-scious. When he awoke, he was able to remember both his own name and the exact reason why he was retiring. Hall of Fame Cowboys receiver Michael Irvin had a less polite word for it on ESPN. Pointing to the tim-ing of Barber's declaration, with most of a season yet to go, Irvin said, "To me, that's not retiring. That's quitting."

COWBOYS

1-10-G14 (shotgun) Jones runs for 5
2-5-G9   Jones runs for 4
3-1-G5   Marion Barber runs for 1

1-G-G4   Barber runs for O

2-G-G4   Bledsoe's pass intended for Glenn is intercepted
  by Sam Madison

The play was called for the right side; Bledsoe threw to the left, ane-mically. "Too much improvising," Parcells grumped. "Too many mis-takes." He switched in the third quarter (in fact, forever) to a backup quarterback covered in cobwebs, Tony Romo of Eastern Illinois Univer-sity, who in four years as a Cowboys employee had thrown exactly two passes. The third one of his pro career was deflected by Michael Strahan and intercepted by Antonio Pierce at the Dallas twenty, brought ahead to the fourteen.

GIANTS

1-10-C14 Barber runs for 1

2-9-C13   Manning passes incomplete

3-9-C13   (shotgun) Manning passes to Jeremy Shockey
  for 13 and the touchdown; Jay Feely's kick is good

New York 19, Dallas 7

Romo's second interception was caught by Fred Robbins. The third one, thrown from the Giants' eleven-yard line, Kevin Dockery returned ninety-six yards for a touchdown. But in the weeks ahead, Romo would blossom into George Clooney, and he would have his revenge against the Giants. Parcells, who looked historically spent on the sideline that Monday night, would pep up for a while.

"What's that, our third win on the road?" Coughlin asked rhetori-cally in the locker room. The coach appreciated Barber's 114 yards but seemed even more pleased with the contribution of Strahan. "Michael was very spry, very active," Tom said. "He pretty much stopped the run on his own in the first half." Ernie said, "That's the thing about Stray. He's famous for rushing the passer, but of all the great sack men in the history of the league, he may be the best one against the run."

"Two weeks ago, we were a bad team," Strahan said. "We were done, we were hopeless, nobody gave us a shot. But now we've beaten the Redskins at home and the Eagles and Cowboys on the road. Who's the class of the NFC East?"

Amani Toomer, who caught three of the twelve passes Manning completed, answered in a much softer voice. "We are," he said, "when healthy." It was a smart comment from maybe the smartest man on the team, who noticed that Arrington wasn't the only player who had to be helped off. Osi Umenyiora, Sam Madison, and Justin Tuck were injured, too. It was just the overture.

On the road, with no tunnel to skulk in, Accorsi watched from the second row of the press box, sitting alongside John Mara, as both of them tried not to slam their fists on the table too often. Ernie saw the games as a general manager would, flashing back to the first time he scouted a player or to the day he drafted him. When Jim Finn, for instance, made a good block that helped Barber, or ran for a short gain himself, Accorsi was almost the only one in the stadium who noticed Jim.

"Finn's just one of those team guys," Ernie said. "He still plays the position that they've basically eliminated in this league: fullback. Burton Catholic High School and Penn. It's funny, I saw him play against Fordham his senior year. Freezing cold day. I took the Saturday off—I'd been traveling so much. 'Oh, hell,' I thought, 'I'll go see Penn-Fordham. It's nearby. You can't not see a college football game on a Saturday.' Finn played tailback that day, but he looked like a fullback to me. He ended up a cap casualty in Indianapolis and now he's seven years in the league. Not a devastating blocker, but a good clutch player. If he's unaccounted for, he'll catch the ball and get as much as he can, every inch of that. Just a great guy to have on a team."

With five tackles, corner Corey Webster had an unusually strong game against the Cowboys. "Second-year guy, LSU," Ernie said. "Was on his way to being a first-round pick when he hurt his foot and played through it. After his stock dropped a little, I considered him the steal of the second round. But he hasn't developed as quickly as we thought. He hasn't gotten there yet. He still may. The talent is there."

Running back Brandon Jacobs: "If we would just spread the field with this big guy [six-four, 264]," Accorsi said, "we could ride him forever. In my opinion, he could be a truly great player. He's got a chance. Brandon's an absolute throwback to the days of Marion Motley in Cleveland. Maybe Rick Casares in Chicago is a better example. Jacobs is big and strong, but he's not a fullback. He's a halfback. I like a two-back offense, you know. I hate the single back even more than I do the I formation. I love the old split formations. The symmetry of them."

Safety Gibril Wilson: "Until he got hurt, he was the best blitzing safety in the league. A little safety—Gibril probably doesn't weigh two hundred pounds—is going to pay a price. Fifth-rounder three years ago. He told Ronnie Barnes, 'Mr. Accorsi never talks to me.' Ronnie said, 'Ernie probably isn't exactly certain who you are in the clubhouse. But he sure as hell knows who you are when you have your uniform on.' So I went around to say hello a couple of days ago. We bet a buck on the Tennessee game. He's a Volunteer. Gibril and Eli played against each other for four years, so now they're rookies together here, and in the very first team drill, Wilson makes a diving interception. 'That's one, Manning,' he whispers to Eli when they're together later on the sideline. Eli laughs. Great kid, Gibril. All football player. Only the injuries have kept him from coming into his own."

Kick returner Chad Morton: "He hasn't done much this year. Hasn't been as explosive. But I like him. He's a competitor. I just wish he'd start making a few big plays."

Safety James Butler: "Great nose for the ball. Great ball skills. Smart as hell. But it was touch and go this off-season, because he suffered a kidney injury and it was questionable whether he should play anymore. That scared everybody a little bit. But it's regenerated. I think he's okay. He's easing back in."

Safety Will Demps: "We used to have Brent Alexander here, who couldn't run anymore at the end but was still smart. We retired him for Demps, but Will has not had a good year. The first season coming off a knee is often shaky. But players develop. You have to have patience for that. I'm an impatient man who's patient with athletes."

Linebacker Gerris Wilkinson: "He's got some talent. They haven't discovered it yet."

Linebacker Carlos Emmons: "At the end of the trail. Very proud, very regal, athlete. He's been hurt a lot, but he's an NFL professional and really helps just being on your team, even if he's not contributing that much."

Linebacker Chase Blackburn: "Great young man, special teams. Suffered a dangerous injury last year, neck. He's just one of those terrific kids. Probably underestimated his whole life. Good special-teamer. Can run a little bit."

Linebacker Antonio Pierce: "Well, I don't even know how to describe him. He's almost as good a leader as I've ever been around in football. He's not Unitas, but he's just as understated. We don't get Arrington without Pierce. We don't get Pierce without Jessie Armstead, the jilted lover. It's the legacy of this organization. Armstead leaves here after the oh-one season, mad. But he calls Pierce when Antonio's a free agent, and tells him, 'If you have a chance to sign with the Giants, do it.' Antonio was in an airport at the time, on his way to Minnesota. Brandon Short called Arrington, too, even though that meant Short might be LaVar's backup. That's the legacy of this organization."

Center Shaun O'Hara: "He's just one of those guys you're always going to remember in your career. Hurt a lot. Plays hurt. A lunch-pail guy. Tough as anybody. Brunswick guy. Rutgers. Loves it here. I hope his agent lets him stay."

Cornerback Frank Walker: "He's not just in the doghouse here. He's got a suite of doghouses here. Not with me. I think he's a delightful character. But he can't stay out of trouble with the coaching staff. They're constantly wanting me to get rid of him, but I won't do it. He's a corner who can run, and they're not easy to find. I talked to him before the season. I said, 'Frank, can you *please* keep your mouth shut and stay out of trouble with the coaches?' Because he just rubs them the wrong way. I saved him about three times. 'Frank's reverting,' Coughlin will say. But then I check it out and the players still love him. He's a character. He's a wacko. He's a great kid."

To someone not in the racket, it sounds like one long list of great, injured kids.

"I have faults and weaknesses," Accorsi said, "probably more than most. But relating to young athletes is not one of my problems. I don't listen to the same music they listen to. I don't enjoy the same movies. We don't share the same hobbies. But I have a good relationship with these kids. I like them. I admire them. Even at sixty-five, a GM has to remember being young. Conspirators will come along, and I don't like conspirators any more than Tom does. But I find a lot more good teammates than conspirators. That's Jerry West's measurement, about as good a single barometer as a GM can have. 'Is he a good teammate?' West has always asked."

Whether in the tunnel or the press box, that's what Accorsi looked for when he watched the games: good teammates.

13

OFF THE STREET

AT SOME BIG MOMENT, maybe in a championship game, a player with an unfamiliar name will make a tackle or an interception and be identified on television as a loan officer at Wachovia Bank who, just a day or two before, was picked up off the street. "Off the street" is a phrase that directors of pro personnel, like the Giants' Dave Gettleman, use to describe replacement parts that come and go almost daily, all season long, through a revolving door that never stops spinning. But it's a misleadingly romantic label. Virtually all of these dreamers were on NFL rosters at one time. Without exception they are former football majors at some renowned cradle of learning still nursing an old college ambition on a loading dock or in a convenience store.

With Tom Coughlin looking on despairingly, his assistant coaches conducted the tryouts in the bubble by the practice field. Gettleman, who rounded up these unusual suspects, stood off to the side with his arms folded, looking exactly like both the prep coach and the small-college offensive lineman he once was. "If you were ever a high school football coach," George Young used to say, "more than a little part of you stays a high school football coach." Even twenty-five years removed from the sideline at Spackenkill High School in Poughkeepsie, New York, Gettleman still wore a figurative whistle around his muscular neck. He said, "I had this one kid"—they all had this one kid—"at Spackenkill, which was a small school of about six hundred and fifty ninth, tenth, and eleventh graders. Later, at a bigger school, Kingston High, I coached all kinds of kids with Division One potential, and a few of them won scholarships—full boats—to colleges large and small. But only this one kid at Spackenkill, a running back named Barry Lewis. Six foot two. About two hundred thirty, two hundred thirty-five pounds. Wonderful family. His father's name was Eli. Blue-collar guy. Black guy. Real quality guy. He worked on the docks."

After Barry's sophomore season, Gettleman visited the Lewis home and laid it out for the family. "Barry has legitimate ability," he told them. "If he applies himself, he has a real shot at a free education." Turning to Barry, he said, "But you can't just *be* in school, you have to *do* school." And to everyone's surprise, Gettleman said, "he did do school. Not great, but much, much better. Good enough." Two years later, Syracuse University came calling.

As Gettleman said, "The assistant coach recruiting our area showed up in my office looking about as harried as anyone I've ever seen, frustrated about something, maybe just exhausted. I guess their dance card was virtually filled. Probably he had just lost a much better recruit somewhere else. But he was ready to bring Barry to the Syracuse campus. Then, if the other black kids gave him a thumbs-up, he'd have his scholarship. I said, 'Terrific, wait right here.' So I went to get Barry out of class. It was an art class, I remember. He was at a potter's wheel. 'C'mon, c'mon, c'mon,' I said, 'wash your hands.' On the walk back to my office, he was very quiet. Barry was a naturally quiet kid anyway. 'Are you okay?' I said. 'I'm okay.' So I introduced the two of them, and the coach asked a couple of friendly questions, but Barry wouldn't answer him. Not even a grunt. The coach said something else. Barry just looked at him. This went on for about five minutes before I said, 'Coach, let me call a time-out here.' Barry and I went into the hallway. 'Please don't be afraid, Barry,' I said. 'You can do this. He's just a guy who happens to be a football coach at Syracuse. He already likes you. He already knows you can play. All he wants to do is converse with you. Are you ready now?' 'Okay, I'm ready.' But, back in the office, he froze up again. It was the saddest thing I have ever seen in my life. Do you know who that coach was? Nick Saban. I ended up getting Barry into North Carolina A and T on financial aid, but he hopped on a bus and came home after three days. I can't even tell you exactly how he died, just that he died very young. 'Barry's dead.' That's all you heard. He had legitimate ability, that kid. I look at all of these kids coming in here to work out for us, and I think to myself, 'Damn.'"

Gettleman was silent for a moment, sitting in his office. But when he switched on his computer to check the day's transactions, he smiled. "Look at this," he said. "Curry Burns is back with the Texans." Burns was a safety who played his college ball at the University of Louisville. "Houston drafted him originally," Dave said. "I think he went to New England from there, then to us, then to Washington, something like that. I know he hooked on with a number of practice squads. He has quite a few stickers on his suitcase. And now he's back where he started, full circle. Good old Curry Burns. He's off the street."

These searches in the bubble for a replacement or two always took Accorsi back to a three-week episode in 1987 when 90 percent of the NFL players had to be replaced. "Just about a year ago," Ernie said, "somebody came up and told me, 'There's a guy I met in Chicago who wanted to be remembered to you.' 'Who's that?' 'A quarterback. He said he played for you.' 'Not very many guys played quarterback—wait a minute, where? Cleveland? It wasn't Jeff Christensen, was it?' 'That's it!' 'Tell him to go to hell the next time you see him! He cost us home field advantage, and that ended up costing us the championship game!'"

Two weeks into the 1987 season, the players union struck for free agency and the owners decided to play on with Hessians, including a prisoner or two, a prison guard or two, and one gentleman under indictment for murder. On the first Sunday of replacement football, four punts were blocked for touchdowns, one kickoff was mistaken for a punt, and a fellow named Anthony Allen caught 255 yards' worth of passes for the Washington Redskins. With a straight face, the Associated Press referred to one of the starting quarterbacks as "an insurance salesman with a history of shoulder trouble."

Some NFL teams, like the Giants, had no heart for this pantomime.

"The Giants were coming off a Super Bowl year," Ernie said, "and George Young was adamant that he'd rather lose all of the replacement games than risk alienating one of the real players. As you might expect then, the Giants did lose them all." Other teams, like the 49ers and Browns, saw an opportunity. From chaos, there is profit. That first week at Giants Stadium, in the middle of the least-watched Monday night game in history, San Francisco coach Bill Walsh slyly inserted a running quarterback and suddenly switched to a wishbone offense. On the opposite sideline, head coach Bill Parcells performed a double take worthy of Casey Stengel and then exploded into laughter. The 49ers won, 41–21.

"I brought Christensen in to quarterback for the Browns," Accorsi said. "He was a guy in his thirties from Eastern Illinois, and he was no bum [originally drafted 137th by Cincinnati in 1983]. He shouldn't have had any trouble outclassing all of these school bus drivers, and he did make it look fairly easy the first week. We went to New England and in front of about fourteen thousand people beat the Patriots, twenty to ten. Larry Mason [*the* Larry Mason, from Troy State] ran for a hundred and forty yards. Our next game was at home against the Houston Oilers, who hadn't beaten us in something like ten straight games. But Christensen threw about a hundred interceptions, and we lost, fifteen to ten. As it turned out, that changed the world. That's how Elway got to be at home against us in the AFC Championship Game—you know, Byner's fumble. Then our third replacement game was in Cincinnati, where we almost never won, and the rumors were flying that this thing might be settled in the eleventh hour. Before we left, I got a phone call from Gary Danielson—he was the veteran quarterback behind Bernie Kosar—and Gary wanted to meet at Art Modell's house. He brought along Ozzie Newsome, the tight end, and Brian Brennan, the receiver, and Ricky Bolden, the left tackle. 'We're all older guys,' Gary said. 'I'm thirty-nine, okay? Let Bernie and the younger guys stay out to avoid recriminations. But if a handful of veterans at just the right positions crosses the picket line, we should be able to steal this game. The guys staying out have heard the plan and they're all for it.'"

Thirteen-year-old Ernie Accorsi's immense love for sports crystallized one day in a football game played on this unassuming little field in Hershey, Pennsylvania. *Courtesy of Ernie Accorsi*

Ernie's first football job was under legendary Joe Paterno (left) at Penn State. His most vital function, at least as far as Paterno was concerned, was to keep a bowl in the coaches' office filled with red licorice, but he managed to bootleg a number of life and football lessons from Joe and assistant coach George Welsh. *© Jerry Pinkus*

Ernie left Penn State to join the Baltimore Colts. "As I was pulling away from Penn State, Paterno gave me a pep talk: 'You're swimming with the real sharks now, Ernie. If you try to play their game, you'll be eaten alive. Just be the way you are.' " *Courtesy of Ernie Accorsi*

After a stint in the league office, Ernie returned to the Colts and in 1982 became General Manager, inheriting Coach Frank Kush (left), who was known as the toughest guy in the league. The Colts owned the top pick in the 1983 draft, but top pick John Elway publicly swore he'd never play for Baltimore. *Courtesy of Ernie Accorsi*

Ernie with Val Pinchbeck, Lamar Hunt, and George Halas. *Courtesy of Ernie Accorsi*

Ernie and Johnny Unitas (left) were so close that when Unitas' career ended in Baltimore, the great QB presented his last Colts jersey to Accorsi, not to the NFL Hall of Fame. *Courtesy of Ernie Accorsi*

Trainer Ronnie Barnes with beloved Giants owner Wellington Mara (right). Barnes sat a thirty-day vigil at Mara's bedside as the owner fought his final battles with cancer. At one point, Ronnie felt derelict enough in his duties to apologize to Coach Coughlin, who told him in a low, cracking voice, "You're doing God's work."
Courtesy of Ronnie Barnes

Below left: When Ernie took over as Giants GM, he soon installed Kerry Collins as quarterback. Many considered Collins—whose personal life had been turbulent— damaged goods. But Accorsi followed his gut, saying, "I've always believed that if a kid was ever a good kid, he can be a good kid again." © *Jerry Pinkus*

Below right: Coming off a 4-12 2003 season, Ernie bet it all on Eli Manning. "I realized that I could turn out to be wrong on this kid. . . . I knew we might not know for sure until years after I leave. But I could live with it. We had a quarterback." © *Jerry Pinkus*

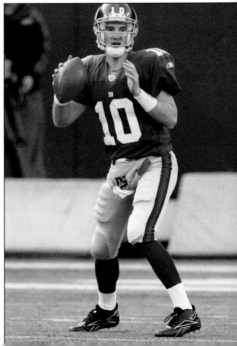

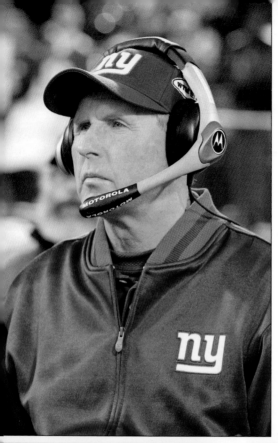

With the new quarterback came a new coach, disciplinarian Tom Coughlin. In time, Ernie would fret that his coach and QB weren't as closely bonded as he expected them to be.
© *Jerry Pinkus*

Eli Manning presents the game ball to John Mara after the Giants' October 30, 2005, victory over the Redskins, their first game after Wellington's death.
© *Jerry Pinkus*

Above left: Coming into the 2006 season, veteran defensive end and team leader Michael Strahan was among the players who "declared" for the Super Bowl. When Strahan was lost to an injury in November, the team was devastated. © *Evan Pinkus*

Above right: Running back Tiki Barber's 2006 season proved spectacular, making him only the third player in NFL history to achieve four 2,000 total yard seasons. Determined to leave the game healthy, Tiki chose to retire at season's end. © *Jerry Pinkus*

After a devastating early loss to the Seahawks, fiery tight end Jeremy Shockey became the star of the postgame show, declaring, "We got outplayed *and outcoached*." A big believer in Shockey, Accorsi had been ambivalent years before when he first watched him play, noticing that Shockey loved the spotlight. "But what a player." © *Jerry Pinkus*

Newly signed linebacker LaVar Arrington, a three-time Pro Bowler who'd never lived up to his potential, was finally learning to play within himself as part of a system, but minutes after knocking down this Drew Bledsoe pass, a ruptured Achilles' tendon ended his season. © *Jerry Pinkus*

Six-foot-five wide receiver Plaxico Burress occasionally earned the ire of fans who questioned his desire, but his rebel reputation and jailyard stare hide a hard-working, dedicated teammate. Plax wears the number 17—an unusual number for a wide receiver—to commemorate the date of his signing with the Giants. © *Jerry Pinkus*

Amani Toomer, the stateliest presence on the team and the Giants' all-time career yardage leader (8,157—nearly 3,000 yards more than Frank Gifford), was lost to knee surgery halfway through the season. © *Jerry Pinkus*

The Giants' "walking miracle," six-foot-three, 305-pound utility man Rich Seubert. He suffered three horrible leg fractures six games into the 2003 season that left him out the rest of that season and the next. Seubert doesn't know why the Giants stuck with him: "I'm pretty sure the coaches didn't really have much to say about it . . . it was Accorsi and the Maras who kept me." ©*Jerry Pinkus*

Despite a solid season, rookie Mathias Kiwanuka earned derision from fans when, leery of a "roughing the passer" call, he failed to bring down Titans QB Vince Young on a sack. Still, Coughlin assured, "Mathias is going to be a great football player." ©*Jerry Pinkus*

When, one week, ailing punter Jeff Feagles was listed as "doubtful," Accorsi called on 45-year-old kicker Sean Landeta to stand by. Just for showing up, Landeta got paid $47,000, "the minimum for a player who's been in the league 403 years."
© *Jerry Pinkus*

The Giants' manager of personnel, Jerry Reese, Ernie's longtime protégé, at the press conference where he was introduced as Ernie's successor. Accorsi had been loud and unambiguous in recommending that Reese replace him, but the situation was delicate. © *Jerry Pinkus*

"What Ernie didn't know," Danielson said, "was that Modell had called me first. Art put me up to coming back. 'We need a quarterback,' he said, 'and I can't ask Bernie to cross the line.' I said I'd do it, but I had to have somebody to throw it to. Okay, I thought—Brennan. You could talk Brenn into anything." Against the Bengals replacements, Danielson looked like a youthful Y. A. Tittle. "It was like watching Notre Dame taking on Hillsdale Junior College," Ernie said. "They were having so much fun. Brennan showed them this move, and then he gave them that move, and he didn't have to make a third move, because there wasn't anybody anywhere near him. I mean, some truck driver was thirty yards down the field. We were leading, thirty-four to nothing, it was pitch-and-catch, and Danielson had completed like twenty passes in a row, when suddenly it dawned on me that all of these records were going to count." Accorsi began to panic on behalf of Dante Lavelli and Paul Warfield, not to mention Otto Graham.

As a matter of fact, at Buffalo the week before, Gary Hogeboom of the Indianapolis Colts threw five touchdown passes to tie a twenty-two-year-old franchise mark that was presumed to be the property of Johnny Unitas but, as Ernie well knew, actually belonged to a dentist who used to back Unitas up, Gary Cuozzo. "I rushed into the coach's booth," Accorsi said. "I'd never done anything like this in my life. 'Tell Schottenheimer,' I shouted, 'to get Brennan the hell out of the game!' There were still seven minutes to go, and Brian needed only about two more catches and twenty more yards to extinguish Lavelli and Warfield.

" 'We have a sacred trust!' I told the coaches, who had no idea what I was yelling about. But Brennan came out. He was pissing and moaning on the sidelines, waving his fist at the press box." "You had to know Brenn," Danielson said. "In The Drive game, he ran a great pattern and caught like a fifty-yard touchdown pass [forty-eight] to give us a twenty-to-thirteen lead with five minutes to go in the fourth quarter. After The Drive, and the overtime, and the terrible loss, all Brenn said was, 'Shit, now nobody's going to remember my touchdown.' "

In the locker room after the 34–0 replacement victory, Marty told Ernie, "I think you should know, I threw you under the bus with Brennan. After all, I have to go on coaching this guy. He says he's going to kill you." "You son of a bitch!" Brennan called out, flying across the room. "I said, 'Brian, Brian, Brian, calm down! I love you to death, you're having a very good career, but I'm not going to let you wipe Warfield and Lavelli out of the record books.'" "You love *me* to death?" Brennan said. "You love Webster Slaughter [the Browns' other receiver] more!"

"Yeah, but he's a better player than you are," Ernie said.

"He's a pain in the ass!"

"You're right, and you are, too. The thing is, he's good enough that I'll put up with him being a pain in the ass, and you're not. You're just not good enough to be a pain in the ass, Brian. Stop being a pain in the ass." Not that day, but soon, they were pals again. "Brian has never completely forgiven me for taking him out of that game," Accorsi said, "but he can almost laugh about it now."

"Ernie may be the only general manager," Michael Strahan said, "who has ever talked to a player that way. Or, for that matter, who talks to players at all. I knew George Young, but my relationship with George really wasn't much. It was kind of like he's the GM, I'm the player. He did his talking to my agent. With Ernie it has always been personal. He'll tell you what's wrong with you, but he'll compliment you, too, which you have to know is rare. Because, when contract time comes around, they're going to try not to pay you. But Ernie violates the GM code. 'Michael,' he'll say, 'you're the best. I've never seen a defensive end do that.' Just among players, I'll bet he leaves with as many real friends as anybody in the NFL."

Such as Sean Landeta.

Because Giants punter Jeff Feagles looked doubtful one week with an arthritic knee, Landeta, a former member of the Baltimore Stars (USFL), Philadelphia Stars (USFL), New York Giants, Los Angeles Rams, St. Louis Rams, Tampa Bay Buccaneers, Green Bay Packers, Philadelphia Eagles, Rams redux, Eagles redux, and Giants redux, was brought back for a single game and technically a twenty-fifth year in professional football. Ernie said, "First of all, we had to get both houses of Congress along with the Armed Services Committee to force Tom to sign on. It was a numbers thing, as usual. He was worried he might have to dress two punters and lose a precious forty-sixth player. I said, 'Tom, if we don't have a punter, the game is forfeited, okay?' Landeta was the obvious choice. He was nearby, on Long Island, and I know where Sean's heart is—with this franchise. And I know he has ice water in his veins. He's a Smoky Burgess. Fat or old, just roll ole Smoky out there and he'll hit you a line drive double into the gap."

As it turned out, Feagles was able to go after all, and Landeta didn't even dress. All the same, Sean's paycheck just for standing by was $47,000. "It's the minimum," Ernie said, "for a man who's been in the league four hundred and three years. For forty-seven grand, Sean got in his car and drove sixteen miles. But don't forget, he had to cross over two bridges, paying his own tolls both ways—seven bucks for the George Washington Bridge alone. And do you want to know something else? He'd have done it for forty-seven dollars. He'd have done it for forty-seven cents."

Landeta said, "If the old rules were still in place, the pre-cap rules, with no minimum salaries, I'd be able to play into my fifties [he was forty-five] because I'd play for less than anybody. I'd be so cheap that I'd be the most unpopular guy among the other punters in the whole history of punting. But I'd perform. Since I was nine, I've just enjoyed doing this. I don't know how to explain it to you. I've loved all of the things that sports are about. Being part of a team, especially. Working toward a goal. Achieving that goal. To make your living, your life, at a game: it's a little boy's dream, isn't it? I'll bet there are a hundred million guys out there who know exactly what I'm talking about."

He marked the starting point at age nine because that's how old Landeta was in 1970 when Jim O'Brien of the Baltimore Colts kicked a thirty-two-yard field goal with five seconds left to beat the Dallas Cowboys in Super Bowl V. "Growing up in Baltimore," Landeta said, "I was like every kid in town, a Colts fanatic. All of us ran outside the moment that game ended, and with our heels made that little dent in the ground—remember?—to tee the ball up and kick it. Every one of us was Jim O'Brien. We didn't have goal posts, so we kicked the ball over a volleyball net and pretended it was to win the Super Bowl."

Fast-forward to 1978. "I had been punting and placekicking on sandlots for eight years, just for the fun of it," Landeta said. He wasn't even on the team at Loch Raven High School. "One morning, I came to school early to have my senior picture taken, and ran into the coach in the hall. 'I hear you can kick,' he said. 'Why don't you come out to the field this afternoon?' That was my only year of high school football. I punted and kicked field goals, both."

Just lately, the serendipity of that brush in the hall had been tumbling end over end in his mind. "What if I hadn't been there at that exact moment? What if the light that morning had been red instead of green? What if the photographer had taken one more shot? On top of which, the coach didn't have to ask me. He hadn't been looking for me. He just happened to see me." *Here comes the snap, and the boot . . .*

A kicking career at little Towson University (formerly Towson State Teachers College) led first to three seasons in the USFL and then to New York. In an NFC Divisional Play-off game against Chicago in 1985, Landeta dropped back to punt for the Giants, and a gust of Soldier Field wind blew the ball right out of his hands. On what was officially called a five-yard punt return, the Bears scored the only touchdown they would need that day. But just one autumn later, New York won the Super Bowl and Landeta joined Lawrence Taylor, Harry Carson, Leonard Marshall, Jim Burt, Joe Morris, Brad Benson, and Mark Bavaro at the Pro Bowl. Four years further on, Sean helped the Giants do it again. He really was Jim O'Brien.

"These days," he said, "I go out four or five times a week to a high school field or to a public park and punt footballs. Occasionally I have the luxury of a college or a high school snapper, but most of the time

I'm by myself. Coaches like to talk about a punter's soft hands, about the techniques of catching the ball, and holding it out there, and punting it. But the truth is, I've never thought about any of those things. I've never thought about rushing linemen, either. It's two seconds. You go out, you get set up, you catch the ball, you kick it. To me, it's the most natural thing in the world."

If he wanted to, Landeta could take a bag of twenty footballs out to the park. But, like a golfer on a practice putting green, he prefers to work with only three. "That way," he said, "I can go back and forth, get a little running in, think about what I'm doing, and just get ready." To Feagles, punting and golf have always seemed similar. "I think of the end zone as a green-side hazard," Jeff said. "I don't want to hit it in the water. I want to drop it on the flag. The way I look at it, the pin is tucked right next to the five-yard line." Landeta said, "I'm not much of a golfer, but I agree that a lot of the basics are the same. Make good contact. Don't try to kill it. Swing smooth. Hit the ball solid."

Considering all he had accomplished and how many memories were already in the bag, what was keeping Landeta standing by? "The possibility of doing it just one more time," he said simply. When will he finally let himself come to a stop? "I guess when there's only one team left that says it will keep me in mind," he said. "That might be next season, but I hope not. By my calculations, I have to have at least three or four GMs tell me that they'll consider me a candidate if their guy goes down or if he doesn't perform. Then it makes sense to stay ready. Only one 'maybe' out of thirty-two teams just isn't worth all of the work. Of course, if a day arrives when I don't feel like going to the park, that'll end it, too. And, obviously, my kicking won't be good enough for this level forever."

Saying goodbye to Ernie in his office, Sean headed back to his car for the drive home to Long Island. He had parked near the bubble, where big men just a little bit out of shape with surprisingly quick feet and astonishingly intent eyes were panting their lungs out and, in a few cases, trying not to faint. "It isn't the money," Landeta said. "Who doesn't like money? And everybody wants a job. But if a rule came in tomorrow that said all of the players in the NFL had to play for a fraction of their current salaries, all of them would still be out there."

Not all of them.

"Okay, ninety-five percent of them," he said. "You can see it, can't you? In their eyes?"

14

REESE

NEW YORK'S DIRECTOR of player personnel, Jerry Reese, was a former high school quarterback and small-college defensive back from the river town, the prison town, of Tiptonville, Tennessee. Reese seemed too small at five foot nine, not to mention too polite and well spoken, to be the fearsome blocker and tackler still whistled about at the University of Tennessee–Martin, where he is in the Hall of Fame. "You know what, I was probably an overachiever," Reese said with a grimace. (Overachieving is not much of a virtue in the scouting trade.) "I had a good coach who made me a better player, that's all. Lacking size and speed, I had to be really, really aggressive, and I guess I was." It was said that Reese *insisted* his high school team win the Tennessee state championship, and just when that perfect season was drifting away, Jerry personally retrieved it by running back a kickoff for a touchdown.

"I come from a single-parent family," Reese said. "My biological father died when I was seven, and I was twelve when my mother married my stepfather. He worked at the park, not as a ranger or anything like that, just mowing lawns, cleaning up. Tiptonville is a poor, rural town, but it's not a bad place to come from." Jerry's real father, J. C. Hillsman, died in an industrial accident at a mill that produced oil from cottonseeds. The seven children that Hillsman had with Jerry's mother weren't his only children in town. "We don't consider them half brothers and half sisters," Reese told John Branch of the *New York Times*. "They're brothers and sisters."

The consistent male influence in Jerry's young life was his great-grandfather, an equally hard and soft man who wasn't anything like his job: shooting, gutting, and skinning hogs in a backwoods slaughterhouse. Just to be with him, Jerry was willing to tie a kerchief over his nose and assist in that putrid and dismal work. Reese also chopped cotton and cut grass. "One summer," he said, enjoying the memory, "a local farmer hired me as a flagman for the crop dusters. I'd march off eighteen rows and then signal for the drop." Eighteen rows and wave for the spray. Eighteen rows, all day long. "If I ever write a book," he said, "that's what I'm going to call it. *Eighteen Rows*." Every child of Ozella Garland—Miss Ozella, as she was still known in Tiptonville—had at least a shot at college, an unusual opportunity in Lake County, and they all took some advantage. Jerry earned a bachelor of science degree in health and education and a master's in education administration. "When your mother works for twenty years at the H.A.S. factory," he said, "standing at a machine all day, making denim, and then she takes a job as a corrections officer in the prison, you're pretty much obligated to succeed at something."

Football was a natural choice. That last year at Tennessee-Martin, Jerry was the Most Valuable Player in the Gulf South Conference, and when he stayed on as a graduate assistant at $400 a week, he fell in with one Jeremiah Davis. "At that time Jeremiah was an assistant coach at Tennessee-Martin," Reese said, "who thought enough of me to let me sleep on his couch. And he wouldn't let me pay him. Jeremiah and I were playing chess late one night when he looked up from the board to say, 'I'm going to work for you one day.' Just like that. I thought he was stalling because I was winning the game. I said, 'Come on, Jeremiah, make your move.' 'Listen to me,' he said, 'I'm serious. I'm going to work for you one day.' I didn't think anything else about it."

Davis, a scout's scout with the Giants now, joined the team as a summer intern twenty years ago. When the internship ended, Jeremiah wouldn't leave. Accorsi said, "George Young told him, 'You did a great job, Jeremiah, and we'd like to consider you for the future, but there's no position here now.' 'That's okay,' he said, 'you don't have to pay me. I can live with my mother. But I'm staying.' 'You don't understand . . .' 'I'm not leaving.' George went to the Maras and said, 'You've got to let me hire this guy.' On top of being stubborn and loyal, Jeremiah was good. He was just a special scout."

Michael Strahan said, "Jeremiah was the one who worked me out at school [Texas Southern] over and over. He was the only one, really, who kept coming back around until I hit the number. He put me on this training exerciser where you had to slam all these pads within a certain amount of time to prove your quickness. Jeremiah worked me like a dog. I kid him now that he tortured me more than anybody. 'And you're the only scout,' I tell him, 'who didn't at least have the decency to take me out afterward to get me something to eat.' "

To Davis, scouting wasn't a matter of arithmetic. "I didn't really care about the score Stray made," Jeremiah said. "I just had to get him to that number in case somebody else cared. It's never a number that you see in a player. It's something else." "It's a conviction," Ernie said. "All you can ask for in scouting is a conviction. After you have that, then you just need the balls. Guys like Jeremiah champion their causes. That's why they want to be in the draft room in April, so they can fight for their guys. I love the scouts. I don't think you could be a GM in this league if you had never done any scouting at all, if you didn't understand what it feels like to believe in a player. There's this peaceful—actually, exhilarating; *peaceful* is the wrong word—moment when you have a guy pegged. You've got him. You've watched him all day, or all season, and now you're ready to sit down and write your report. Some people will still protect themselves in the gray areas, but not guys like Jeremiah. Not guys like Reese."

"Years later," Jerry said, "when Jeremiah was with the Giants, he called me up. 'Jerry, we need a scout in the Southeast, are you interested?' I was, like, 'Are you kidding me? No way! I'm out of graduate school now. I'm the assistant head coach at UT-Martin. I'm making thirty-five thousand dollars a year—I can be the next head coach. I'm not going anywhere.' But he kept bugging me. My wife and I started talking about it, praying about it. Our daughter was only two—our son wasn't born yet. I already had a nice deal. I didn't want to mess that up. Then again, the NFL was the biggest game in the world. Gwen, also a UT-Martin graduate, finally said, 'Let's give it a shot,' and all of a sudden I'm a scout for the New York Giants."

The first thing you have to know about the scouting life, maybe the only thing, is that you will be on the road some 185 to 200 days a year. Get up in the morning, drive to the school, watch the videotape, talk with the contact people—trainer, strength coach, head coach, position coach—watch practice, take notes, get back in the car, drive three hours to the next economy motel, type up your report, go to bed, get up and do it again, and again, from Cracker Barrel to Cracker Barrel, on an endless highway.

"It's not digging a ditch," Reese said, "but it's hard work." It's hardest on the heart. "I'd go out for fourteen or sixteen days at a time, and when I'd get back, little JR wouldn't know me. He was just starting to walk. I'd reach out for him and he'd pull away. That kind of stuff can kill you."

Reese had very good eyes for the task. "I think some guys just have an innate ability to see it," he said. "If you work at it, I guess you could develop it. But I believe, even as a young scout, I had a pretty good fix on it. I could see things. Then you have to be able to express it, put it on paper, without writing a novel. You know, get to the point. What can he do? What can't he do? Can this guy contribute to our football team? Can he make it? Why will he make it? Why won't he make it? It's neither a science nor a crap shoot. It's an understanding. I don't know, I just had a feel for it, and a love for it."

Accorsi noticed. In fact, he saw a general manager in the making. Talking Reese into leaving the frontier and coming into the front office was the tricky part. Even New Jersey real estate prices scared Jerry and

Gwen. But Ernie made the sale. Then twice he jumped Reese over more experienced men, first to assist Dave Gettleman with pro personnel, then to handle the college personnel himself. "The best three years of my career was in the pro department," Jerry said. "When you're on the road scouting, you kind of forget who's actually playing in the NFL, who's good enough to contribute, I mean. 'Wow, this guy's really helping? I didn't think he was even close to good enough when I saw him a few years ago.' You stop thinking all of the time about the stars. You learn how a medium-level player, even a low-level player, can chip in something valuable. When you think about it, there really aren't that many great, great football players. Most are developmental projects. Picking out the top guys and the bottom guys isn't all that difficult. It's seeing those guys in the middle who can play a little—that's where you make your money. Maybe he's fast and nothing else. Maybe he's just big. But then, maybe he has something—the makings of something—that you just can't quite put your finger on. But you like it."

The few black executives in the National Football League in 2006 were mostly former stars like the tight end Ozzie Newsome, the quarterback James Harris, and the receiver Gene Washington. "Here was a guy," Ernie said, "who wasn't even a player in the league, who started off at the very bottom, like most of us, and worked his way up the same way, step by step." Accorsi was loud and unambiguous in recommending to John Mara and Steve and Jonathan Tisch that Reese replace him, but Ernie had to be careful not to push too hard. It was a situation of some delicacy.

Chris Mara, the Giants' vice president of player evaluation, wanted the GM job desperately, and he was eminently qualified. Since 1979, Chris had worked in player personnel for his father's team. When Wellington's second son didn't rise to the position of head of player personnel—"We can't have any fireproof heads of player personnel," George Young snorted—Chris went off on his own for a while to run a scouting service and eventually to be the president and general manager of the New Jersey Gladiators of the Arena Football League. They finished first in the Eastern Division of the National Conference. To be near his father for Wellington's last years, Chris returned to the Giants' front office in 2003. He had the skills absolutely to be an NFL GM, if only he had a different last name.

Chris' daughter, Kate, was a film actress with mounting credits (*Random Hearts, Brokeback Mountain, We Are Marshall, Shooter*) in increasingly juicier parts. She was both a Mara and a Rooney—Chris and the former Kathleen Rooney represent something of a Giants-Steelers merger— which is a little like being by the Triple Crown–winning sire Secretariat out of the Triple Crown–winning dam Genuine Risk. They could have called Kate or any of her three siblings "Six Crowns." But she was putting her dad in obvious danger of going straight from being Somebody's Son to being Somebody's Father, and the urgency of his campaign to be the next GM was a watercooler topic all season long in the New York front office. Outsiders like former Redskins GM Charley Casserly would be interviewed pro forma. That's standard. Scott Pioli of New England would make a small news item out of declining to be interviewed. But neither of them ever had a chance. There were only two serious candidates to replace Accorsi.

A few days after Halloween, on a windy Sunday in Giants Stadium, New York beat Tampa Bay, 17–3, in a punter's game. "It's been my experience," punter Jeff Feagles said, "that if there are a lot of reporters standing around my locker after a game, it isn't good news for me." And Feagles was more experienced than almost anybody else in the business. The Tampa game was the 295th without a break for this balding, forty-year-old island in the middle of a sea of twenty-two- and twenty-three-year-old men. Jim Marshall's fallen record of 282 games continued to be slightly more impressive, because Marshall had been a position player— a defensive end for Minnesota (who sometimes picked up the ball and ran the wrong way). Still, a punter has to stay employable for an awfully long while to head the NFL's all-time list for durability, sixty games in front of Brett Favre.

Actually, Feagles tried to retire during the last off-season, returning with his wife, Michelle, to their hometown, Phoenix, Arizona. But Ernie told Jeff, "You can't retire until I retire," refusing to submit his papers. And then an even funnier thing happened. The Feagles' four sons, ages six to sixteen, voiced a preference for Jersey over the Valley of the Sun, and Jeff came back to the Giants. Like Jim Bowie and Davy Crockett, Feagles and Accorsi were in it together until the end, trying not to strike out swinging at the Alamo.

"Usually when there are this many people around my locker," Feagles repeated after the Bucs game, "the smart money is on a blocked punt, although a high snap is well within the realm of possibility, too, or maybe it's just a good old-fashioned dropped ball. Whatever it is, you can be pretty sure it's a screw-up of some kind."

But no, this time the attention was on two coffin-corner kicks that qualified as the plays of the game in a forty- to fifty-mile-per-hour windstorm. "And we knew it would be this way when we went to sleep last night," center Shaun O'Hara said. "That's what you get when you play in the swampy Meadowlands. I thought to myself before I went to bed, 'Sunday might be a Jeff Feagles day.'"

On practice days, whenever the elements became uncomfortable enough for the team to seek shelter inside the bubble, Feagles always stayed outdoors to experiment with the wind currents in Giants Stadium. "It's a great place for punting in swirls," he said, "if you know the prevailing tendencies; in other words, if it's your home. The visiting punters look at the flags flapping atop the stadium. I've learned to ignore them. The twisting winds at field level are the important calculations. You have to time the gusts and adjust your drop. Today was a two-step drop, instead of a regular two-and-a-half-stepper. It's fun to see the ball hit at the five and back up like a sand wedge. It's fun to get up in the morning and know you're going to have a chance to make a real contribution today. Hell, I've always loved the Giants Stadium winds."

The Buccaneers were less enraptured. Antonio Pierce said, "On the field, they kept talking about how cold they were, how they had gone from a hundred-and-five-degree heat to this. 'Welcome to New York,' I said. 'Why don't you see a show while you're in town?'"

The battle of the Barber twins, Tiki and Ronde, was scored a draw. Neither stood out. Tiki won the game, while Ronde wrapped up their lifetime series, three victories to two. Twice in the course of the day's events they collided—Ronde is a defensive back—but only one rhubarb resulted. "He was mad that I hit him so low the first time," Ronde said. "So, nailing him again, I said, 'Is that high enough for you, Tiki?' 'Yeah, man,' he said. 'Thanks. That's perfect.'"

Ronde had less conversation and success trying not to be pancaked by Brandon Jacobs on the goal line ("I don't know who that number twenty-seven is," said Tampa coach Jon Gruden, "but he made a difference"). In an even less felicitous match-up, Ronde was hopelessly alley-ooped by Eli Manning and Plaxico Burress. "When you're five-nine-and-a-half," Ronde said specifically, "you might be able to cover a six-five guy in the end zone, but not if he can catch a ball one-handed—and left-handed—without even looking at it."

Two Giants series were sufficient to win, an extended one in the first quarter and a shorter one in the second that followed a fumble by Tampa's rookie quarterback Bruce Gradkowski.

GIANTS

1-10-G47 Barber runs for 4
2-6-B49   Manning passes to Burress for 13
1-10-B36 Barber runs for 4
2-6-B32   Manning passes to Jim Finn for 8
1-10-B24 Barber runs for 1
2-9-B23   Manning passes to Visanthe Shiancoe for 13
1-G-B10   Barber runs for 3
2-G-B7   Manning passes to Burress for 7 and the
          touchdown; Jay Feely's kick is good.

New York 7, Tampa Bay 0

GIANTS
1-10-B28 Manning passes to Burress for 25 yards

"In the locker room before the game," Plaxico said, "Eli told me, 'This might be a day when catching the ball is enough. Forget about getting yards after it. Just go down. No turnovers is the deal today.' And we had none."

1-G-B3   Barber runs for 2

"Evidently it's not my job to score touchdowns anymore," said Tiki, still without any for the year.

2-G-B1   Jacobs runs for 1 and the touchdown; Feely's kick is good
New York 14, Tampa Bay 0

Two field goals came later, one for the Buccaneers in the first half, one for the Giants in the second. As Kate Mara would say, when the punter plays the lead, the movie is usually a short subject.

Starting off the season with five straight losses, the Bucs had put together a pair of victories on their way to New York, including a stirring last-second one over Philadelphia. But now they were depressed again. The winners weren't overly ecstatic, either. They were professional. "The object is to win," Tom Coughlin said prosaically. About the growing roster of injuries—linebacker Brandon Short strained a quad muscle—Strahan said to the cameras, "The guys who came in all looked like starters to me." But, off to the side, he conceded, "There are reasons the starters are the starters and the backups are the backups."

Used to seeing more joy in a winning locker room, O'Hara delivered the day's punch line: "Hey, you can't go home with the prom queen every night."

15

GOODBYE, TOOMS

OR AN ILLUSTRATION OF expectations in New York, consider
how loudly the Giants were booed at home in the course of winning
their fifth consecutive game. The level of the opponent—a second
straight 2-and-5 team, the Houston Texans—had something to do with
that.

And the Texans were ahead in the fourth quarter, 10–7, as Eli Manning started a drive on his own thirty-three-yard line with an incompletion. Not because they were so pressed for time, just to stir the tempo in
the hope of reinvigorating their logy quarterback, the Giants switched
to a no-huddle offense.

GIANTS

1-10-G33 Manning passes incomplete

2-10-G33 (no huddle, shotgun) Manning throws to Tiki
Barber for 13

1-10-G46 (no huddle, shotgun) Barber runs for 12

1-10-T42 (no huddle, shotgun) Manning passes to Michael
Jennings for 5

2-5-T37 (no huddle, shotgun) Manning passes to Jeremy
Shockey for 14

1-10-T23 Offside, Houston

1-5-T18 (no huddle, shotgun) Manning passes incomplete

2-5-T18 (no huddle) Barber runs for –1

3-6-T19 (no huddle) Barber runs for 7

1-10-T12 (shotgun) Manning passes to Amani Toomer
  for 10
1-G-T2   Brandon Jacobs runs for −1
2-G-T3   Manning passes to Shockey for 3 and the
  touchdown; Jay Feely's kick is good

New York 14, Houston 10

Houston had only one turn left, but it was looking like that would be enough.

TEXANS

1-10-T30 David Carr passes to Wali Lundy for 2
2-8-T30 Carr passes incomplete

At this point rookie Mathias Kiwanuka, in at right defensive end for injured Osi Umenyiora, drew the first roughing-the-passer penalty of his professional career. "Talk about the difference between college and the pros," he said. "In college after making a play like that, you're getting head slaps and high fives on the sidelines. In the pros, you can expect a big fine, I'm told." Three games hence, this minor event filed away in the back of Kiwanuka's consciousness would lead to a major catastrophe.

1-10-T47 Lundy runs for 8
2-2-G45   Lundy runs for 3
1-10-G42 Lundy runs for 4
2-6-G38   Carr passes to Jameel Cook for 3; Cook fumbles
  to Corey Webster; the Giants survive the game, but
  not intact

Joining the burgeoning list of the infirm and ill, Plaxico Burress (back) and Kareem McKenzie (migraines) did not play. With no notice, grizzled pro Bob Whitfield, thirty-five years old and in his fifteenth (and final) NFL season, started at right offensive tackle for McKenzie. "I hear you're starting," Ernie said to him in the locker room. "Yeah, I got the memo," Whitfield said. Later, he confessed, "I was trying to find my game face. It wasn't in my bag. It's been so long since I needed it, I couldn't remember where I left it."

In the second quarter, wrestling with right tackle Zach Wiegert, Michael Strahan took an awkward step and had to leave the field with what at first was called a midfoot sprain. Adrian Awasom, just two weeks removed from the Giants' practice squad, replaced him. "I'm not talking about the foot," Strahan said afterward, filling the locker room with a sense of foreboding. "You lose Strahan," Antonio Pierce fairly whispered, "and you lose the face of the Giants' defense. Tiki, offense. Michael, defense. They're the Giants." Barber, by the way, finally broke through—on a sixteen-yard dash—to score his first touchdown of the season.

In Strahan's rookie year of 1993, he missed ten full games with a strained Lisfranc ligament in a foot. Jacques Lisfranc, a field surgeon for Napoleon, might be surprised to know how many men were still catching their feet in the stirrups while being thrown from horses on the Russian front. Strahan's Lisfranc suspicions would be confirmed in a few days, and that wouldn't be the worst news for the team.

At the same time, there was some silliness afoot. During the game, both Carr and top draft choice Mario Williams threw the Giants' basketball jump shots back in their faces. Wasn't that inevitable?

"There was almost a fistfight over it," said Williams, a six foot six, 293-pound defensive end from North Carolina State, whom the Texans preferred to Southern Cal running back Reggie Bush and Texas quarterback Vince Young in the last draft. But Chris Snee, Tom Coughlin's son-in-law, argued for leaving Mario alone, saying with undisguised admiration, "He's bigger than I thought he was before I actually saw him." Shaun O'Hara, a skilled hand at satire, especially for a center, said, "This is *our* basketball court. Nobody shoots jump shots on *our* court."

Chicago was next up in Giants Stadium, but no longer were the Bears undefeated. As New York was edging Houston, the Bears weren't just losing to 1-and-6 Miami in Chicago, they were basically being exposed, 31–13. Mike Singletary, William "the Refrigerator" Perry, Jim McMahon, and Walter Payton hadn't been reincarnated after all. As a result, quarterback Rex Grossman was under siege at home. His four interceptions and two fumbles in a slender victory over Arizona had been aggravated by three interceptions and a fumble against the Dolphins. Grossman's ratings were barely registering on the scale of quarterbacks, and, next to Rex, Manning appeared confident. "Eli's got confidence," Whitfield said sagely, "but he doesn't yet have what I call savvy confidence. It's how you walk and talk. The quarterback is a leader by default, but Eli still has to work on walking and talking."

Because Burress was out and Amani Toomer was reduced to just two short catches by a throbbing ankle and a nagging knee, Shockey served as Manning's primary target against Houston. Jeremy caught eight passes for sixty-six yards and a touchdown, and on a call in the end zone close enough to be challenged, Shock had a second touchdown slammed out of him by kamikaze safety Glenn Earl. Jeremy ran back to the huddle to tell Eli, "I have to make that catch, man."

Three days after the game, Toomer learned that his left knee wasn't merely sore. He had partially torn the anterior cruciate ligament and needed immediate surgery. Amani's season was over. "Man," Barber said, "where is the sniper hiding?" Toomer, the stateliest Giant, was the team's all-time career yardage leader (8,157) by nearly three thousand yards over Frank Gifford. Amani needed just two touchdown passes to overtake Kyle Rote (forty-eight) at the head of that list, too. Nobody— not Rote, not Homer Jones, not Del Shofner, not Earnest Gray—could touch him for hundred-yard games (twenty-two). "This is bad," Tiki said. "Unassuming. Quiet. Great. Whenever we needed a big play, Amani was there to make it. He isn't a player who came into the NFL guaranteed a great career, either. He's a guy who had to fight for it. That's why it's always meant so much to him."

On September 9, 1995, Accorsi scouted Toomer of the University of Michigan in a game against Memphis at Ann Arbor:

STRONG POINTS—EXCELLENT HANDS . . . ELUSIVE, CLEVER . . . WIGGLES ON THE QUICK SCREEN . . . MAKES PEOPLE MISS . . . BREAKS TACKLES, TOO . . . TALL AND RANGY . . . EXCELLENT SIZE, 6-3, 194 . . . WILL CATCH IN A CROWD . . . TAKE A HIT AND HOLD ONTO THE BALL . . . QUICK AND EXPLOSIVE OFF THE LINE OF SCRIMMAGE . . . BIG PLAY RECEIVER.

WEAK POINTS—THE ONLY QUESTION I HAVE ON HIM IS DURABILITY, AND THE FACT THAT THERE IS NO CONFIRMED SPEED. HE LOOKS FAST ENOUGH FOR HIS SIZE.

SUMMATION—BIG, RANGY RECEIVER WITH ENOUGH SPEED AND MORE THAN ENOUGH EXPLOSION . . . CAN RUN AFTER CATCH WITH THE ABILITY BOTH TO ELUDE AND BREAK TACKLES . . . HAS COURAGE TO CATCH IN A CROWD AND MAKES BIG PLAYS . . . EXCELLENT HANDS.

QUICKNESS 68, AGILITY 68, BALANCE 70, STRENGTH 68, EXPLOSIVENESS 70, COMPETITIVENESS 70, DURABILITY 66, QUICK FEET 68, HANDS 70, INITIAL QUICKNESS 70, RELEASE 70, SEPARATION 70, PATTERNS 68, FIND OPEN AREA 68, RECEIVE SHORT 70, RECEIVE LONG 70, ADJUST TO BALL 70, REACT TO CROWD 70, RUN ABILITY 70, BLOCK 66.

FINAL RATING—70. FINAL DESCRIPTION—THIS GUY'S A DIFFERENCE MAKER.

"That day," Ernie said, "he went up for a badly thrown ball, caught it and got hammered, broke two ribs, but came down with the catch. When I got back to the office, I told George Young, 'I probably shouldn't write a report on just one play, but I saw all I needed to see on that play. Hands, courage, got open, took a hit.' Toomer didn't have numbers, but nobody has numbers at Michigan." Just the fact that he went to

Michigan demonstrated that Amani was his own man. His father, Donald, played for Woody Hayes at Ohio State. Hayes once said that if his car
ran out of gas in Michigan, he'd push it across the state line before he'd
buy anything from those bastards.

The Giants selected Amani in the second round of the 1996 draft,
using the thirty-fourth pick overall. That first season, they assigned him
tight end Mark Bavaro's old jersey number, 89, and set him to work fielding punts. Amani returned two of them for touchdowns but missed
the last nine games of the season when the other anterior cruciate ligament, the right one, blew. He returned from reconstructive surgery to
become the definitive New York Giants receiver. In a princess-and-the-
pea moment, Toomer switched to number 81, explaining that the 9 on
the right side of his back felt a tad heavy; it was interfering with his equi-
librium. Playing as many as 127 games without a pause, Toomer turned
out to be a standard for durability and dependability as well. "He's been
everything for us," Barber said. "He's Toom."

Soaking in a hot tub in the training room, Toomer said, "Sometimes
I feel like I've been doing this eighty-five years. Other times it feels
like I've just begun. I was watching a Monday night game recently, or
maybe it was a later game after ours—I can't remember—but it was just
another football game. And something dawned on me that I never even
thought about before. The TV cameras can look inside our helmets! They
can see inside our eyes! I thought, 'Man, I don't want to show them that
much.' I always thought I was hiding out there. But that camera takes away
your protection. I've been making a conscious effort to control my body
language on the field, to develop a poker face at the bench, so as not to
give away everything that's inside me. It's too personal. It's embarrassing.
I'm going to work on that while I'm rehabbing. I hope to come back a
complete mystery to the announcers in the booth."

Professional athletes who shrink from cameras or attention are fairly
rare in the New York area, where a player without his own column or
radio show is an object of pity. "It takes a certain kind of person to play
well here," Toomer said. "It has nothing to do with whether he's from a

rural area or a cosmopolitan area; it's inside him. Can he shoot for the stars? Can he stand daily pressure? You can't lay back here and just have a nice career. I had a rough start, but I just knew I'd make it, and I was sure I'd end up being a longtime Giant. Every now and then they'd draft a guy who looked like he was going to be my replacement, but those guys always tried too hard. In the pass-catching business, if you have to try too hard, something's wrong. When it's feeling good on the field, there's this amazing comfort level. You're primed at the line of scrimmage. You actually kind of hum, like you're a race car at the starting grid—five thousand RPM and shaking, shaking, shaking, and then all of a sudden, whoosh! You really get to know yourself on a football field. I know I've got some Giants records, but I'm not ready to look at them yet. I'm not ready to stop."

Not surprisingly, Manning took Toomer's loss the hardest. "He's the most consistent great player on our team," said Eli, deciding not to go into who was the least consistent. "You always know what you're going to get out of Amani. He does the right thing on every play. If the quarterback doesn't trust his possession receiver, if you have the slightest doubt that he'll get open, it makes you just a split second late, and that's when you commit your biggest errors." Toomer was the one who told him, way back when Eli arrived, "New York is for the strong-willed." Like a game plan, Manning had made a study of New York sports, immersing himself in the Knicks and Nets and even the Devils and Rangers. "I had never been to a hockey game until I got here," Eli said. "Those are good fun, too." A New York athlete can't ever get down, either on himself or on the team. "Because if he does," Manning said, "the media are going to go for the kill shot. They'll say, 'He's not strong enough to be here.'"

But a quarterback who loses his Raymond Berry can't help but feel a little down, at least momentarily. In the weeks to come, the *New York Times* would plot a steady decline in Manning's passing rating, especially on third-down plays, from the last short pass to Toomer that allowed the Giants to run out the clock against Houston.

Only for about a half a day did the players allow themselves to talk about the many injuries. After that, the dear departed were spoken of no more. "You can't talk about injuries in the NFL," said Brandon Short, another Penn State linebacker. "It's not just that it's an insult to the backup players, it's a built-in alibi for everyone on the team. It's a self-fulfilling prophecy. You just can't talk about it. You just can't think about it. You just have to keep on playing."

The first half of the season was over and the Giants stood 6–2. New Orleans, that team starting out in the opposite direction, was also 6–2. Their new quarterback, Drew Brees, was no longer being described as damaged goods from San Diego. Their rookie coach, Sean Payton— once a replacement quarterback in the strike year of 1987—was about to become the toast of the league.

"He was an assistant coach for us," Ernie said, "who never even got an interview. I blew it."

16

TIME-OUT, GIANTS

THE FIRST DOMINO FELL, the season began to be lost, on a time-out called by New York with 1:30 left in the opening half of a Sunday night game versus the Chicago Bears. Not one player, not one coach, not one reporter, not one fan—even in retrospect—would cite this as a significant event, let alone a seminal one, but Accorsi did, the moment it happened. "He didn't second-guess you, Tom," I told Coughlin many weeks later. "He first-guessed you. He first-guessed the hell out of you."

"Ernie picks his spots," Coughlin said.

Unable to decide between a drizzle and a downpour, the night was wet and cold, especially in Accorsi's Giants Stadium tunnel, which leaks. "Do you know who that is?" Ernie said, trying to dodge the heaviest drips. He nodded toward a Bears bystander, number 4, who in the pregame hour was also working hard to stay moderately dry. "Brad Maynard," Ernie said contemptuously. "He's a punter from Ball State. We had him here with us in the Super Bowl year, 2000. Every time we exchanged punts with the Ravens, they gained about six yards on us." When the other Bears players had joined Maynard in the tunnel, they put their fists together, and Thomas Jones, a running back, hollered, "We're the best team in the NFL! We've got to show them that right now!" Someone with a more modulated voice in the center of the scrum said, "Take it to the house on two, baby," and they all screamed, "Take it to the house!" and stampeded under the goalpost onto the field. Number 23 brought up the rear.

"That's the rookie Devin Hester," Ernie said, "a University of Miami guy. Wait till you see him. He was a little weird at the workout, but he's got a lot of ability. His father played at Florida State with Deion Sanders, who was coaching Hester in the workout. 'What's Deion doing here?' I asked the kid. 'Oh, he's my mentor, he's my guru.' But that wasn't really what worried me. Hester kept saying, 'I'm a defensive back, I'm not a receiver.' Well, they tried him at both positions, and he looked like a hell of a receiver to me. Great hands. But he didn't want to play there. He wanted to be Deion Sanders. And anyone could see he didn't have the instincts or the experience for that. The Bears are listing him as a cornerback, but they're using him as a kick returner. He sure has the instincts for that."

Taking the opening kickoff, the Giants wasted a nine-play drive with a missed field goal of thirty-three yards in a tricky wind. But on Chicago's third snap of the game, quarterback Rex Grossman made the exact mistake for which he was becoming infamous. "The book on Grossman," Accorsi said, "is that if you put pressure on him in his own territory, he's going to give you the game. He shows a lot more talent on your side of the field than he does on his, kind of like the hitter who can kill you when the count is three and one but has no chance at oh and two. Let Grossman get into a comfort zone, though, and he can play."

On third and nine at his own twenty-five, Rex threw a pass to the right side that was easily intercepted by Mathias Kiwanuka and returned to the one-yard line, from where Brandon Jacobs forced his way into the end zone. With neither quarterback shining in the rain, an exchange of turnovers—an interception of Eli Manning, a Jones fumble—brought about a swap of field goals. After the Giants struck for another three points, their scoring "drives" amounted to one yard, three yards, and nine yards.

Eli was not just struggling but foundering, especially since the two-minute mark of the first quarter, when left tackle Luke Petitgout limped out of the game. Still, the Giants had a 13–3 lead and it was raining hard.

BEARS

1-10-B26 Grossman passes to Mark Bradley for 6
Two-minute warning
2-4-B32   Grossman passes to Jones for 8
1-10-B40 Grossman passes incomplete
2-10-B40 (shotgun) False start, Chicago
2-15-B35 (shotgun) Another false start, Chicago
2-20-B30 (shotgun) Grossman passes to Jones for –2
3-22-B28 . . .

That's when the Giants called time-out with a minute and a half to go until halftime, to save some clock for themselves.

"No, no, no, *no!*" Accorsi cried out, turning into Rumpelstiltskin, startling the spectators in the seats above. "Don't be too smart! Don't be too smart!" This was a Paterno-ism. "The Bears are ready to settle for thirteen to three at the half! It's raining! Let them settle for thirteen to three at the half!"

Then came the second domino.

3-22-B28 Jones runs for 26 yards

"Third and twenty-two," linebacker Antonio Pierce said later, disgustedly. "It was a give-up play. Everybody in the league runs a draw or a screen in that situation. It was just a simple draw play." But the Giants, especially safety Will Demps, couldn't stop it; or didn't, anyway.

1-10-G46 Illegal shift, Chicago
1-15-B49 Grossman passes incomplete
2-15-B49 Grossman passes to Muhsin Muhammad
for 22 yards
1-10-G29 Grossman passes to Mark Bradley for 29 yards
and the touchdown; Robbie Gould's kick is good
New York 13, Chicago 10

With the thirty-five seconds they had preserved, the Giants ran their own give-up play, a Barber plunge, and went off to the locker room looking like the trailing team. Both of Chicago's long passes at the end victimized corner Sam Madison, who tried bravely to come back from his hamstring strain but plainly had no legs. The latest injury, maybe the worst of all, walked right past Accorsi on a bare left foot. Petitgout, the left tackle, the quarterback's main protector, was limping to the locker room on a broken fibula. He was finished for the night and for the season. In fact, he was finished with the Giants forever. After every snap from center the rest of the year, Manning would move almost imperceptibly to his right before he did anything else.

"It's broken; he's out," Accorsi said, returning from the X-ray room to his tunnel just before the teams poured through for the second half. "Tiki is saying sprained, but his right thumb is broken, too. Tiki just doesn't have the time to have a broken thumb right now, God bless him. He only has a half a year left to go. Me too."

Chicago took the third-quarter kick and drove to the Giants' two-yard line before fumbling. But New York couldn't move an inch and Jeff Feagles had barely enough end zone space to launch a punt.

BEARS

1-10-G43 Jones runs for 2
2-8-G41 Grossman passes to Jones for 4 (plus roughing the passer on William Joseph)
1-10-G22 Illegal contact, R. W. McQuarters
1-10-G17 Jones runs for 7
2-3-G10 Jones runs for 10 and an apparent touchdown, nullified by John Gilmore's hold
2-7-G14 Jones runs for 4
3-3-G10 Grossman passes to Muhammad for 10 and the touchdown; Gould's kick is good

Chicago 17, New York 13

Old Bob Whitfield, the first-round draft choice from yesteryear (for Atlanta), who hadn't been as nimble since breaking his own leg in 2003, moved into Petitgout's position and was outclassed horribly by defensive end Alex Brown. One of Brown's two sacks caused a Manning fumble that left the Bears just twenty-one yards from another touchdown and a 24–13 lead. In his comfort zone, Rex Grossman certainly could play. Then a forty-six-yard sprint by Barber set up an eight-yard run by Jacobs for Brandon's second touchdown. The Bears led only 24–20, with 11:49 left in the game, when the last domino fell.

GIANTS

1-10-G21 Barber runs for 5 (personal foul, Chicago)
1-10-G41 Manning passes to Plaxico Burress for 10
1-10-B49 Barber runs for 8
2-2-B41   Manning passes to David Tyree for 12
1-10-B29 Manning sacked by Brown
2-24-B43 (shotgun) Barber runs for 9
3-15-B34 Manning passes incomplete

"Do you believe we called a pass play there?" Ernie asked. "Now we can't even try a field goal."

Wanna bet?

4-15-B34 . . .

"Oh, no," Accorsi whispered as Jay Feely came out to attempt a fifty-two-yarder. "Oh, God," Ernie said, "no!" Hester dropped back into the end zone. "Now we have all of our fat guys on the field," the GM said in a normal and resigned voice. "Watch Hester run it back all the way for a touchdown." And he did. As Deion's protégé crossed the goal line, he leaped into the air and fired an imaginary jump shot at the Giants.

Afterward, Whitfield was the most distraught. "I was watching to see the ball sail through the uprights," he confessed, "rather than running down there and covering the kick. Counting that play and the two sacks, I feel like I lost this game single-handedly." In days to come, in a poignant moment during a players-only meeting, Whitfield would rise to tell his teammates that he hadn't expected to have to come in and play such an important role. He beseeched the backups to the backups to try to be readier than he was when the call came.

In the locker room after the Chicago game, center Shaun O'Hara said of Hester's 108-yard run, "The last thing you think of is that it's going to be short and they're going to return it for a touchdown. Even if you had a crystal ball, you might not see that one."

The final score was 38–20. After that night, for any observer not too emotionally involved, the only unknown about the 2006 Giants was whether they would keep playing or quit. Maybe never in the NFL's history had there been so few good teams at the top and so few bad teams at the bottom and so many average teams in the middle. Where New York might fit at anything like full strength no longer mattered. Like the Super Bowl, full strength was out of the question now. The season, as a season, was over.

Walking into a pro football front office on a Monday morning, you wouldn't have to have seen or heard about Sunday's game to know the score. You don't have to pass a second desk to realize how good or bad it was. After a victory, any kind of victory, the workers are dancing in the aisles. After a loss, any kind of loss, the women and men darting here and there with a pen or a sheaf of paper aren't just depressed, they're despondent. The morning after the Bears game was worst of all.

"This is a scrambling day," Ernie said darkly. "We're waiting for the official word on Petitgout. We already got some bad news on Justin Tuck, who didn't play last night. His separation is worse. Ronnie Barnes is flying with him to Charlotte tomorrow for an operation, so Justin's lost. He has no family to go with him, and Ronnie doesn't want him to have to go alone. We need a left tackle, and of course Tom is looking for [the great 1950s pass blocker] Roosevelt Brown. You can imagine what's out there at this point in November with all of the injuries. There's nothing. Is there a tackle out there? Is there anyone even on a practice squad? It's hard to pry people from practice squads. The player has to notify his club, and the club immediately makes a counteroffer, or tries to arrange room for him on the roster, especially if it's a team not going to the playoffs. I doubt Petitgout will be back, but I'm not going to be in a hurry to put him on injured reserve. John Fox almost committed suicide in Carolina after he put running back Stephen Davis on IR and ended up going all of the way to the Super Bowl. By then, Davis was a hundred percent healthy and ineligible to play. If only to show our team I'm not quitting on them, I'm going to hold out that same hope for Luke."

Immediately after the game, Petitgout had said, "I'll be fine . . . a couple of weeks. Guys have played with this before."

"He would say that, wouldn't he?" Accorsi said, chuckling. "God, these guys are great. Luke's dreaming, of course, but I love dreamers."

At the moment, Ernie was not in love with his head coach. "I did a lot of bitching in the tunnel last night," he said, "and, frankly, when I think about that game, twenty-four hours later, I'm *more* angry. When Tom was hired, I asked him, 'Is there a bunker mentality among head coaches?' and he answered, 'I'm going to count on you to be blatantly frank with me and give me your slant so that I can always have a fresh point of view.' They all say that, but they don't really want to hear anything but what they want to hear. I'm going to write it out for him today in a memo. 'This is what I think.' I'm going to put it on paper, not for the record, just because I don't have time today to wage a running debate. Tom can look at it if he wants. He can throw it away if he wants. But here's my view.

"What we did last night, it violated everything I *ever* learned about football. It violated every principle Paterno taught me. Joe had two things that he screamed, I'm telling you, twenty times a day—I'm not exaggerating. One is field position, field position, field position. Number two, don't try to be too smart. Be sound. You're not going to outsmart anybody. It's going to blow up in your face, especially if you're trying to outsmart someone. If you're sound, you're going to win.

"I look at players' eyes in the tunnel. I learn a lot in that tunnel. It's thirteen to three—the Bears don't think they're going to win the game because they have to beat us by intercepting the ball or causing some other turnover or, somehow, unleashing Hester. What do we do? We give them the opportunity. Why do we want the ball back for thirty-five seconds to begin with? It's raining. We could fumble the kick, we could commit a holding penalty. We could give them life. Our quarterback is having a terrible night. What was to be gained? Had there been a single sign that we could take the ball and march it down the field in thirty-five seconds? After that, it's third and twenty-three. Chicago's giving up the ghost, right? Get in the locker room, Tom, with our thirteen-to-three lead! And when the Bears ran into the locker room, they were a different team. On the road in the NFL, it isn't long before you don't think you can win. 'We're not going to win this game, okay?' And they were getting awfully close to that. But no, we were too smart.

"Now we've come back to twenty-four to twenty and we're first and ten on their twenty-nine. We've got control of the situation. We're running the ball and they can't stop us. We ran for a hundred and fifty yards—no one has stopped us from running the ball all year in those conditions—and why we're not using Jacobs, I have no idea. He was unopposed on both touchdowns. We're wearing them down. The weather is bad. Maybe we won't be able to hold them later, maybe we'll screw up on defense later—six starters are out, after all—but we're going to go ahead in the game for the moment at least, if we just play smart. But instead, for some unknown reason, against *that* pass rush, with Eli having a bad night, we try to throw. Now it's second and twenty-four. We've changed the game. We get to third and fifteen, and Hufnagel says, 'Oh, I think I'll try this pass play to Plax. That's part of my philosophy.'

"Finally, rather than hand the ball to Feagles and trust the best plus-punter in the league to spin the ball inside the twenty and give Grossman a chance to give away the game in bad weather, we try a fifty-two-yard field goal in the same direction a thirty-three-yarder had already been missed. Our big, slow field-goal protection guys then get to watch Devin Hester dance a hundred and eight yards untouched. He would have scored in a two-hand touch football game.

"We could have won a thirteen-to-ten game. That's our kind of game."

The rush of words seemed to be over. A little chagrined, Ernie smiled. But he was just taking a breath.

"Tom said, 'I told Eli today that you don't score points by running the ball, you score points by passing it.' That kills any chance of me sleeping tonight. Tom had this long talk with Eli in which he basically told him, 'You're the reason we lost and you're going to have to play much better or we won't win.' Do you think Bill Cowher ever said that to Ben Roethlisberger? Pittsburgh never asks Roethlisberger to win a game by himself. They ask him not to lose by himself. 'I told Eli,' Tom said, 'You know why I made that stupid decision on the field goal, Eli?' Now listen to this. 'Because you weren't playing well and I didn't know how we'd get down there again.' Now I have to go to Manning sometime today and try to reassure him that it's not all his fault."

Ernie had one other thing on his mind.

"Do you know what all this takes me back to?" he said. "Alabama beat Penn State in the Sugar Bowl, fourteen to seven, to win the national championship in 1978. That was the goal line stand game. In the pregame, Penn State kicker Matt Bahr was booting one sixty-yard field goal after another. He'd never been in a dome in his life. He was laughing. 'How easy is this?' But every time they were in range for a long field goal, about seven times, Paterno kept calling for a third-down drop-back pass, and Bear Bryant, who never, ever blitzed, blitzed the hell out of them and knocked them back out of range every time. Following the game, Jim Tarman says, 'Why don't you come up to Joe's suite?' 'Thanks anyway, Jim,' I said. 'C'mon, Joe wants you up there.' Just a few people, Paterno's wife and brother, a couple of others, were in the room. Joe was staring out the window at the Mississippi River. I was almost afraid to go up to him, he looked so wounded. He turned to me and said, 'I did a bad job, Ernie. Maybe I can't do this at this level.' What? 'Maybe I'm not good enough to coach against a guy like Bryant'—whom he never beat, by the way. Back home, Joe told Sue, 'I think I'm going to quit.' In kind of a play on the advice Joe gave me, she told him to go back to New York, rent a car, drive to the old streets of Brooklyn, and walk around for three days.

"'Think of what you wanted when you were a kid,' she said, 'and then come home.' Walking the old streets, Joe said, 'What am I doing? When I was a kid, I would have killed for the job I have now. I had a bad game, and it was my fault. It was no one else's fault but mine. But I'm not quitting.' Paterno told me he has gone back there subsequently a few more times. And I do it, too, in Hershey. It clears your head. I've packed up a lot of my stuff already. Maybe in the next couple of days I should drop off a few of these boxes in Hershey."

Other than for a left tackle, Ernie had one great wish on this Monday morning.

"To hear some other head football coach," he said, "any other head football coach, say, 'I had a bad game, and it was my fault. It was nobody else's fault but mine.'"

17

"IT'S A FABULOUS GAME"

BOXES OF MEMORIES WERE disappearing from Accorsi's office and reappearing at his town house in Hershey. As Ernie was hauling a couple of heavy files up some steps at home, the contents shifted and he tumbled back down headfirst into a wall. Neither Chuck Wepner nor Carmen Basilio ever sported a shinier black eye. "My head was out to here," Ernie said a few days later. "It was like a baseball. So I called Ronnie Barnes right away. It was a Wednesday night, when the doctors regularly come to Giants Stadium for their midweek update of the players' conditions. One of the specialists asked me what day it was, what was the score of last week's game—hadn't I suffered enough?— what was my mother's maiden name. Then came the really scary questions: 'Do you have any feeling in your fingers and toes?' 'Yeah.' 'Are you sure?' *'Yeah!'* " Nobody could understand why he didn't have a broken neck or at least a fractured skull, but he didn't. What a year the Giants were having. Even the general manager was lining up for a CAT scan.

Two of the boxes he gave to me to deliver to Ron Wolf. The best gauge of whether Ernie would miss this work was probably Wolf, the former Green Bay Packers GM, who was a little older than Accorsi and retired on a similar schedule after about thirty-five seasons. For many years, they were each other's closest friend in the GM trade. "Wolf is from New Freedom, Pennsylvania," Ernie said. "When I first met him, he was traveling the East, scouting for the Raiders. He was their only scout. We'd see each other five or six times a year, and have a meal at this little luncheonette by the bus station." Now Wolf lived with his wife on a finger of water near Annapolis, Maryland, mostly ignoring the NFL. These days, Wolf said, he was less likely to watch a live football game than an old black-and-white tape from what he considered a much happier era. "I liked sports a lot better," he said, "in the days before ESPN."

It was Ernie's and Ron's shared habit to search out vintage and obscure pro and college films and pass them back and forth. "Wolf's a lot like I am," Accorsi said. "We speak the same language." Yeah, quarterbacks.

Ron was the assembler of the original Tampa Bay Buccaneers, the unchallenged worst team in the history of the league, loser of its first twenty-six games. After one of those losses, head coach John McKay was asked a question about his team's execution and replied, "I'm in favor of it." But, blessedly, Wolf was better remembered for his days in Green Bay. Between those jobs, he served the New York Jets as a player personnel man, and at one point was far and away the leading admirer of a Southern Mississippi quarterback named Brett Favre. The summer before Favre's senior year, an automobile accident took something out of him: thirty inches of intestine. "He was raw and took the darnedest chances, but I liked him," Wolf said. "He didn't play as well as a senior as he did as a junior, not too surprisingly." But he held himself like a great player, and Wolf believed he was.

Unfortunately, the Jets' best draft choice that year was a sixth pick in the second round. Favre went fifth in that round to Atlanta, where he sat on a shelf. Well, he didn't just sit on the shelf. He also went out on the town and had a hell of a good time.

After securing the Green Bay job, Wolf stood before the board of directors of the publicly owned Packers and heard himself tell them there was an obtainable player who was so gifted that he would make the citizens forget anybody else who had ever worn a Green Bay uniform. There was a gasp in the room, even before Wolf named the player, a third-stringer for the Falcons. "That's the fun of what I used to do and Ernie still does," Wolf said, "but I think it's less fun than it used to be. I don't miss it. I don't think he will, either."

And yet, in the middle of lunch on the Annapolis waterfront, not responding to a question, germane to nothing at all, Wolf suddenly looked up and said softly, "It's a fabulous game." No, he didn't miss it.

Back in the front office, an old man and a young man represented two other good measuring sticks for Accorsi. Harry Hulmes, the 1960s Colts GM who spoke kindly even of agents, was still standing up for decency, as now Ernie played the part of George Young. "Harry is probably the purest human being I've ever been around," Ernie said. "There's no guile. There's no con. He has empathy for absolutely everyone, and now I'm the one trying to talk him out of it."

Hulmes: "Oh, what a great punt!"

Accorsi: "No, Harry, that's not a great punt. That punt just pinned us down on the ten-yard line. It's a bad punt for *us*, Harry. Okay?"

Later—

Hulmes: "My God, that's one of the greatest runs I've ever seen!"

Accorsi: "Harry. That's the other team. It's a bad run. Bad. Very bad."

Ernie said, "With Wellington gone, Harry's my connection to the past, just like Matt's my connection to the future."

Matt Harriss was a kid in his twenties, the Giants' youngest front office worker, who already knew what he wanted. "Going on the road trips, just being part of the Giants, is wonderful," he said. "Ernie has taken me under his wing since the day I came over from the league office this year. I arrived in April. My last day with the league was a Wednesday, my first with the Giants was a Thursday. It was the day we signed LaVar Arrington. About three hours later, Ernie and I were just kind of getting to know each other, and Kevin Abrams walks out of his office. Ernie yells down the hallway, 'Hey, Kevin, what have you done today?' 'What do you mean?' 'Kid's been here three hours and has already signed us a linebacker. What the hell have you done?' I felt comfortable right off the bat. The more I'm around Ernie, the more sure I am that this is what I someday want to be. The losses are terrible, I know, but they don't make me want to be a GM any less."

"Matt gets my batteries charging, too," Accorsi said. "He takes me back to Upton Bell and those days. Showing him little things reminds me of them at the same time."

"He'll sit with me and watch a tape," Harriss said, "and just talk about what he sees, and suddenly I can see it, too. 'Look at this,' he'll say. 'Look at that.' The best things, though, are just little pieces of history or advice that he passes along. He called me in to show me the Pittsburgh Steelers' Christmas card. You open it up and it's just the team with signatures. Nowhere does it say 'world champions.' 'That's Rooney class,' Ernie said. He told me a story from the 1970s, when the Steelers were champions a lot. Walking into the office, Mr. Rooney heard a receptionist answering the telephone, 'World Champion Steelers.' He waited until she hung up the phone, and then told her in a kind way, 'You don't have to say that. They know.' Ernie loved that. I do, too."

"Ron is a reminder to me that it's okay to retire now, I'm ready," Accorsi said. "Harry is a reminder that it was never just the winning and the losing. Matt reminds me that this has always been a good thing to be. I've been lucky."

The game in Jacksonville, a 26–10 loss, was a reminder that Eli was still fogged in (nineteen of forty-one), and when Antonio Pierce expressed his solution, "We just need to get our guys back," was he speaking of this year or next?

18

TITANIC, HINDENBURG,

JOE PISARCIK . . .

WARMING UP AT LP Field in Nashville, home of rookie quarterback Vince Young and the 3-and-7 Titans, Jeremy Shockey had his first look at the skeleton inside the ring finger of his left hand. It was neither an inspiring sight nor a favorable omen. "It's a little frightening, to tell you the truth," Shockey said after catching a ball wrong, "to see the bones coming out of your hand like that. But the doctors pushed them right back in, sewed me up tight, numbed me up good, and I was ready to go. Hell, I was going to play, even if they cut it off."

And on Eli Manning's first completion of the game, Jeremy caught a seven-yard pass for a first down and laughed. The short stuff was key to the Giants' strategy. Narrowing Manning's responsibilities seemed to be the order of the day, until the end. "We knew exactly how they were going to play," Coughlin said. "We had a great game plan." It worked so well at the start, and for such a long time, that the entire New York team finally seemed to relax. "The Titans were asleep the whole game," Tom said. "Sound asleep. Willing to let us do whatever we wanted to do, until . . ."

That first Giants scoring drive of fifty-two yards was built on Tiki Barber and Brandon Jacobs runs plus Manning's twenty-yard pass to Plaxico Burress, who then scored the touchdown on just a three-yard Eli throw across the middle. New York's second good drive of seventy-six yards included quick completions to Burress, Shockey, and Barber, along with two blasts by Jacobs, for fourteen yards on a third down and for ten on the touchdown. Two more short Manning passes to Barber and David Tyree figured in the third success, capped by Jacobs' second touchdown on a four-yard run. The score was 21–0 at halftime, 21–0 throughout the third quarter, and 21–0 at 5:25 in the fourth. But there was a New York series that started in the third and ended in the fourth that was worth reviewing later.

GIANTS

1-10-G11 Manning passes incomplete
2-10-G11 Offensive holding, Kareem McKenzie
2-16-G5   Manning passes to Jacobs for 9
3-7-G14   (Shotgun) Jacobs runs for 10
1-10-G24 Barber runs for 9
2-1-G33   Barber runs for 6
1-10-G39 Manning passes to Burress for 11
1-10-50   Barber runs for 3
2-7-T47   Manning passes to Barber for 9
1-10-T38 Offensive holding, David Diehl
1-20-T48 (shotgun) Manning passes to Shockey for 7
2-13-T41 Jacobs runs for 5
3-8-T36   (shotgun) Manning passes to Jacobs for 5
4-3-T36   (shotgun) Manning passes incomplete;
   14 plays, 53 yards, no points, no field goal
   attempt, no coffin-corner punt

Over three seasons, the Titans were 1 and 21 in games they were losing after three quarters by so much as one point, let alone three touchdowns. "Tennessee went three and out then," said Accorsi, who was sitting in the press box next to John Mara. "So, on first down at our twenty-nine, Eli hands off to Tiki and he carries for six yards. It's second and four at the thirty-five. There are twelve minutes and some seconds to go, and Tennessee is basically on the brink of *no más.* We got a quarterback who's been shaky, but nonetheless, we're in complete control, and we're not playing the Bears either. What do we do? We empty the backfield and go into the shotgun. They know we're going to pass. You can't hand off to air. We throw a takeoff to Plaxico, who's covered by their best corner—their only corner—who intercepts the ball, and the game turns. 'Everything's changed now,' I whispered to John. Later I said to Tom, 'Why, Tom? I just would like to know why.' First of all, every time you run the ball, it's forty-five, fifty seconds off the clock. Let the time run out. The Titans wanted no more of number twenty-seven [Jacobs]. Just grind them down and send that big bastard straight at 'em."

The corner who made the interception and returned the ball twenty-six yards to the Giants' forty-six was Adam Bernard Jones, known as "Pacman" since childhood for the video game and its industrial efficiency he emulated while gobbling up rivers of milk. Pacman had changed drinks since, and when it came to legal scrapes involving gunfire and strip clubs, Jones was single-handedly holding his own against the entire fifty-three-man roster of pro football's Hole-in-the-Wall Gang, the Cincinnati Bengals. Incidently, a suspension for Pacman was on the way.

Significantly, the field position that accompanied Pacman's interception could only be put down to carelessness, in the worst sense of the word—apparent lack of caring—by Burress. Plaxico blatantly quit on his pass route—"I thought the ball was over both of our heads"—and made a quarter-hearted attempt at tackling Jones. "I guess I should have jumped on his back," Burress said, "and taken a penalty."

TITANS

1-10-G48 (shotgun) Young passes incomplete
2-10-G48 (shotgun) Young passes to Bobby Wade for 25
1-10-G21 (shotgun) Young runs for 2 (unnecessary
    roughness, Tennessee's LenDale White)

2-23-G34 (shotgun) Young passes to Travis Henry for 5
3-18-G29 (no huddle, shotgun) Young passes to Wade
    for 9
4-9-G20   (no huddle, shotgun) Young scrambles for 7
    (unnecessary roughness by New York's Frank Walker)
1-G-G6   (shotgun) Henry runs for −1
2-G-G7   (shotgun) Young passes to Bo Scaife for 3
3-G-G4   Young passes to Scaife for 4 and the touchdown;
  Rob Bironas' kick is good

New York 21, Tennessee 7

Walker, the Giants defensive back with his own "suite of doghouses," started at left corner because Corey Webster had a swollen toe. Frank's hit on Young at the sideline probably would have qualified as assault even if the target hadn't been a quarterback. "When he crosses the line of scrimmage," Walker said, "he's just a regular football player to me. If I let him lean forward, he gets the first down."

Soon, Tennessee had the ball again, still behind by two touchdowns with about seven minutes to go. Without Plax's help this time, Pacman again flipped the field position by returning a thirty-nine-yard Jeff Feagles punt twenty-three yards to the New York thirty-six.

TITANS

1-10-G36 (shotgun) Young passes to Wade for 9
2-1-G27   (shotgun) Young passes to Wade for 11
1-10-G16 Henry runs for 9
2-1-G7   (shotgun) Young passes to Scaife for 5
1-G-G2   Henry runs for 1
2-G-G1   Young scrambles for 1 and the touchdown;
  Bironas' kick is good

New York 21, Tennessee 14 (4:24 remaining)

Manning converted one third-down play with his own freelance run, but on third and nine at the Giants' thirty-three, Eli passed to Barber for only four, and Feagles punted again (3:07 remaining).

TITANS

1-10-T24 (shotgun) Young scrambles for 24 yards (offsetting penalties, no play)

1-10-T24 (shotgun) Young passes incomplete

2-10-T24 (shotgun) Young passes incomplete

3-10-T24 Young passes incomplete

4-10-T24 (shotgun) Apparently sacked, Young slips the grasp of Mathias Kiwanuka and scrambles for 19 (2:44)

1-10-T43 (shotgun) Young passes to Roydell Williams for 20

Two-minute warning

1-10-G37 (shotgun) Young scrambles for 16

1-10-G21 (shotgun) Young passes to Drew Bennett for 7

2-3-G14 (shotgun) Young passes to Brandon Jones for 14 and the touchdown; Bironas' kick is good

Tennessee 21, New York 21 (:44 remaining)

On second and one at his own twenty-eight, thirty-two seconds from overtime, Manning dropped back in the shotgun and aimed a deep pass at Tyree that again settled in the soft fingers and palms of Pacman Jones. Three plays later, Bironas kicked a forty-nine-yard field goal to complete either a sensational comeback or a hideous collapse, depending on how you looked at it. The city of New York looked at it only one way. The *Titanic,* the *Hindenburg,* and Joe Pisarcik were all back in the headlines.

"We're going to be sick about this one," Coughlin said in the locker room, "for, for, forever."

Of the final pass, Eli said, "If you miss, you have to miss high and away, not short. Throw it away. Get to overtime at least. I thought I had a chance to reach Tyree. There just wasn't enough on it." At one point

Manning was sixteen for twenty-one for 132 yards and a touchdown. But he ended up eighteen for twenty-eight for 143 yards and two interceptions. Much later, sitting by himself, Eli said, "If the media wants to put all of the blame on me, that's fine. I can handle it. I can take it. It doesn't bother me. The important thing is to continue trying to earn the respect of the players, to get to the point where they trust you. That's what really matters. That's what I'm striving for. The really important thing is to stay together in the meantime, while we're all learning, even through terrible, terrible losses. I know I sound pretty vague and stupid to the media, but I'm trying to be careful, measuring my words. They keep asking the same question a hundred different ways, trying to get me into fights with my teammates, hoping I'll throw somebody under the bus. Then they can slam me for that, too. 'Hell, don't feel sorry for yourself,' Dad called to say, 'I dealt with losing for fifteen years. Three losses in a row used to be a winning streak for the Saints!' That didn't make me feel all that much better, but it did make me laugh. 'Keep fighting,' he said."

"Eli was very, very affected by that last interception," Coughlin said many weeks later. "That was heartbreaking." But the Kiwanuka play was the one that reverberated not just through the Giants' clubhouse but throughout the league. "That's the one the media really killed me on, too," Coughlin said, looking back, "for my reaction on the sideline, you know, running back and forth. But think of this: I'm being told on the earphones by the defensive coordinator, 'We've got him! He's down! The game's over!' Only I look up and the son of a bitch is running out of bounds right in front of me! If we had him and he's down, what happened? What happened? What happened? The ball's almost to midfield. 'Kiwanuka let him go! He just let him go!'"

"I had my head down, buried in Young's chest," Kiwanuka said. The rookie imagined he could feel the throwing motion of the quarterback's arm across his body. Remembering the roughing penalty of a few weeks earlier, he let go. ("Thank God, thank God!" Young said. "He let me loose!") "I worried it might be a fifteen-yard penalty," Kiwanuka said, "if I didn't let him go. I didn't know he still had the football in his hand. As a pass rusher, you work all game long to get to the quarterback . . ."

Coughlin couldn't help but think of Steve McNair, the former Titan scrambler, who made so many Sundays so uncomfortable back when the coach was working in Jacksonville. "I had to play all those games against McNair," Tom said, "and now this guy does this. The game isn't in balance with these guys [running quarterbacks], and they tell you these guys can't survive in the NFL. Young runs for seventy yards against us. He's a runner! But we hit him on the sidelines and it's unnecessary roughness. Because he's a quarterback. A six-foot-five, two-hundred-thirty-five-pound quarterback. The league has got to do something about this, but they refuse to recognize that a few of these guys aren't your regular quarterbacks. They're just not the same."

In that cause, Coughlin found an unexpected ally in fellow Syracuse alum Keith Bulluck, a linebacker on the Tennessee side. Bulluck said, "We won, so I'm happy. But I think the NFL has a silly attitude about running quarterbacks. 'Whatever you do, don't hurt the quarterback, even if he's steamrolling your ass, about twenty yards at a clip.' It worked to our benefit today, but I still don't get it." Receiver Scaife, Young's old Longhorn teammate, said, "Vince did this same thing to Oklahoma State my senior year at Texas. We were down thirty-five to nothing, scored just before the half, then came back to win it. So I've seen it before. Nothing new to me. The whole NFL better get ready. It's going to be seeing this a lot."

If Tom looked a bit panicked on the sideline, he contended that he was panicking on behalf of Kiwanuka. "Mathias plays very, very hard," Coughlin said. "He's going to be a great football player, I think. But a play like that one can define a veteran, let alone a rookie. That's Jim Marshall of the Vikings running the wrong way. The next day, every team in the league made a point of calling every defensive player together and showing them that play. A new message went out. 'Don't throw the quarterbacks down on the ground, but grab them, hold them, squeeze them until the whistle blows.' The moment it happened, honestly, my first thought was that it could end up being this poor kid's identity."

Immediately following the loss so stunning that it literally rang in the losers' ears, Coughlin asked someone to go get John Mara. "You know John," Tom said. "He's a guy who always sticks his hand out to you after a loss. I'm still not used to that. He came in and sat down. 'John,' I said, 'I'm sorry, I'm sorry, I'm sorry.' I said, 'There's no explanation. I can't tell you what happened.'"

"Wow!" was all Titans head coach Jeff Fisher could say, over and over. "Did that really happen?" Young promised, "This is just a sneak peek into what's coming for me and for our team." But Fisher couldn't stop shaking his head. "I expected the Giants to grind the ball out," he said. "For whatever reason, they decided to go no back and throw the ball down the field. We were fortunate."

"I never thought they would go on to win the game," said Antonio Pierce in a daze, "until they went on to win the game."

"Let's face it," Brandon Jacobs said, "that's a team we should beat the shit out of. We pissed it away. They suck."

"Chill out, Brandon," Gibril Wilson said. "If they suck, what does that say about us?"

That made three New York losses in a row (one more to come). In 1994, Lawrence Taylor's first season of retirement, the Giants lost seven consecutive games to stand 3 and 7 with six to play, and their Hall of Fame linebacker returned to the locker room to deliver a pep talk. It wasn't Knute Rockne but it was memorable. At the height of his oratory, during what may have been a world record for profanity, Taylor shouted, "Even your bitches are ashamed of you!"

And the Giants won their last six.

19

K BALLS

TEAMS ON BAD STREAKS are often said to find entirely new ways to lose, but the way New York found next had such a trivial nature and such a terrible consequence that it probably *was* unprecedented. It had to do with two old-time employees in an officious mood (who were fired by Accorsi the following day) and with the football itself. Jay Feely, the Giants' placekicker, began to explain.

"Five or six years ago," he said, "my first year in the NFL, K balls came in, just for kicking. The reason for that, honestly, was because guys were working up the balls. They'd put them in an oven, they'd put them in a sauna, they'd do all kinds of stuff prior to the games to get the balls in the best kicking shape so they would fly as far as possible. The catalyst for the new rule, I've always heard, was a game between Green Bay and Minnesota, when Mitch Berger apparently kicked every ball through the end zone. At the same time, Gary Anderson made all of the Vikings' field goals with a little too much room to spare. Mike Holmgren, the Green Bay coach, was not too happy about it, and he was a member of the competition committee. Now, that's the story I heard. This was the genesis of the K balls coming in."

Reaching into his locker, Feely pulled out an average-looking football. "Here's a ball from last week's game," he said. It was stamped below the laces with a capital K.

"They all come from the same factory, but you can get a ball where the seams stick up more than others, and some are nubbier than others. They add that nubbiness to the balls when they're making them. I don't know if it's little stones or what, just some kind of a pebbling process. Now, the quarterbacks like the nubbier balls, because that gives them a little more grip. But a kickoff guy prefers them real smooth without a lot of pebbles, so they'll go farther. If the ball boys on the sideline know a good kicking ball from a bad one, they can make sure you get the decent ball to kick off. All of the balls are brand-new, but some of them will go at least ten yards deeper."

A designated ball preparer from each team—not a kicker, though—may rub the footballs down for thirty minutes before the game. No longer than that. But one is sure to be smoother than another. "Then the referee will take the balls and make his little mark," Feely said. "Some of them have a stamp, some write their initials. He also puts a little drawing on the nose, in ink, like the pennant on this one. See? So when the ball is tossed into the game, he can tell at a glance that it's one of the ones he's checked. It's a legal ball."

The men in charge of the balls on the sideline strut around like officials and sometimes forget that they aren't officials. Feely said, "The guys here don't want to be too proactively on the side of the kicker, for some reason. They won't go above and beyond a certain point. I'm not sure why." On the road, he'd never experienced any difficulty exchanging one K ball for another. But at a particular juncture in the Cowboys game at Giants Stadium—an important juncture—Feely asked if he could have a different K ball and was refused.

"When you have a bad ball in your hands," he said, "you can feel it right away. 'C'mon, give me the other ball,' I said. 'No.' I couldn't believe it. 'You've got the right ball, go ahead and kick off,' one of them said. 'You get the ball *I* choose,' the other one told me."

Shouting to his right and left, Feely alerted the other special-team players, "This isn't going to go very far! It's a bad ball! It's going to be short!" "Here's where your adrenaline is up," Feely said, "and you have a real chance of kicking the ball into the end zone and starting them off on their twenty. But I knew, even if I hit it as good as I could, this was not going to be a great kick." It wasn't. Why didn't Feely say something after the game? "In the NFL, kickers get made fun of all the time," he said. "We're these idiosyncratic little people who sort of play football. Everything is fodder for how ridiculous we are. I didn't even want to mention it to anybody."

Ernie said, "Feely's a great guy, the player rep, and he wasn't going to blow the whistle on the ball boys—I say 'boys,' they're seventy years old. One's a truck driver. But the good Lord gave me a big nose for a reason. Something just looked wrong about that last kickoff. So I called Jay into a side room. A few equipment men were there, too. 'I smell a cover-up here,' I said. 'What's going on?' Feely's really sheepish. After some prodding, he finally says, 'Well, the guys in charge of the balls wouldn't give me the K ball I wanted.' 'What?'

"'They've been with the Giants since Yankee Stadium,' one of the equipment guys says. 'What?' 'We tried to fire them a few times, but they used to go straight to Wellington.' 'What?' And then I find out that the game officials had been begging us to replace these guys for years. 'They're so obstinate,' one of the referees says, 'we can hardly get the ball into the game on time. They act like it's their private domain.' Now, I ask you. Is there anything else that can go wrong?"

Had he told Coughlin?

"Yeah, he went ballistic."

Dallas came to New York in the midst of its own kicking rumpus. Six days earlier, Bill Parcells had dumped high-priced free agent Mike Vanderjagt in favor of old Martin Gramatica, who immediately missed a forty-four-yarder against the Giants but wasn't finished for the day. New York took possession at the thirty-four.

GIANTS

1-10-G34 Tiki Barber runs for 6
2-4-G40 Eli Manning passes to Barber for 6
1-10-G46 Barber runs for 7
2-3-C47 Manning passes to Jeremy Shockey for 5
1-10-C42 Barber runs for 1

2-9-C41	Manning scrambles for 7
3-2-C34	Brandon Jacobs runs for 11
1-10-C23	Barber runs for 5
2-5-C18	Barber runs for 1
3-4-C17	(shotgun) Manning passes to Shockey for 17 and the touchdown; Feely's kick is good

New York 7, Dallas 0

Three plays into the second Cowboy series, quarterback Tony Romo looked for wide receiver Terry Glenn but found defensive end Mathias Kiwanuka instead. Kiwanuka returned the intercepted ball twelve yards from his own twenty-eight to the forty before, inexplicably, untouched by anyone, he dropped the ball. He just dropped it. "He's got the ball! He's got the ball!" Coughlin reenacted the play several weeks later in his office. "In plus territory! He loses the ball! He drops it without getting hit! That's two colossal game-changing plays two weeks in a row! Those things can define a player, I'm telling you!"

DALLAS

1-10-G40	Romo passes to Terrell Owens for 10
1-10-G30	Julius Jones runs for 3
2-7-G27	Romo passes incomplete
3-7-G27	Defensive pass interference, Antonio Pierce
1-G-G1	Marion Barber runs for 1 and the touchdown; Gramatica's kick is good

New York 7, Dallas 7

Gramatica and Feely matched field goals for a couple of quarters until the score was 13–13, but there are good field goals and there are bad field goals, and the Giants' field goals were rancid. Third and goal at the five after one long drive, third and goal at the four after another, they reaped just six points. Fourth and one at the Cowboys' twenty-four got them nothing.

With under ten minutes to go in the game, Dallas took possession
and maintained it for six minutes and eleven seconds.

DALLAS

1-10-C34 Romo passes to Owens for 11

1-10-C45 Jones runs for −3

2-13-C42 Romo scrambles for 10

1-10-G48 (shotgun) Romo passes to Owens for 11

1-10-G37 Romo passes to Owens for 6

2-4-G31   Romo passes incomplete

3-4-G31   (shotgun) Romo passes to Patrick Crayton for 11

1-10-G20 Jones runs for 3

2-7-G17   Jones runs for 2

3-5-G15   Romo passes to Glenn for 10 (personal foul,
          Jason Bell)

1-G-G2   Barber runs for 0

2-G-G2   (shotgun) Romo passes incomplete (false start,
          Owens)

2-G-G7   Barber runs for 7 and the touchdown;
          Gramatica's kick is good

Dallas 20, New York 13

Now about four minutes remained. Stood up for measurement next
to another young quarterback whom the Giants fans were thinking they
might prefer, Manning had outperformed Romo to that point. Eli had
two touchdown passes to Tony's none. Romo had two interceptions to
Manning's none. And now Eli had the ball. In a sixty-three-yard Giant
offensive, Manning's arm would feature in fifty-nine of them, as he
threw six passes and completed them all.

GIANTS

1-10-G37 (shotgun) Manning passes to Plaxico Burress for 8

2-2-G45   (shotgun) Barber runs for 4

1-10-G49 (shotgun) Manning passes to Barber for 2
2-8-C49   (shotgun) Manning passes to Burress for 9
1-10-C40 (shotgun) Manning passes to Barber for 28
1-10-C12 Manning passes to Barber for 7
2-3-C5   Manning passes to Burress for 5 and the
   touchdown; Feely's kick is good
Dallas 20, New York 20

Feely's shallow kick with the wrong K ball only gave the Cowboys nice field position. It didn't complete the twenty-six-yard pass from Romo to tight end Jason Witten that really won the game. Slipping left, Romo saw Witten break off his route into a vacuum between Pierce and Will Demps. "It was nobody's fault," Pierce said. "It was just a great play." It was a splendid read and throw. Then, reconfirming Parcells' genius, Gramatica kicked a forty-six-yard field goal to win the game.

One of the reasons Romo could so easily sprint to the left side was that Michael Strahan was still in street clothes. He had spent the week sitting at his locker chewing on peanut butter sandwiches and reporters. "Two and a half hours before the game," Coughlin said, "we worked Michael out. But he couldn't go." Accorsi, the sentimentalist, thought Stray might be worth dressing just for the "Willis Reed effect." Tom looked at Ernie like he was Kiwanuka.

Parcells, whose nickname for Romo was Pancho Villa ("Sometimes he shoots at the first thing he sees"), took a soft look around Giants Stadium before he departed, saying, "Most of the great memories I have are centered at this place."

Hours even before Strahan's workout, maybe six hours before the game, Parcells sat with a former Giants colleague in a car in the parking lot. They didn't want to draw any attention to themselves. Old friends, they just wanted to talk. What Bill supposedly said became the lead item on the front office grapevine: "I'm available to be the Giants' GM if they get stuck. Keep me alive with John Mara, will you?"

That phrase blew around the front office like a prairie fire "if they get stuck." Weeks later, Parcells complained about the rumors flying that he was interested in replacing Accorsi. Bill asked John Mara to issue a press release denying that they had ever talked about the GM job. Mara had no trouble doing that.

But the reaction in the front office was hilarity. "The rumors started with the same guy who's upset that they're out there," everyone said. "Bill's the one who blew up all those trial balloons. He's the one who set them all loose. Now he wants us to pop them for him." Some men take so many different positions that it must be hard to remember them all.

Pat Hanlon said, "When Bill asked me if he and his grandson could watch some Giants games from the press box, I told him, 'Sure, Bill. I'll always have a space for you.'" Though not for a fact, Pat probably was the first one who knew Parcells wouldn't be returning for another season in Dallas.

Leaving the field after losing to the Cowboys, Manning and Burress had a significant exchange. The inconsistency of Plaxico's effort had been a topic since the Tennessee game, but Manning voiced no complaints.

"That last catch for the tying touchdown against the Cowboys," Burress said some days later, "was one of those catches I was telling you about, that I don't really understand. I reached back behind me with both arms, pulled my hands back over my head, and the ball was in them. Now we're walking off the field after another bad loss, the fourth in a row, and Eli looks over at me and says, 'Great catch, Plax.' He's heading to the locker room to face the music again, and he says that to me. I can't tell you how that made me feel."

"After the Jacksonville game, after the Tennessee game," Accorsi said, "Tom screamed at the players at the top of his lungs. *'How could you do this? How could you do that? You did this wrong! You did that wrong! Where did the penalties come from?'* 'Well, since you've been here, Tom, we've been leading the world in penalties, that's where they came from.' He couldn't see what a shattered state they were already in. But after the Cowboys game, Coughlin was great. First off, he said, 'Everybody close it up here.'

He pulled them all in. 'I just want you to know, we did some things I didn't like. But you played your hearts out and I'm proud of you. We didn't win and I know how much it hurts—and it should hurt. But this is a team full of winners. There's not one loser in here. We're still in this thing.'"

Incidentally, when Romo was promoted to starting quarterback, he continued in his previous job as the holder for extra points and field goals. In what probably qualifies as irony, the Cowboys' season would end in a 21–20 loss at Seattle, just one yard from a first down, just two yards from the goal line, on a nineteen-yard field goal attempt that neither Gramatica nor Vanderjagt could have missed. But a shiny K ball slipped through Romo's fingers. Those things can define a player, I'm telling you.

20

"NUMBER SIXTY-NINE

IS REPORTING . . ."

EVERY FOOTBALL TEAM has what Accorsi calls "a walking miracle." The Giants' version was a six-foot-three, 305-pound utility man named Rich Seubert. "He suffered the all-time broken leg six games into the 2003 season," Ernie said, "three horrible fractures, the worst Ronnie Barnes had ever seen. Go take a look at that leg. [The right one, he meant. Its scooped-out wound was covered over by a graft of nonmatching skin, as shiny pink as the neck of an auto racer who has been on fire.] Rich missed the rest of that season and the next. We just hung with him. You talk about patience. But you don't give up on a character like that."

"Fractured tibia, fractured fibula, shattered ankle—they didn't just break, they exploded," said Seubert, an undrafted free agent who from Western Illinois University walked onto the National Football League in 2001 to become New York's starting left guard the following season. "I don't know why Ernie stuck with me. I was in the hospital for three weeks, then on the injured reserve list for half a year, then on the physically-unable-to-perform list for a full year. With a skin graft, you know, you really can't do anything until it takes, and mine didn't take right away. I just lay in bed, losing weight. I went into the hospital weighing three hundred and came out maybe two-seventy. There wasn't much meat on me." Pro teams don't usually stick with a player that long just on the *chance* that he might be able to rehab himself enough to make some

kind of lesser contribution than he was making before he was so badly
hurt. "I'm pretty sure the coaches didn't really have much to say about
it," Seubert said. "Put it this way, if they'd had something to say about it,
I guess I would have been gone. I don't mean this bitterly. That's just the
way it is in pro ball. It was Accorsi and the Maras who kept me. They
could have just cut their ties and said good luck. But they gave me
a chance to play again. Do you think I'm not going to play hard for
this team?"

Seubert had to adjust everything, especially his own dreams. "I never
thought I was going to be a Hall of Famer or anything like that," he said,
"but I was having a good year, my second year starting, and then everything suddenly came to an end. I always figured football was like riding
a bike—I've played football my whole life. It was the only thing I was ever
really good at growing up, and I loved being good at it. I just loved the
game of football. But it's not like riding a bike. I had to learn it all over
again from scratch. Waiting for that first game back, and that first serious hit, I wondered how I was going to respond. You really don't know
how you're going to feel. I had been lucky with injuries before."

Well, he broke a femur in high school. "But other than that," Rich
said, "I was injury-free. I never missed games, never missed practices. I
liked the hard work of football, I enjoyed it. But I can't say I always
enjoyed the rehab. Different things kept going wrong. I had to have the
screws taken out, and my toe was stuck up in the air, so they went and cut
the tendons for that, so I could push down at least. I got into bad moods
from time to time, sort of 'to hell with it' moods. But I always snapped
out of them and I just kept grinding away. A lot of the guys on this team
helped keep me going. Like Jeremy Shockey. We've been training camp
roomies since I've been back. Players talk about their college teams as
though they were their families. They're too embarrassed to talk about a
pro team that way. But the truth is, a pro team is even more of a family, I
think. I know for sure that an NFL team has no chance to succeed unless
you want to play for the guys you're sitting in the room with. You don't
have to like absolutely every guy. Just don't hold any hard feelings

towards the ones you don't like. And play your heart out for the ones you love."

For the first twelve games of the season, Seubert's most visible role had been as an eligible receiver in short-yardage situations, whose entry into the game for some reason had to be announced over the stadium loudspeaker by the referee. "Number sixty-nine is reporting as an eligible receiver." Sometimes, when the official was slow switching off his microphone button, seventy-eight thousand people could hear Rich say, "Sixty-nine reporting, right. Thank you, sir." He was there to block, of course. Though technically Seubert was a third tight end, he lined up in the backfield like William "the Refrigerator" Perry.

Only once in Seubert's pro career, back in 2002, did he ever actually go out for a pass. It was the last down of the wild card play-off game. The Giants were losing in San Francisco, 39–38, and about to attempt what would have been the winning field goal when the snap was botched and Seubert took off downfield. With the ball in the air, he was interfered with blatantly by 49ers defender Chike Okeafor (the league's head of officials said so the next day) but nothing was called.

In the thirteenth game of 2006, against the Carolina Panthers at Bank of America Stadium in Charlotte, because of a chain reaction of in-game injuries, Seubert played center ("for the first time in a real game since sixth grade," he said), guard, and tight end, "and I stunk at all of them," he lied afterward.

Before the game, it had seemed that the Giants were finally going up against a team more damaged than they were. Panthers quarterback Jake Delhomme's right thumb looked like he had hit it with a hammer while hanging a picture. For the first time in four years, thirty-four-year-old Heisman Trophy–winning quarterback Chris Weinke was getting the start.

During those clipboard seasons, Weinke threw exactly thirteen passes, but before this day was done, he would heave sixty-one more. The last time Weinke was their regular quarterback, 2001, the Panthers won 1 game and lost 15.

Star linemen Mike Rucker and Julius Peppers aside, it seemed that an army of total strangers had taken over the Panthers' defense. "Who *is* that guy?" Plaxico Burress asked Eli Manning, nodding in the direction of number 27, the safety on Plax's side. That was Dion Byrum, an undrafted rookie just signed off the Tampa Bay practice squad, a refreshingly honest man. Referring later to the Giants' first touchdown, a twenty-eight-yard pass from Manning to Burress, Byrum said, "I was caught completely out of position. I was trying to get the call from my safety on what coverage we were supposed to be in. But by the time I could get his attention, the Giants had snapped the ball, and Plaxico being six-five with that long stride of his, he already had me by those eight or nine yards."

That made the score 10–0 early in the second quarter, but then Weinke struck consecutively for twenty-one yards (Steve Smith) and thirty-six (Drew Carter) to make it 10–7; that is, to make it a game. During the next series, center Shaun O'Hara turned an ankle and Seubert brushed off his sixth-grade memories and picked up the ball. "The shotgun snaps were what really scared me," he said. " 'Can't you just stay under center for a while?' I asked Eli, but he smiled and said, 'You'll be fine, Rich. Anywhere between my knees and my chin will be cool.' That gave me confidence." (There's the Eli the public has never seen.)

Sometimes the center has a defensive player right on his nose. Other times, there's absolutely nobody. "Yeah, I like it when there's absolutely nobody," Seubert said. "But there's a beauty to the center position, like every position. You've got two guys next to you and one of them is usually working with you. And, unlike me, Chris Snee and David Diehl knew what the hell they were doing."

With a thirty-seven-yard field goal, Carolina tied the game, 10–10, but the Giants had the last word of the first half. Manning was having a nice game.

GIANTS

1-10-G21 Manning passes to Sinorice Moss for 7

2-3-G28   Tiki Barber runs for 18

Two-minute warning

1-10-G46 Offside, Panthers

1-5-P49   (shotgun) Manning scrambles for 9

1-10-P40 (shotgun) Barber runs for 5

2-5-P35   (shotgun) Manning passes incomplete

3-5-P35   (shotgun) Manning passes to Shockey
for 25 yards

1-G-P10   (shotgun) Manning passes to Visanthe
Shiancoe for 9

2-G-P1   Brandon Jacobs runs for –1

3-G-P2   Manning passes to Shockey for 2 and
the touchdown; Feely's kick is good

New York 17, Carolina 10

When Reggie McKenzie sprained his neck in the third quarter, Diehl had to move to right tackle for the first time all season, Seubert shifted to left guard, and O'Hara returned injured to the center position. ("Hurt enough to be questionable a week later," Ernie said, "that's how much guts O'Hara's got. High-ankle sprain. Do you know how much that hurts? But there are some guys you just can't keep off the field.") Among all of the Giants' offensive linemen, only Snee hadn't missed time or switched positions.

Throwing, throwing, and throwing some more, Weinke accumulated 423 yards passing but was intercepted three times, twice by Gibril Wilson. The second brought about another New York touchdown.

GIANTS

1-10-P14 Jacobs runs for 6

2-4-P8   Manning passes to Barber for 6

1-G-P2   Manning passes incomplete
2-G-P2   Jacobs runs for –1
3-G-P3   Manning passes to David Tyree for 3 and the
    touchdown; Feely's kick is good
New York 27, Carolina 10

So the proverbial month of Sundays was over, 27–13. The Giants' four-game losing streak was ended. Barber had run for 112 yards and quietly slipped over the ten thousand mark in yards rushing for his ten-year career. "Despite the perception," Tiki said, "we actually have been having a pretty good time trying to practice our way out of this mess."

The Giants improved to 2 and 11 in games Michael Strahan had missed with injury, this being his fifth DNP of the season. "I never even heard of that stat until this year," Strahan said. "But somebody better do something about it next year. Like Ernie, I'm not going to be around forever." Eli completed seventeen of thirty-three passes for 172 yards, three touchdowns, and no interceptions. "It wasn't the prettiest second half in the world," he said, "but we didn't make any really big mistakes." On top of being thirty-four for sixty-one, Weinke set an unofficial but still imposing record when six different potential Panther receivers dropped balls that were right in their hands. You had to hand it to the Panthers. Dion Byrum, the honest safety, was credited with making seven tackles.

"You forget how good it feels just to win a game," O'Hara said. "It feels so good to win."

Coughlin said, "I give our players credit. They're a closer team than you know."

"It's not just a relief for Tom," Antonio Pierce said. "It's a relief for all of us. If anything bad happens to the head man, it runs down to us."

The snapshot of the game that fit in the family album was taken when Seubert was in at center and momentarily had the wind knocked out of him. As Seubert was being tended to in the middle of the field, off to one side of it, Grey Ruegamer was practicing a few snaps. In the NFL, one center usually hunkers down and stays put for a decade, if not a generation. Here were the Giants with their sixth-grade center on the ground and a second understudy in the wings trying to learn his lines during a time-out. In what was almost an exquisite injustice, Ruegamer also took one turn as the hippopotamus in the backfield ("Number sixty-five is reporting as an eligible receiver")—his only appearance in that capacity all season—and son of a bitch if Manning didn't try to throw the ball to him in the end zone. But a blitzer bumped Eli's arm at the last instant and the pass fell just slightly short. "Rich and Grey are good friends," O'Hara said, "but I'm not sure Rich would have ever forgiven him." "A better athlete would have caught the ball," Seubert said with a wink in his voice.

A couple of days later, Rich was sitting alone, panting, recovering from a wrestling match with one of the exercise machines. "This second life of yours," I asked him, "is it worth it?"

"Oh, a hundred percent worth it," he said. "I'd be back in Wisconsin probably doing something with my wife and child, and I'd be happy enough. I'm a happy guy. I'm a lucky guy. Maybe I'd be hunting, come to think of it. Shit, I could be hunting. But I wouldn't have this feeling of last Sunday inside me now. I couldn't sleep Sunday night. Of course I never sleep Sunday nights. None of us do, I don't think. You lie down and think about all of the plays you were involved in, the bad plays more than the good ones. I played three different positions Sunday, and I guess I'm proud of that. But who cares? Somebody gets hurt, I've got to play. If they come back and somebody else gets hurt, I've got to play. That's my job now. When you have one position—I'd love to be the left guard again—you get used to it, it becomes kind of your own. I don't like it on the other side of the line. Different stance. Different footwork. It's not as natural. I'm not as comfortable. But it's still football. As I said, I'm a guy who loves football."

Obviously Accorsi was thrilled to win the Panthers game, but there was a small catch, the old one. Carolina was one of the other National

Conference teams still alive for the wild card spot in the play-offs. "After you're in this league awhile," Ernie said, "everywhere you go, there's somebody you care about on the other side of the field." In Charlotte, it was the Panthers head coach, John Fox, the former Giants defensive coordinator who predicted that 41–0 shutout of the Vikings.

"Foxy's a great coach," Ernie said, "a pain in the ass, but a great coach. You have to love him, and I do. I certainly don't enjoy watching him lose a game he needed. That year the Panthers went to the Super Bowl [after the 2003 season] and just barely lost to the Patriots, I called him up after the conference championship game. They beat the Eagles to get to the Super Bowl. I knew he wouldn't be home; it was a road game. But I left him a message, or tried to. I started to congratulate him and just broke down. I couldn't finish. He called me back the next day to say, 'That's the greatest message I've ever received from anyone.' 'In golf terms,' I said, 'I withdrew. Did not finish.' 'I know,' Foxy said. 'That's what made it great.'"

21

STILL WATCHING FOOTBALL

GAMES ON TV

BILL WALSH, THE Hall of Fame coach and GM from San Francisco, spent the 2006 season fighting leukemia, the disease that took his forty-six-year-old son, Steve, in 2002. "My attitude is positive but not evangelistic," Walsh said on the telephone. "I've had a number of blood transfusions; they're exhausting. I have a bad stomach all the time. But otherwise I'm functioning pretty normally. I'm pragmatically doing everything the doctor recommends, working my way through it. Thank God for Stanford. Not only are they giving me the best treatment, they have a lot of volleyball and basketball games going on every day, and I'm enjoying watching these young people play. For a while there, I thought I was dead. I put all of my stuff in order. But I'm not dead. I'm still watching football games on TV. I'll accept my fate as it unfolds. I've always felt that way. I have no regrets."

The late-season emergence of Jeff Garcia in Philadelphia, who took over for injured quarterback Donovan McNabb in the eleventh week, delighted Walsh. "Do you remember that day we were talking about Jeff in my office?" he said. Of course I did.

During the 1990s Walsh left the football business for a few years to take a shot at television commentating for NBC. He worked the Notre Dame games mostly. But Bill was never at home in the broadcast booth. I ran into him when he was with the NBC Olympic party on a cruise ship in Barcelona harbor. "I know what you're doing here," he said. "What am I doing here?" As the century ran out, Walsh was more than glad to reclaim the GM chair in San Francisco.

During those years when Bill was out of football, he fell in love with this undersized and underpublicized quarterback, Garcia, at Walsh's alma mater, San Jose State. Though famous for schooling Joe Montana, Steve Young, Dan Fouts, and Ken Anderson, truth be told, Walsh derived an even greater satisfaction molding competent quarterbacks out of much lesser clay: Sam Wyche, Guy Benjamin, Virgil Carter. Carter was a brainy runt with petite hands who broke in with the Chicago Bears. Go check out the passing numbers Walsh pulled out of him in Cincinnati. With the 49ers, Steve DeBerg set an NFL record for completions the year before Bill traded him away to get his shadow off the new starter, Montana.

Though the San Francisco papers were still touting Jim Druckenmiller, Walsh told me in 2000, "Have a look at Garcia at practice today."

"The only thing I ever learn at practice," I said, "is not to go to practice."

Ignoring that, Bill said, "When I was out of the league, I tried to sell Garcia to one NFL team after another. Most of them didn't even answer my letter. So he went off to Canada instead, and played nicely. I'm not saying he's the quarterback of the future, but he's got instincts."

After five good years in San Francisco—a couple of them very good—Garcia wandered away to Cleveland and Detroit. Removed from the Walsh system, he looked less than ordinary. But when the Eagles came to Giants Stadium for Game 14, Garcia was the talk of the league. Philadelphia was on a two-game winning streak with the backup, and he would run that string to six.

Thanks to a thirty-eight-yard Chad Morton punt return, New York had a short path to the game's first touchdown.

GIANTS

1-10-E21 Eli Manning passes to Tiki Barber for 5
2-5-E16   Offside, Eagles
1-10-E11 Barber runs for 11 and the touchdown;

Jay Feely's kick is good

New York 7, Philadelphia 0

But Garcia asserted himself then—twice. The second time he was aided by a Manning interception.

E A G L E S

1-10-E20   Garcia passes to Donté Stallworth for 5

2-5-E25   Brian Westbrook runs for 9

1-10-E34   Correll Buckhalter runs for 4

2-6-E38   Garcia passes incomplete

3-6-E38   False start, offense

3-11-E33   Garcia passes to Westbrook for 11

1-10-E44   Westbrook runs for 6

2-4-50   Garcia passes to Reggie Brown for 20

1-10-G30   Buckhalter runs for 7

2-3-G23   Garcia passes to Westbrook for 14

1-G-G9   Buckhalter runs for 3

2-G-G6   Garcia scrambles for 4

3-G-G2   Buckhalter runs for 2 and the touchdown;

David Akers' kick is good

Philadelphia 7, New York 7

E A G L E S

1-10-G41   Garcia passes to Westbrook for 8

2-2-G33   Buckhalter runs for 11

1-10-G22   Offside, defense

1-5-G17   (shotgun) Garcia passes to L. J. Smith for 9

1-G-G8   Westbrook runs for 6

2-G-G2   Westbrook runs for 1

3-G-G1   Buckholder runs for 0

4-G-G1   Westbrook runs for 1 and the touchdown;

Akers' kick is good
Philadelphia 14, New York 7

In the fourth quarter, the Giants were still within seven points, 29–22, when Eli's second interception was returned nineteen yards by Trent Cole for the clinching touchdown. The final score was 36–22, and Garcia wasn't finished with the Giants. They would see each other one more time.

New York was the loser of five of six, all without Michael Strahan. Now, of the fourteen games Strahan had missed since 2004, New York had lost a dozen. Someone with a sense of timing dug out a rookie photograph of Stray and pinned it up on the locker room bulletin board. This was intended to give the players a laugh, but that wasn't the effect. "It doesn't look a thing like me," Michael said. "Players keep saying, 'That's not you, that can't be you.' 'Yeah, it is.' But even I looked at it and saw a totally different person, a child." It turned into an object lesson for the whole team, and not a cheerful one. "Time is flying by," Strahan said.

One of the players observed, "As old as you look, Stray, maybe you should apply to replace Accorsi as GM."

"You know what," Strahan said, "just knowing the little bit I know about what it takes to do it, I don't want to even think if I could. Because I know I would never want to. Negotiating with a man about his financials, his livelihood, all of the little details that are mind-boggling to me anyway? No thanks. I'd be an honest GM, though. I wouldn't BS the players. A player would rather hear he's not good enough and what he has to work on than all the BS. Nobody has to tell the players what's happening to us now. We just have to keep going. That's the challenge from here on in, and everybody knows it. Keep going."

The most interesting thing that happened around the Philly game occurred on the floor of the New York Stock Exchange two days later when Steven Mara and another trader had a contretemps that reportedly involved at least one mimed jump shot and a couple of curse words. The Giants players were actually impressed. Somebody out there was fighting for them.

22

DOUBLE SAFETY DELAYED BLITZ

I F A H O M E G A M E started to go really sour, Accorsi might abandon his tunnel and begin moving around the stadium in search of a luckier vantage point. The television networks had monitors set up in back rooms. Maybe he'd stare at those for a while, or go to the TV set in the players' lounge of the locker room, or climb up to his office, switch on the game, turn down the sound, and continue packing his boxes. When John Mara stuck his head into Ernie's office a couple of days before the Saints game, Mara was startled by how barren it already looked. "Oh, man," John said. "You really *are* leaving."

The crate Accorsi was filling, with one eye on the television screen, would have made a perfect time capsule of the NFL over the last almost forty years. Included were two poems written by the tender and tough Giant Kyle Rote ("Where laden clouds nudge into winds, / Beneath an azure sky— / To soften sunlight's dancing on / A mountain stream nearby"); a letter from Weeb Ewbank, the winning coach for the Baltimore Colts and the New York Jets in the two most important pro football games ever played ("Dear Ernie, I'm sending you a hat I found in my basement. It's at least old and brown. Remember the string of victories we had in Baltimore because I kept wearing that same brown suit? That suit plus Art Donovan, Gino Marchetti, Raymond Berry, Jim Parker, Lenny Moore, John Unitas, Alan Ameche, Jim Mutscheller, and several other great guys did the job"); a note from Olivia Manning ("Thank you for the beautiful flowers—so pretty, so bright—and the kind words on my mother's passing. I must say that Eli's calm nature was probably inherited from his grandmother. That and some other good traits as well. She loved following Eli and the New York Giants—and probably still is"); a "Kosar the Viking" campaign button; a cigar still in its cellophane wrapper.

"Mr. Rooney gave me that," Ernie said. "I'd never smoke it, of course. I consider it a holy relic, a piece of bone from St. Francis of Assissi. If I unwrapped it now, it would crumble."

As part of the ceremony of leaving, Accorsi had made a pilgrimage to the Pittsburgh Public Theater to see an actor named Tom Atkins portray Rooney in a one-man play called *The Chief*. It was co-written by Rob Zellers and Gene Collier, a former *Post-Gazette* sportswriter.

"Atkins had him down cold," Accorsi said. "He walked like him, talked like him. Even smoked like him. Collier told me afterward that they had to get permission from a hundred fire wardens just to let him light the cigar onstage for one second. 'Oh, is this bothering anyone?' he says to the audience. 'I'll put it out.'" The playbill went into the capsule.

"Look," Ernie said, handing over a 1987 note from Jim Kensil in the league office. Next to Pete Rozelle, Kensil was the best executive the NFL ever had, another old sportswriter. "After all of my years in this business, with the league and the Jets," Kensil wrote, "you might think I'd do a book. But I'm not going to. I have no axes to grind, no kisses to tell. Sure, I've met and had to work with a few people I didn't like, but I'm certain there are many who feel the same about me. It's a wash. Anyway, pleasant memories need not be recorded publicly. Better to savor them privately with friends like you. If I did write a book, here's some of the things I'd say: 'Mike Ditka is my all-time favorite player, there's never been another coach as impressive as Lombardi, Pat Summerall makes for awfully easy listening, I miss the late Dave Brady of the *Washington Post*, my favorite movie is Red River. (Are you surprised?) George Halas's feistiness, Well Mara's dignity, Dan Rooney's patience and Jim Finks' candor are qualities I wish I had . . .'"

"You know what that is, don't you?" Accorsi said. "That's Jimmy Cannon in the old *Journal-American*. 'Nobody asked me, but . . .'"

"'. . . I never saw an ugly woman in a polka dot dress,'" I finished an old Cannon line, and we laughed, despite what was happening on the muted television.

"When this season is over," Ernie said, "I'm going to sit down and do the same thing Kensil did. 'Nobody asked me, but . . .'"

Reams of yellowed old sports columns fell into the box. "When I broke into sportswriting," Ernie said, "there were lyricists like Red Smith. If you enjoyed a big game, you couldn't wait to pick Red up in the morning and see what he thought of it and how he wrote about it. The best columnists in those days almost put sports to music. It was wonderful to read. There isn't as much emphasis on lyricism today. It's all reporting. The rumors seem to count for more than the writing now.

"After the Colts beat the Raiders in the AFC championship game, January of 1971—I was still the PR guy in Baltimore—Smith came up to me in the press box and said, 'Young man, could you help me get a cab back to the hotel? I'm with Jimmy Cannon.' I said, 'Mr. Smith, I would be happy to take you back myself.' As I drove, I listened as they recapped the game. They got to talking about Unitas [who was near the end]. 'Jimmy,' Red said, 'it used be like watching Bob Feller.' 'Now,' Cannon said, 'it's Eddie Lopat.'"

One of those color-coded play charts was a must for the capsule—"Denny's menus," Accorsi liked to call them. While he ragged the coaches for needing their chart, he didn't blame them for hiding behind it when plays were being called. On that subject, Ernie was the man who knew too much. "In the last game of the seventy-seven season," he said conspiratorially, "the Colts had to beat New England at home to win the division, and we just did, 30–24. A lip-reader named Bobby Colbert, who had been the head coach at the Gallaudet School for the deaf in Washington, 'saw' the Patriots' defensive coordinator say 'double safety delayed blitz.' It was third and eighteen, and we were on our own twelve.

"The word was flashed in to Bert Jones, who checked off to a pass down the middle for tight end Raymond Chester. He went eighty-eight yards for the winning touchdown. There have been binocular-wearing lip-readers in the league ever since. I'm not kidding."

Though no binoculars were handy, a slip of paper with X's and O's on it fell into the collection neatly.

"Back when the PR guys used to advance the road games," Accorsi said, "I was in Foxboro at practice on a Thursday. The cabbie who brought me all the way out there from Boston said, 'While I'm here, I think I'll buy a ticket.' I'm pretty sure that's the only ticket I ever sold advancing a football game. Following practice, I was introduced to the Pats' head coach, John Mazur. 'How long have you been here?' he asked. 'The whole practice,' I said. 'You spying son of a bitch!' he said, being a typical paranoid coach. Now I'm mad. I called our coach, Don McCafferty, as I normally would, to check on injury reports and to tell him the weather and read him anything interesting out of the Boston newspapers. 'You know, Mac,' I said, 'Mazur jumped down my throat at practice, so I might as well tell you what I saw there. In a full-house back-field, they put a receiver in at fullback and then motioned him out.' 'What day did you see this?' McCafferty asked. 'Today, Thursday.' 'You stupid son of a bitch,' he said. 'Don't you know that Wednesday is every-body's offensive day, and Thursday is everybody's defensive day? That's *our* offense you saw. The receiver at fullback motioning out is Ray Perkins.' "

In his desk Ernie found faded copies of the twenty-three ballots the owners needed to elect Rozelle commissioner in 1960. On the third go-round, a San Francisco attorney named Marshall Leahy missed being anointed by one vote. Baltimore favored interim commissioner Austin Gunsel, Chicago passed, Cleveland wanted Leahy, the Cardinals Leahy, the Lions Leahy, the Packers Leahy, the Rams Leahy, the Giants Leahy, the Eagles Gunsel, the Steelers Leahy, the 49ers Leahy, the Redskins Gunsel. "Ten years later," Accorsi said, "Tex Schramm [of the Cowboys] was presiding over a secret owners' meeting at the Hilton in Baltimore. Don Klosterman asked me to get a document out of his office desk and bring it to the hotel. I knocked on the door of the NFL suite. It was pretty easy to find. Smoke and noise were pouring out of it. A guy opened the door, took one look at me, and slammed the door in my face. That was Marshall Leahy."

A Pro Bowl program from Ernie's days with the league office surely fit. "Val Pinchbeck and I were running the two teams in New Orleans," Ernie said. "This is 1976, when no one cared about the Pro Bowl and the players wouldn't play. Val and I were walking along Bourbon Street one night when we heard shots—coming at us. Bullets were ricocheting off everything around us. We dived into an ice cream parlor on the floor, and Pinch was on top of me. He was heavier then. I ran the NFC team. Jim Hart of the Cardinals was one quarterback, but Fran Tarkenton didn't show and Archie Manning and Roman Gabriel were hurt. So I called Mike Boryla. He had taken over for Gabriel and won five straight games for the Eagles. My coach was Chuck Knox; Val's was John Madden. When Boryla arrives at practice, Knox comes up to me and says, 'Ernie, this guy can't play. I'm not playing him. So don't expect to see him. How did you come up with him?' I said, 'Coach, there was no one else.' In the fourth quarter, we're down by ten or so and Hart gets hurt. In comes Boryla. He throws two long touchdown passes and is named the MVP. I walk into the locker room and there's Chuck hugging Boryla and telling him how great he was."

Ernie took a little replica of Brooklyn's Ebbets Field off his bookshelf and tossed it in the box. "My greatest regret in sports," he said, "is I never saw Ebbets Field." Then he threw in a lot of books and photographs, one with Pinchbeck, Lamar Hunt, and George Halas. Halas, with one foot balanced on the running board of a Hupmobile in Canton, Ohio, was the man who started the National Football League in 1920.

"Because of Brian Piccolo," Accorsi said, "Papa Bear and I had a connection. I asked Halas once about playing right field for the Yankees just before Babe Ruth. He said, 'Ernie, I was lousy. I lasted one year. Couldn't hit. There were two other right fielders between me and Ruth. They were getting rid of me, anyway.'"

Accorsi decided to leave behind the old-fashioned Boy Scout hat, the kind Baden-Powell used to wear, a gift from a local troop and an unending source of laughter in the Giants' front office. But he packed the caps that said NYPD and NYFD, remnants of 9/11. "On the fourth anniversary, some of our players wanted to wear them on the sidelines," Ernie said. "You know the NFL and dress codes. 'Go ahead,' I told them. 'Sometimes it's better to ask for forgiveness than permission.' The league called me Monday morning to say, 'Don't do it again.' Unbelievable."

An old 8 mm film taken in 1958 joined the stack. "My dad and I," Ernie said, "took a post-Christmas trip to the Breakers Hotel in Palm Beach to play in the national father-and-son golf tournament. We bought tickets to the Orange Bowl at a department store in Miami. Oklahoma versus Syracuse. The worst seats in the house, or maybe the best, as it turned out. I had gotten the movie camera for Christmas and, on the opening play of the game, from the absolute perfect angle, a back for Oklahoma ran sixty-five yards for a touchdown straight to my lens. Do you know who it was? Prentice Gautt, the first black to play in the Orange Bowl. It's a little faded, but it's there."

It's all a little faded, but it's there.

Meanwhile, there wasn't really any game against New Orleans. After an early Eli Manning to Jeremy Shockey touchdown strike, the Giants were never again on the Saints side of the field. The final score was 30–7. "There was obviously some frustration," Tom Coughlin said, "and some despair." "I stood in the locker room and watched Tom afterward," Ernie said, "collecting himself to talk to the players, deciding what he was going to say. I have to admit, my heart went out to him." "After a bad loss," Bill Walsh said for all football coaches, "you're drained physically, mentally and emotionally. There's nothing left of you. You kneel down for the prayer and you can't get up, and somehow you make it back to the coaches' room and just break down, sobbing."

"Tom was good again, though," Ernie said. "He knows the difference between getting the hell kicked out of you by a healthier team playing a lot better than you are, and quitting. They still didn't quit." Now the Giants had just six days to find out if they could go the distance.

The next morning, Christmas morning, Coughlin took the play calling away from John Hufnagel and handed it over to quarterback coach Kevin Gilbride. Hufnagel offered to stay and help, but a day later he decided to go. "There's no offensive coordinator," Coughlin said. "If there would be one, it would be me." Soon, Gilbride would have the title as well as the Denny's menu.

When Tom made the decision on Hufnagel, he called Ernie. Dialing Accorsi's cell number on Christmas, the coach didn't realize that Ernie was right next door. "A second later, when I walked into Tom's office," Ernie said, "he did the all-time quadruple take and almost fell over. I tried to reassure him. I certainly agreed with the decision."

"I just hope the change gives us a spark," Coughlin said. "We've got to win a game."

"Yeah, do me a favor," Ernie said. "Just win a game, will you?"

23

REAL LIFE IN

THE SPORTS WORLD

DECEMBER 28, TWO DAYS before the last game on New York's regular schedule, was the forty-eighth anniversary of the sudden-death championship game between the Baltimore Colts and the New York Giants in Yankee Stadium. On that date every year, from the early 1970s until Johnny Unitas died in 2002, Accorsi always telephoned Unitas to remind him of what day it was. This time Ernie was the one being reminded, via an e-mail message. The Giants GM e-mailed back: "I thought of John this morning. Talked to him a little bit. Asked him to help Eli Saturday night. I miss calling him."

If the 7–8 Giants lost to the Redskins, Tom Coughlin was certain to be fired. This wasn't written down anywhere, but everyone in the front office knew it. (Everybody in town knew it.) The game was in Washington, two days before New Year's, and the only question was whether Coughlin would be fired on Sunday afternoon or Monday morning. The leading candidate to replace him was Charlie Weis, despite a multi-million-dollar buyout clause Notre Dame had built into Charlie's contract as an NFL moat. The second name on the list was Bobby Petrino of the University of Louisville, who, as the industry used to say of Sid Gillman, knew how to complete a pass.

Neither Weis nor Petrino nor anyone else had been contacted or sounded out or so much as whispered to. The Maras don't operate that way. If Coughlin was to be dismissed, Tom would have to be told first. So, by definition in a Mara organization, no potential replacement *could* have been called before then. Ernie offered to check out the landscape quietly, but John Mara declined, ghost-walking around the office all week with an anguished expression. He had to be the last of the NFL owners who worried about the assistant coaches' children maybe having to change schools. Win in Washington and the Giants were guaranteed to make the play-offs by the thickness of a membrane; lose and they were all but mathematically eliminated.

The Redskins were 5–10, but they were better than that. They employed too many $30 million players not to be a little better than that. Iconic head coach Joe Gibbs had returned from Canton and Gasoline Alley in 2004, for the money probably, which wasn't like him. It was more like Bill Parcells, who had to replenish his coffers following an expensive divorce. But Gibbs seemed almost as detached as Parcells on the sideline, and the Redskins looked nothing like their former selves. In the earlier game at Giants Stadium, a 19–3 New York victory, the *Washington Post* noticed that the Skins ran the ball just twenty times, including only six carries in the second half. Every third-down play with five yards or fewer to go was a pass play. Even at third and one on the Giants' twenty-four-yard line with a minute left in the third quarter, quarterback Mark Brunell tried a short pass to Chris Cooley. After the fourth-down field goal was missed, the score stayed 16–3.

That's not Joe Gibbs, John Riggins, Joe Bugel, the Hogs, or the Redskins.

"I don't know what's going on over there," Coughlin said. "They've got a cast of characters on that coaching staff, all different kinds of people, all different kinds of money. It looks to me like they've got a defensive coordinator who thinks he's the head coach. And an offensive coordinator who's got to be a little sensitive about making two million dollars a year. [Coughlin was making $3.3 million.] All kinds of staff, all kinds of people. Joe's in another role. He's not calling the plays. He's kind of stepping back, watching things. But they're not easy to beat,

I can tell you, especially in Washington. They play hard. Gibbs' teams always play hard."

Speaking of not calling the plays . . .

"I know, I know, Ernie is always getting on me about that," Coughlin said. "I've been the play caller; I've not been the play caller. It's not harder; it's not easier. It just—it's like this." He cupped his hands to his forehead and looked out at the narrow world as though through the turret slit of a Sherman tank. "You're in a conclave anyway," he said, "but when you're calling the plays, you're deep in a tunnel. You can't see anything else. You can't do anything else. You can't be involved in special teams or in what your defense is doing that week. It can be done. It's been done. I did it. But, I guess I've learned, you shouldn't try to be all things to all people."

Marty Schottenheimer told Accorsi that Coughlin had been a difficult man to coach against when Tom was in Jacksonville and Marty in Kansas City. "Sometimes you just match up well against certain teams," Coughlin said with a shrug. "We had great success against them." He went on to say, "I hated taking the play calling away from Hufnagel. I have a tremendous respect for John. He's the greatest worker you've ever seen. Unbelievable. I don't think the guy sleeps. I don't know. I really don't. I don't think he sleeps."

When the word came that Hufnagel had been forced to hand over the offense to Kevin Gilbride, the first thought was that at least in part it must have been Accorsi's doing. "No, it was entirely mine," Coughlin said. "We couldn't even cross midfield against New Orleans. We had to change something."

The night before the Redskins game, Roy Posner made Accorsi go to dinner with him in Washington. "Usually, the night before a game," Ernie said, "I never leave the room. I'm a room service guy when the kickoff is approaching. But on the road lately, Roy had been dragging me out. 'Come on, you're having dinner with me tonight.'" Once, and for a long time, Posner was the chief financial officer of the Loews Corporation. In retirement he had become an unofficial moneyman for both partners, Tisch and Mara. Roy was seventy-three, ate steak at every meal, and smoked like the old Camel sign in Times Square, more than Paul Henreid and Bette Davis combined. "Roy, I don't know whether I should leave my suite," Accorsi told him. "It's possible that this is the last suite I'll ever stay in. I'm not going to be staying in suites on my own nickel." But they went to dinner with Kevin Abrams and a couple of others, and Ernie enjoyed it. " 'Kevin, you don't know me very well,' Posner said when Abrams passed the spinach. 'I have never eaten, nor will I ever eat, a green vegetable.' " The Giants players were fond of Posner, a grandfatherly figure with snowy hair. They weren't exactly sure who Roy was, but he was a familiar presence on the New York sidelines, from where he watched the game that Saturday night.

Bill Walsh, who sat down to view it on television from northern California, said, "To be honest with you, I expected the Giants to be packing up their cars and getting ready to drive away. But no, they played their hearts out." So did the Redskins, who took the opening kickoff and went fifty-five yards before Ladell Betts fumbled. Giants tackle Fred Robbins scooped up the ball and brought it back sixty-seven yards to set up a field goal. Yet, fielding a second kickoff, Washington didn't look at all discouraged, Betts especially.

REDSKINS

1-10-R20 Betts runs for 9

2-1-R29 Mike Sellers runs for 2

1-10-R31 Jason Campbell passes incomplete

2-10-R31 Betts runs for 21 yards

1-10-G48 End around to Antwaan Randle El, who passes to Santana Moss for 48 and the touchdown; Shaun Suisham's conversion is good

Washington 7, New York 3

Pressed up against their own end zone, the Giants needed a thirty-two-yard run by Tiki Barber just to move out of the shadow. In what could have been his swan song, Tiki was warming up for something glorious.

GIANTS
1-10-R42 Eli Manning passes to Barber for 7
2-3-R35   Manning passes to David Tyree for 5
1-10-R30 Barber runs for 1
2-9-R29   Manning passes incomplete
3-9-R29   (shotgun) Manning passes to Plaxico Burress
   for 14
1-10-R15 Manning passes incomplete
2-10-R15 Barber runs for 15 and the touchdown;
   Jay Feely's kick is good
New York 10, Washington 7

In the next Giants series, Barber slipped off-tackle for fifty-five yards and a second touchdown. The score was 27–7, New York, when Washington started to make its fight with extended marches in the back of the third quarter and the front of the fourth.

REDSKINS
1-10-R31 Betts runs for 17
1-10-R48 Campbell passes to Moss for 3
2-7-G49   Betts runs for 4
3-3-G45   (shotgun) Campbell passes to Cooley for 16
1-10-G29 Betts runs for 4
2-6-G25   Face mask penalty, Redskins
2-21-G40 Campbell to Cooley for 12
3-9-G28   (shotgun) Campbell scrambles for 15
1-10-G13 Betts runs for 2

2-8-G11   Campbell sacked for –3

3-11-G14 Campbell passes to Betts for seven

4-4-G7   Campbell passes to Betts for 7 and the
touchdown; Suisham's kick is good

New York 27, Washington 14

REDSKINS

1-10-R34 Betts runs for 1

2-9-R35   False start, offense

2-14-R30 Campbell passes to Randle El for 24

1-10-G46 Illegal shift, offense

1-15-R49 Campbell passes to Randle El for 13

2-2-G38   Betts runs for 1

3-1-G37   Sellers runs for 2

1-10-G35 Campbell passes to Moss for 17

1-10-G18 Campbell passes to Moss for 13

1-G-G5   Betts runs for 4

2-G-G1   T. J. Duckett runs for 1 and the touchdown;
Suisham's kick is good

New York 27, Washington 21

Then came another Tiki tour de force.

GIANTS

1-10-G25 Barber runs for 10

1-10-G35 Barber runs for 3

2-7-G38   Barber runs for 2

3-5-G40   Defensive holding, Washington

1-10-G45 Barber runs for 5

2-5-50   Barber runs for 50 and the touchdown;
Feely's kick is good

New York 34, Washington 21

All but 7 of Barber's 234—count 'em, 234—rushing yards were in the book, but if Tiki was about done, the Redskins were not.

REDSKINS

1-10-R32 Betts runs for 4

2-6-R36   (no huddle, shotgun) Campbell passes to
    Randle El for 16

1-10-G48 (no huddle) Campbell passes incomplete

2-10-G48 (shotgun) Campbell passes to Moss for 10

1-10-G38 (shotgun) Campbell passes to Betts for 34

1-G-G4   Duckett runs for –5

2-G-G9   Campbell passes to Cooley for 8

3-G-G1   Campbell passes to Sellers for 1 and the
    touchdown; Suisham's kick is good

New York 34, Washington 28

Second-year quarterback Jason Campbell was having a breakthrough game. "I was never impressed by him at Auburn," Accorsi whispered, though. "His problem is just about the worst one a quarterback can have, accuracy." When Campbell was momentarily knocked out of the game in the second quarter and the veteran Brunell replaced him for a play, Ernie actually shuddered. Coming back, Campbell demonstrated character. All the same, the Giants' GM was glad to see him. With 2:18 left, seventy-eight yards from a victory, Campbell threw four straight inaccurate balls and New York was in the play-offs.

"At least that's something," Accorsi said softly in the locker room.

It's everything.

"Our defense is so bad," he said, "so hurt or so bad, however you want to put it, we can't stop anybody. Every time we had the game won, they came right back down the field. You know, I don't like the Redskins any more than I do the Eagles or the Cowboys—or any of their fans, either. But I'll say this. Saturday night. December thirtieth. A five-and-ten record. No play-off possibility. And the stadium is not only packed, but at twenty-seven to seven nobody's leaving. And on that drive that got them to twenty-seven to fourteen, the people are going absolutely crazy. You've got to give it to them. They have a passion that's unbelievable."

So did at least two others in the building: Barber ("playing his last game, as far as he knew," Accorsi said, "playing for his life. I don't think I've ever seen a performance quite like that") and John Mara. If you think of owners only as money guys who aren't really competitors, you should have seen Mara standing off by himself in a corner of the underground, balling both fists. John was overjoyed. "We're off the Schneider," he said. For the first time since 1990, the Giants had qualified for the play-offs in back-to-back seasons. "I've never thought of myself as a money guy," he said when that term was suggested. "Competition. That's what my whole life has been about. I live and die every weekend. This has been true for me since I was a child."

He was nine in 1963, when a Y. A. Tittle–to–Frank Gifford touchdown pass wasn't quite enough to beat the Chicago Bears and win the NFL championship in frigid Wrigley Field. "We went from 1964 then," Mara said, "to 1981 before we were in the play-offs again. That comprised the balance of my childhood, my teenage years, and my young adulthood. For the most part, we had pretty lousy teams, too. I took that very personal. This notion of my father being such a revered figure, which he certainly was for most of his life, forgets that there was a down period, when he was subject to so much criticism. That was difficult to take, for his family and for him personally. I'm a very competitive person by nature. Yes, we want to be a well-run business. We want to make money and everything. But that's not why we do this. It never has been. My grandfather was walking down the street with the politician Al Smith—this is one of the stories I grew up on, from the days when the Giants lost money for years and years—and Smith said, 'Why don't you give it up. It's never going to amount to anything.' 'Well, you know,' Tim Mara said, 'I would. But my boys would kill me.'"

To be in the play-offs a second straight year may not sound like very much to others.

"In the interview room after the game," Coughlin said, "some guy tried to get in my craw. Did you see that? He said, 'You act like you're vindicated.' I said, 'How do you expect me to act? I'm supposed to act some other way to please you?' We'd just won a game, a hard-hitting, honest-to-God, real football game, to make the play-offs, and this guy says, 'Well, they're just a five-eleven team.' If these people would only watch the games, which they don't, they might understand what happened. That's the problem. Do you think winning there is easy? No. Winning a game to go to the play-offs, winning a game that changes everything—that is not easy. And if you want to know the truth, being asked day after day whether you're going to be back next year—it gets to you after a while. You get scarred up a little. It's tough. Your kids are waiting for you when you get home, saying, 'Dad, Dad, don't just stand there and take it! Fight back!' I've always tried not to read the papers or watch the TV too much. The only thing I allow myself to do, I listen to ESPN radio at five in the morning so I can get the scores. Well, this idiot, Jason Smith, is on, saying, 'How can the Giants bring Coughlin back? There's a mutiny in the locker room!' What mutiny in the locker room? Where does all this stuff come from? Then you win a big game, and somebody says, 'Well, what did you really win, anyway?'"

The players could have fired him that night. "I know," Michael Strahan said. "We all knew." George Welsh said, "But guys like Tiki Barber have too much pride ever to go in the tank, for any reason."

"That's it," Strahan said. "Being out of the lineup all these weeks, I've learned that you can't lead from the sideline or in the meeting rooms. Everybody knows what happened to us this season. We won five in a row and then started dropping like flies. Not just losing our best players, losing our most vocal players. You can't be a leader in street clothes at the bench. You have to be on that field. Toomer, Luke, even LaVar—LaVar was new, but he was verbal. Osi's a young guy, but he's verbal. He goes down, I go down." A snowball goes rolling down the hill.

"Losing four games in a row," Strahan said, "the guys who were left could have said, 'Man, what's the use?' This season, there were valid reasons for the Giants not to be good. But telling yourself that is just another kind of quitting. And the bottom line for this whole year, I think, is: nobody quit. I don't care what anybody says, I think Washington was a hell of a win."

"No matter how you cut it," Walsh said, "it was a kind of compliment to Coughlin." Getting out of the way for Tiki, Manning attempted twenty-six passes, completing twelve, for 101 yards. Walsh, the quarterback specialist, didn't like to say what he thought on balance. "Eli has looked passive to me this year," Bill said, "almost fearful."

After the game, Accorsi, Mara, and Roy Posner, standing beside the Giant buses, were squirted by five flying lemons. "Roy was smoking," Ernie said, "as we were waiting to go to the train station at New Carrollton. 'As nice a compliment as it is to have fruit thrown at you,' John said, 'I think we better get on the bus.' 'You need six more lemons to make eleven!' I shouted at the fans. 'Which is exactly how many games you lost this year!'" Arriving at the train station, Roy and Ernie became separated for a moment. "And I heard Ronnie Barnes call out, 'Get the defibrillator, Roy's gone down!' He was surrounded by a huddle of team physicians and players. "Fight, Roy," center Shaun O'Hara exhorted him, "you've got to fight!" And the first report was hopeful. Posner could tell the doctors exactly how many yards Tiki had gained. Roy seemed to be back, he appeared to be okay. As he went off to the hospital in an ambulance, the Giants boarded their chartered train to go home.

In 1948, when Ernie was six, his father and mother took him on a train ride from Harrisburg, Pennsylvania, to Phoenix, Arizona. It was his first grand adventure. They had a compartment. The second, six years later, was a trip to New York City to stay at the Taft Hotel, to sail on the Circle Line around the five boroughs past the Polo Grounds and Yankee Stadium, then to go to the Roxy Theater and see a live entertainment followed by the movie *Three Coins in the Fountain*. On every train ride

Accorsi had taken since, these memories seemed to be spinning in the wheels.

"I was sitting there in the dark," Ernie said, "thinking about the season and looking out the window at the lights and homes and towns passing by when the message came that Roy was dead. He had gone back into cardiac arrest." Ernie didn't wake Mara or any of the others. He just kept looking out the window. At 2:35 A.M., he sent a note on his Black-Berry:

> You know Roy Posner, I think. Heavyset, white-haired retired Tisch moneyman who as a hobby takes all of the trips with us. Sweet, gentle man. Great guy. Drags me to dinner sometimes on the road. On the way to New Carrollton to get the train, everyone was hustling from the buses up the escalators to the platform, and Roy went down. We thought he just fell at first, but he had a heart attack. Six doctors and Ronnie were right there. They were able to revive him. He regained consciousness. Roy was aware of things, even how many yards Tiki had gained—234. They took Roy to the hospital, but he went back into cardiac arrest. He passed away a few minutes ago. Real life in the sports world.

24

"THERE'S A CHAMPIONSHIP
IN THIS ROOM"

I N THE DAYS LEADING up to the play-off game in Philadelphia, Ernie told Coughlin, "Tom, if we lose, I'd like to address the team on Monday." "I don't want to think about that," Coughlin said. "Tom, Dwight David Eisenhower was a five-star general. He had a backup plan at Normandy. You can have a backup plan too, okay?" "Well, what is it you want to say to them?" "Tom, I'm not asking you, I'm telling you. What do you think I'm going to do? Rip your development of Visanthe Shiancoe?"

On the second play of the wildcard game, four-thirty on a Sunday, Eli Manning and Plaxico Burress collaborated for twenty-nine yards and the Giants seemed to be picking up right where they'd left off in September. On third and one at Philadelphia's thirty-four, Manning was replaced by the hefty lefty, 297-pound quarterback Jared Lorenzen. To the Eagles and everyone else at Lincoln Financial Field, this telegraphed a quarterback sneak. But those who had been attending New York's practices all week became momentarily excited. A lot of interesting Lorenzen variations had been installed for the game. "Lorenzen had a good preseason," Ernie said. "He scares me—he's got a rocket arm, very slow release. He's the best quarterback sneaker in the history of the National Football League. He moves the pile."

A sneak it was. Eli returned, and on his first two plays back he completed fifteen- and seventeen-yard passes to Tiki Barber and Burress, the latter for a touchdown.

The game could have been won by New York in the next two series, when the Giants started first at the Philadelphia forty-nine and then at their own forty-eight. False starts by David Diehl and Kareem McKenzie helped scuttle the initial opportunity, but Manning's inconsistent arm was the main reason New York never got close enough even to try field goals. Along with a rain cloud, those squandered chances hung over the team the rest of the game.

Archie Manning had traveled to Philadelphia to see Eli play. From behind the press box in a cafeteria, Archie sat at a table with a cowboy hat tilted over his eyes, hearing the crowd reactions and the public address announcements before the delayed picture flashed on a screen in front of him. "It took Eli a while to take charge at Ole Miss, too, you know," Archie said. "It wasn't until he was a senior that it was really his team."

By now the common, almost universal description of Eli was "a deer in the headlights."

"I know," Archie said, "but it's not fair. He's a quiet kid. He's always been a quiet kid. But it's not from fear. I don't see any fear. And I know him pretty well."

Brett Favre could throw four interceptions and still appear completely convinced that he was the best player on the field that day, and not only that day, any day, any field. Johnny Unitas, my ass. Even if Favre couldn't have been more wrong, he was sure of himself and showed it. The Tennessee rookie Vince Young was already acting a little like that. Every move he made seemed to shout, "Who's the man?" Even in Eli's most brilliant moments, the tantalizing ones that showed absolutely it was in him to do this, he never looked anything like the two of them.

"In this department," his father said, "I expect him to take a giant step forward in the off-season. He's a guy who identifies the problems and works to correct them. If you can practice being more assertive, Eli will practice it this spring and summer. I won't talk to him about it— well, I might talk to him about it, but I'm not going to work with him on it. But Peyton will, I bet you. Eli will never be a screamer, but he's got a lot more fire in him than most people know. Of course he wants to be more consistent. He wants to be more of a leader. Next year, I'm serious, might be his senior year."

Matching Tiki Barber with Brian Westbrook step for step (the two five-foot-nine backs would split 278 rushing yards almost down the middle), Philadelphia tied the game at the start of the second quarter and took a 17–10 lead at halftime. The score was 20–10 in the fourth when, after a Manning incompletion at Philadelphia's six-yard line, the Giants settled for a short field goal. Their next and last drive of the game and the season took four seconds shy of ten minutes and, counting two false starts and a hold, covered a full one hundred yards.

GIANTS

1-10-G20 Barber runs for 13

1-10-G33 Barber runs for 5

2-5-G38 Defensive holding

1-10-G46 Manning passes to Jim Finn for 3

2-7-G49 Barber runs for 3

3-4-E48 (shotgun) Manning passes to Tim Carter for 14

1-10-E34 Barber runs for 3

2-7-E31 Manning passes to Barber for 6

3-1-E25 Barber runs for 2

1-10-E23 False start, David Diehl

1-15-E28 False start, Chris Snee

1-20-E33 Manning passes to Barber for 19, nullified by offensive holding on Snee

1-30-E43 (shotgun) Manning passes incomplete

2-30-E43 (shotgun) Manning passes to Burress for 18

3-12-E25 (shotgun) Manning passes to Burress for 14

1-10-E11 Manning passes to Burress for 11 and the touchdown; Jay Feely's kick is good

New York 20, Philadelphia 20

With about five minutes left in the game, Reno Mahe returned the kickoff to the Eagles' thirty-four, where Westbrook lifted the team onto his square shoulders and carried it home.

EAGLES

1-10-E34 Westbrook runs for 11

1-10-E45 Jeff Garcia passes to Matt Schobel for 6

2-4-G49 Westbrook runs for 5

1-10-G44 Garcia passes to Reggie Brown for 7

2-3-G37 Westbrook runs for 5

Two-minute warning

1-10-G32 Westbrook runs for 13

1-10-G19 Westbrook runs for –1

2-11-G20 Westbrook runs for 0

3-11-G20 Garcia keeps for 0

4-11-G20 David Akers kicks a 38-yard field goal as time
   runs out

Philadelphia 23, Giants 20

The second that the game and the season ended, Marty Schotten-heimer left this message on Accorsi's phone: "Ernie. Marty. I know you're very, very disappointed. I share your disappointment. I also know this: you're a champion. You and I spent a lot of years together, the best years of my coaching experience, and I'm ever grateful for that. But I want you to know I'm thinking about you. When you look back on it, it's been a great career. I love you. You're one of the all-time best. I cherish you as a friend. Thanks, Ernie. Bye."

Schottenheimer was now the head coach in San Diego, the NFL's top seed in the play-offs. Over the last three seasons, his Chargers had posted the league's third-best won-lost record, behind only Indianapolis and New England. But in contrast to his coach-GM relationship with Accorsi, Marty and Chargers general manager A. J. Smith not only weren't warm friends, they worked in an icebox; they didn't even speak.

Schottenheimer said, "A couple of years ago, six or eight times over the period of a year, I went to him and said, 'What's the problem here? Let's talk about this.' But all he ever said to me was, 'I don't want to talk about it.' 'What do you mean? That's childish.' If the coach and the GM aren't on the same page, you have a dysfunctional organization. When Ernie and I hit an impasse in a draft, it was Ernie's call. I was fine with that. The problem here is, they don't even ask me. When they traded [backup quarterback] Cleo Lemon, I found out about it reading the newspaper the next day. Ernie and A.J. are totally different people. Ernie did not ever care who got the credit. I can leave the rest unsaid. It speaks volumes. I say no more."

After the Giants' last loss, most of the attention in the New York locker room fell on Barber. "It's fitting that it ends for me in Philadelphia," Tiki said, "because this is one of the hardest places I've ever played. Give Brian Westbrook credit today. When they needed a big play, he made it for them. He reminds me of myself when I was younger. After the game, [Eagles safety] Brian Dawkins came up to me and said, 'You're a warrior,' and that means a lot to me, coming from him. Because that's his mentality when he plays the game. It made me feel good."

Barber had generous words for teammates and opponents alike, even for Coughlin. "If it wasn't for the guys around me picking me up and keeping me going," Tiki said, "I don't know what would have happened. And that includes the coaches. Tom Coughlin was instrumental in that. I can remember a Philly game when I had three fumbles. It could have killed my confidence. But he kept pushing me upward. Coach Coughlin has done great things in his three years here."

In weeks past, Barber had complained about the way Coughlin was apportioning the ball. In days to come, he would condemn Coughlin for overworking his players, practicing too much in pads. Like a lot of politicians, Tiki had trouble keeping his stories straight. Hell of a player, though.

In conclusion, Barber said, "I told Eli Manning—and Eli's already well aware of this—'Use your voice next year. It doesn't have to be loud and screaming or demeaning. But use your voice. Tell people what you feel and what you need. Be honest about it. They might dislike you for a moment, but if you're honest, they can never fault you.' Eli has to find a comfort level still, but he's well on his way to finding it. I'm excited about what he'll be for this organization for years to come."

Moving from locker to locker, Accorsi touched every player and had a few words for some. He advised Brandon Jacobs, "Don't let anyone tell you that you don't have the stuff to be a great running back, because you do. Don't let them make you a short-yardage back, either." "I just want to be here," Jacobs replied. "That," Ernie said, "I can't do much about."

Accorsi told Plaxico Burress, "You're the best free agent signing of my career." ("You know, it's interesting," Ernie said. "Ever since Plax gave up on that play against Pacman Jones in the Tennessee game, he's been unbelievable. His body language. The big plays. No drops. I think that changed him.")

Ernie shook David Tyree's hand, saying, "You're the best special-teams guy I've ever been around." "You've got the talent," he told Sinorice Moss. Accorsi said to Tim Carter, "You didn't have a great year, Timmy, but don't let them beat you down. Trust your ability. You've certainly got the ability."

Throwing his arms around the punter Jeff Feagles, placekicker Jay Feely, and long snapper Ryan Kuehl, Accorsi said, "You are the three guys who allow a GM to sleep at night." A little sheepishly Feagles informed him, "I'm breaking our retirement pact, Ernie. I'm going to go for a twentieth season." "Well," Ernie said with a laugh, "you're on your own now, Jeff."

Center Shaun O'Hara had yet to be re-signed—Shaun's representative was historically fascinated by free agency. "You should think about staying, though," Ernie told the center. "You fit here." O'Hara was the one bent over the fallen Roy Posner at the Washington train station, urging, "Fight, Roy. Don't give up, Roy." "What a man O'Hara is," Ernie said.

To Rich Seubert, the walking miracle, Accorsi said, "You're one of the toughest guys I've ever been around." "Fuck Philadelphia," Seubert said.

"If I make up an all-time list," Ernie told Jeremy Shockey, "you're on it." "Do you like fishing?" Shockey asked. "No, but I'll go fishing with you as long as you're not the one driving the boat."

"Boy, am I glad we brought you back," Ernie said to Brandon Short. ("We drafted Short, lost him, then brought him back. He played his heart out this year. We knew his knee was shaky when he came. Then he got that ankle. But he played hard all the way through it. He's classic Penn State. Everything about him is Penn State.")

"Thanks again for not giving me up," Osi Umenyiora told Accorsi, who wouldn't even discuss Osi when San Diego sought him in the Manning deal.

Jim Finn put out his hand. ("Finn gets every molecule out of his body," Ernie said. "Whatever's there, he gets. Every time you throw him the ball, he's not going to get any more than he's supposed to get, but he gets every inch of that. If there's eight yards there, he'll get all eight and be fighting for the ninth.")

Ernie's message to Manning was whispered. "I'd do it all over again, Eli," he said, "and you're going to win a championship." "Ernie wants me to be the best decision he ever made," Manning said later, "That's what I want to be, too."

"I'm making my rounds," Accorsi said, "and all of a sudden I look over my shoulder and Carter's standing behind me. 'Yeah, Timmy.' 'Mr. Accorsi,' he said, 'I didn't know you were retiring.' Someone in the background yelled, 'Where the fuck have you been?'" "Thanks for believing in me," Carter said. "You're the only one who did. Thanks for picking me." Two months later, Carter would be traded to Cleveland for running back Reuben Droughns.

Monday morning, when the Giants players mustered in the big meeting room, Accorsi thought of asking the coaching staff to leave. But tight ends coach Mike Pope beat him to the punch, saying for all of them, "I ain't missing this."

"Good morning, men," Coughlin said.

"Good morning, Coach," the players responded.

"*Good morning, men!*" he sang louder.

"*Good morning, Coach!*" they sang back.

Tiki was right; Tom did treat them like schoolchildren.

"The last time I heard anything like that," Ernie said, "was in Sister Veronica's second-grade class at St. Joan of Arc elementary school in Hershey. Before I started to talk, I looked hard around the room, into every player's face. Their eyes were unbelievably attentive."

This is what he said: "I wanted to say goodbye to you before I left. You are my thirty-fifth and last team. I've been with two Super Bowl teams, one that won the championship. Twelve play-off teams. Six teams that went to the conference championship game. Nine divisional champions. Some of those teams that went farther than you did, I didn't really like that much. Some I loved. But there was no team that I liked more than this one. I know some of you better than others. You younger guys, who haven't been around as long, I don't know quite as well, obviously. But I had something to do with acquiring every player in this room except Michael Strahan, and I made sure Michael never left.

"Tiki, I have been with six NFL Hall of Fame players: Johnny Unitas, Ted Hendricks, John Mackey, Franco Harris, Jack Ham, and Ozzie Newsome. You will be the seventh and Michael will be the eighth. Tiki, you have been the most remarkable back I have not only ever been with but that I have ever seen. You have defied every rule of reason in this game, every actuary law in the game of football. You have gotten better and faster as you have gotten older at a position that has the lowest career expectancy in the National Football League. It's been an honor to watch every play of your great career.

"This team has endured more than any team I've ever been with. If I were an objective observer and had been told last August, 'Here is a team that is supposed to be a contender. It's going to be given the most difficult start of a schedule perhaps in history. It's going to lose two All-Pro defensive ends, one of them a Hall of Famer, plus its number one backup, an All-Pro linebacker, both starting corners, the left tackle, and the greatest receiver in the history of the franchise. What do you think its record is going to be?' I would have said four and twelve, or five and eleven. You have endured an incredible amount of criticism from *all* quarters ["That," Ernie said later, "was directed at the coaches"], and yet you made the play-offs and played your hearts out to the last second of the last game. You're good kids. Stay together. Trust each other and be good teammates to one another. I believe there is a championship in this room. I won't be here with you, but I will be cheering for you. Thank you for giving me a lot of great moments."

He saluted them and walked out to a standing ovation.

25

COUNTDOWN

A s the days dwindled down, Accorsi took an inventory one morning. Precisely forty-two remained in his general-managing career. Naturally, that made him think of Jackie Robinson. When forty-one days were left, he remembered Whitey Ford had drawn that unfamiliar number first, before 16. Gale Sayers and Hopalong Cassady both wore 40, Roy Campanella 39. It became a game in Ernie's head, a countdown for an old sports fan getting ready to leave the field.

"Why couldn't he have started at eighty?" said Jeremy Shockey, meaning his own jersey numeral.

"That would be the old Baltimore Colt defensive back Andy Nelson," I told him.

"Really?" he said in a subdued voice.

"No, it would be you, Jeremy," I said, "and Andy Nelson."

Franco Harris and Billy Packer, 34; Bob Turley with the Orioles, Bill Dickey as a coach, 33; Elston Howard, 32; Brian Piccolo at Wake Forest, 31; Bobby Shantz and Eddie Lopat, 30; Bobby Richardson, first number, 29; Jimmy Orr, 28; Clyde "Smackover" Scott, 27; Lydell Mitchell, 26; Hank Bauer, first number, 25; Lenny Moore, Willie Mays, Matt Guokas, 24.

When John Mara announced that Tom Coughlin was returning, and a year would be tacked onto the year he had left, Mara said, "I think there is substantial support for him in that locker room. That's the feedback I have received, and that's what I've observed with my own eyes. There's this notion out there that he's lost the locker room, that there's a mutiny going on down there. That is definitely not the case."

The reporters were so disappointed that one of them, noting that Accorsi hadn't as yet been replaced, plaintively inquired if the new general manager could still fire the coach. "No, Tom Coughlin is our coach for 2007," Mara said, "and hopefully for many years after that. That's the final decision."

"How does it feel," Pat Hanlon asked Mara in the front office that afternoon, "to be even less popular than George Bush?"

It did no good to tell the fans that coaches of consecutive play-off teams in the NFL were almost never fired, especially by a Mara. For many fans, this was a decision beyond explanation. "I'm certainly sensitive to what the fans think," John said. "I have received a lot of mail. But at the end of the day, you can't make decisions on what the fans say, but what your eyes tell you and what your experience in the game tells you."

Shockey, of "outcoached" fame, said, "Everyone on this team, no matter what anyone from the outside says, understands that nothing is more important to Coach Coughlin than winning, and that's what you want from your coach. He deserves to be the head coach of the Giants. I'm glad he's coming back, and I've told many people over the last few days that I hoped he'd be coming back."

"I had some of my best conversations with Tom this season," Michael Strahan said. "We're getting there."

Those like Tiki Barber who contended that Coughlin was too much of a disciplinarian were contradicted by, if nothing else, the cold statistics. With eighteen personal fouls, the Giants led the league in lack of discipline.

For a moment, just a moment, Coughlin was giddy enough to be out of the guillotine's shadow that he started to bring up the subject of a raise. But, hearing distant thunder, he took it back as fast as he could before the stonemasonry came down on top of him. Even the patience of a Mara has limits. "We did not consider an extension for more than one year," John said pointedly.

Tom and Ernie still had a few rounds to go, too. "Pro football is a game that can feed on and profit from antagonistic attitudes," Ernie said. "It's not *My Fair Lady*." When Coughlin neglected to mention to Accorsi that he was firing defensive coordinator Tim Lewis, Ernie couldn't resist lumping Tom with Robert Irsay. "That's the last time I had to get news of that sort on the television," he told the coach. Tom apologized profusely but just wished Ernie would take back the word *classless*. "It was a classless act," Accorsi said, "but you're not classless, Tom. Your class is your saving grace, as a matter of fact."

"I just would like a pat on the back now and then," the coach said.

"You shouldn't need it," said the departing GM.

"We weren't two and fourteen, you know."

"That makes me wonder if you aren't satisfied with eight and eight."

But just a few weeks later, when Coughlin brought spice to the league meetings with a quotable illustration of how unpopular he was with the New York media ("Hitler and then me, in that order," he said), Accorsi called him from retirement to say, "Leave Hitler out of it, will you please?" "I usually say, 'Genghis Khan,'" Tom told him. "Leave him out of it, too," Ernie said. The point is, Accorsi was calling because he was still on Coughlin's side. He was for him. And, of course, Ernie was going to back John Mara in the end, whatever he did, both his decision and his reasoning. If you ask me whether it was lucky for Tom that Ernie wasn't staying, I can't say for sure. But I have an opinion.

Recalling the day of the Coughlin job interview and what Ernie had said afterward ("If we can't win with this guy, I'm taking up tennis"), Mara told me, "For a going-away present, I thought of giving Ernie a tennis racket."

Bobby Thomson, 23; Allie Reynolds and Don Mueller, 22; Bob Kuzava, Tiki Barber, and Roberto Clemente, 21; Frank Robinson, 20; Johnny Unitas, Bernie Kosar, and Alvin Dark, 19; Don Larsen, 18; Vic Raschi, 17; Frank Capitani and Whitey Ford, second number, 16; Thurman Munson, 15; Bill (Moose) Skowron and Otto Graham, 14; Wilt Chamberlain,

13; Gil McDougald and Roger Staubach, 12; Johnny Sain and George Welsh, 11; Phil Rizzuto and Eli Manning, 10.

An e-mail to Tom Webb, an old Accorsi friend, in Baltimore: "Tomorrow—Hank Bauer, the Splendid Splinter, Maurice Richard, Gordie Howe, Bobby Hull, Joe Grabowski (remember him?), Gino Cimoli, Hank Sauer, Johnny Callison (with the Chisox), and Joe Adcock. In other words, nine days left."

Five days after Coughlin was retained, Accorsi sent this e-mail to me: "Jerry Reese just came into my office and told me they gave him the general manager's job five minutes ago. I'm so happy I could cry. In fact, when he came in to hug me, we both cried. What a wonderful day."

Many of the writers, like Vinny DiTrani of the *Bergen Record,* wrote variations of "The Giants must think the team is on the right track. Last week they decided to retain Tom Coughlin as head coach. Today they will introduce Jerry Reese as their new vice president and general manager." But Shaun Powell, a black columnist at *Newsday,* had a different take.

"In the NFL," Powell wrote, "bold is a white executive hiring a scout who happens to be black, then grooming him as a trusted apprentice, then recommending him over the team president's brother to take over as general manager . . . Accorsi knows just about everyone in football and could have gone the usual route by tapping into the old boy network . . . The lack of black head coaches and GMs has less to do with racism and more to do with indifference. Accorsi took the road rarely traveled and convinced a young assistant coach at tiny Tennessee-Martin that the big city was worth a try. Reese started as a scout, then was an assistant in pro personnel, then took over the Giants' college scouting operation four years ago. Pretty soon, Accorsi found the man to lead the Giants. Accorsi saw potential where others didn't bother to look. But that's what the good talent scouts do."

Yogi Berra and Willie Marshall, 8.

* * *

The Reese announcement was made on January 16, the day after the Martin Luther King Jr. holiday. Mara had put off the news twenty-four hours to avoid exploiting the coincidence. Jerry wasn't being hired for his blackness.

At his press conference, Reese said, "I live to put my eyes on the players. I'll never stop being an evaluator. That's what I am. That's what I know. But it's really my time to carry the torch and I don't take it lightly. I have to be successful on a lot of levels, to keep the dream alive."

Doug Williams, the first black quarterback to win the Super Bowl, was one of the first to telephone Reese. Harry Carson, the Giants' Hall of Fame linebacker, attended the press conference. Chris Mara didn't.

"I'm ecstatic," Carson said. "I feel like a little kid. I'm glad for Jerry, and I'm proud of my organization, my old team, for making this statement. It's a huge statement throughout the league."

When Reese came back up the winding staircase to the front office, I said to him, "The GM."

"Ernie won't tell you," he whispered, "but we both cried."

On each end of a small town in Tennessee, road signs were going up: "Welcome to Tiptonville, Home of Jerry Reese, General Manager of the New York Giants."

Peyton Manning finally won his Super Bowl, 29–17 over Rex Grossman and the Chicago Bears. The TV announcers emphasized Grossman's shortcomings, making him sound like an utter neophyte who could barely transact an exchange from center. "Did they notice it was raining?" Bill Walsh asked. Bill still tended to stand up for young quarterbacks.

Eli watched most of the tournament with Archie, Olivia, and the rest of the family upstairs in a private box, and was later introduced with them by Peyton to the audience of *Saturday Night Live*. "Maybe," Walsh said, "it's time for Eli to stop being Peyton's little brother and to start being the quarterback of the New York Giants."

After fourteen victories and just two losses, Marty Schottenheimer's top-seeded San Diego Chargers were ousted in their only play-off game when once again, as the sportswriters say, New England quarterback Tom Brady "found a way to win." The way he found this time was, on fourth and desperation, to throw the ball to the Chargers and rely on them to fumble it back. Safety Marlon McCree had only to bat that ball down, but he obliged. "Brady's Steady Hand Points the Way Again," blared the banner headline in the *New York Times*. Though nobody wanted to notice, the Patriots' estimable quarterback had been in full interception mode for some time, and would throw another one at the end against Indianapolis.

"Sometimes," said Schottenheimer, who was now 5 and 13 in NFL play-offs, "the football gods step in and say, 'Not today.'" Like Coughlin, Marty was offered a second year to go with the season that remained on his contract (in Schottenheimer's case, a $4.5 million per year contract). But club president Dean Spanos and GM A. J. Smith, Marty's nemesis, attached a $1 million buyout clause, which Schottenheimer rejected. "I'm very comfortable fulfilling the contract I signed several years ago," he said coldly. After both of his coordinators departed, Schottenheimer, fourteen wins and all, was fired. Four and a half million dollars will pay a lot of greens fees.

"Talk about a killer loss, that San Diego–New England deal was about as bad as it gets," said Coughlin, who knew of such things. "Brady tried to throw interception after interception down the stretch. You don't think of Bill Belichick's teams getting fifteen-yard penalties and having twelve men on the field, either. This game can turn around on you pretty quickly."

To Coughlin I said, "When Ernie and I visited Charlie Weis at Notre Dame, I told him, 'I like you, Charlie. You remind me of me. You're the hero of all your stories.'"

"Did he get it?" Tom asked. "Did he laugh?"

"He thinks he can fix Eli."

"Maybe Charlie should fix Notre Dame," Coughlin said, "because Eli doesn't need fixing. He just needs the maturity that comes with time."

"The blind-side tackle, Luke Petitgout, goes down. Eli's Raymond Berry, Amani Toomer, goes down. And everyone wants to know, 'What's the matter with Manning? He doesn't look as happy as he used to.'"

"Yeah," Coughlin said, laughing, "and he's drifting to the right on every play."

It's a hard job, quarterbacking in the NFL. "It's so much the hardest job in sports," Don Shula said, "nothing else is even second."

Joe Namath, an expert on quarterbacking in New York, said, "Eli's biggest problem may just be the way he looks. Maybe if he changed his mannerisms or facial expressions just a little bit."

The image of an NFL quarterback now is Peyton at the scrimmage line, gesticulating like an auctioneer. "I think Peyton's theatrics are just a little exaggerated," Walsh said. "He doesn't have to do all of those things at the line before every play." Coughlin respectfully disagreed. "Even with Eli," Tom said, "Ernie would often say to me, 'Why is it so slow at the line? What's all this pointing about?' But an unbelievable chess game is going on. The kid has a thousand things to do. He's got to make the mike [middle linebacker] call. Who's the mike? That's the starting point for all your protection. Then the defense shifts and he's got to make another mike call, and the clock's running down on him. So now they bring a safety up and he's got to rename the mike again. Okay, so how do you want to designate that guy over there, number ninety-three, an end the last time with his hand on the ground, who's now standing up? What is he, a linebacker? Is he a defensive lineman? Where do you want to send your people? And who's the mike now? Okay, fifty-seven is the mike. Good. But, wait a minute. Another safety has moved to the side. You've got to change the call again. Five, four, three, two . . . it ain't easy."

Making himself the mike, Coughlin said, "Here's what's going to happen with Eli. This is what I really believe is going to prevail. Eli will look back on this year and realize that next season, the first person that

will be condemned to death is me. And the second person they're going
to come for is Eli. It's going to toughen his ass up. I really believe that. I
think you're going to see a different guy next year, one with just a little
more seriousness about the consequences that go with this job. We both
might look back on 2006 as the season that made us. That's what I think."

"We played a tough schedule," Eli said, "and we lost a lot of tough
games in almost the absolute toughest ways. We just weren't finding ways
to win at the end. But it's not like we were playing hopeless football. We
were making awful mistakes, but we weren't beaten. We weren't beaten
down, anyway. Out on that practice field, it was high energy, full speed,
every day. After the worst losses, after Tennessee, after the Cowboys, I
never stopped seeing hope on the practice field. We were still having not
just good but great practices. Players weren't down and out. They
weren't just jogging around. They were running, laughing. Enjoying
being on the field again. We hadn't quit. Not one guy. Couldn't the
media see that? Maybe they are just so pissed off that Coughlin has
restricted them to one corner of the practice field that they don't look at
the football. They never seemed to see us. You don't have to know the
players to see the enthusiasm. For as bad as a loss was, for all the rough
things that were being written and said, not only didn't anybody quit. It
was even better than that. Nobody stopped enjoying being a football
player. I think we gained a lot of respect for each other this year, and
something deeper, too. But it starts with mutual respect."

Schottenheimer said, "The quarterback question is, and always has
been, just this: When all hell breaks loose and nothing is going right,
where does your guy stand? That's what you've got to know. Is he
even there? I like Eli, but he's now in a crucible. Now we're going to find
out. The classic example of the quarterback in the crucible was Ryan
Leaf. I'm not comparing Eli to Leaf, believe me. On his worst day, Eli is
worlds better than Leaf. But Ryan is the classic example of the guy in the
crucible. I went to watch him work out. I studied all of the tape, I talked
to his parents, the whole bit. The guy could make every throw a quarterback needed to make. He was the whole package, he could do it all. But

when he got into that crucible, the flame was turned up, and up, and up, and he completely melted. That's what happens at that position."

Truth be known, Schottenheimer fought in San Diego to keep quarterback Drew Brees, rather than let him go to New Orleans. "But I wasn't winning any fights then," Marty said. Brees led the Saints to the final four. Schottenheimer said, "We drafted Eli in San Diego because he was the value in the draft, but I coached Philip Rivers in the Senior Bowl and I liked him, too. So did Ernie."

"I know," I said. "One of the signature things about Accorsi is that he believes what he believes, and he never second-guesses himself. Without even pausing to take a breath, he'll say, 'I love Philip Rivers. Wonderful kid. He had a lot of success this year. I hope he has a lot more. Eli's better.'"

"That's Ernie," Schottenheimer said. "I happen to think Philip Rivers is going to be a very, very fine, winning NFL quarterback. But I'm not betting against Manning because I don't root against, and I don't bet against, Accorsi."

When Ben Roethlisberger won a Super Bowl with the Pittsburgh Steelers, people said Ernie should have picked Roethlisberger instead of Eli. But after Ben took his helmetless, not to say mindless, fall from a motorcycle and began threatening the league lead in boneheaded plays and interceptions, that talk quietly dissipated. Then, people said, Ernie should have kept Rivers instead of Eli, although Rivers never got off the bench for two years behind Brees, when Manning was winning a division title. "Rivers is one of the nicest guys I've ever been around," Ernie said, "but I didn't consider him for three seconds. I saw him against Wake Forest, and with *their* defensive backs, it took forever for the ball to get there. I mean, I hope Philip has a great career because there's no better kid on the face of this earth. But there was no doubt in my mind about the three then, and there's no doubt in my mind now."

Tony Romo, nailed to the Dallas bench for four years, was another budding quarterback the New York fans began to think the Giants should have gone for. "I got the guy I wanted," Accorsi said with a comfortable laugh. "In all of my retirement interviews, everyone asks, 'What was your best deal?' 'Manning,' I say, just to drive them crazy. But, the funny thing is, it's true."

Mickey Mantle and Bobby Sollinger, 7; Stan (the Man) Musial, Al Kaline, and Willie "Puddin' Head" Jones, 6; Joe DiMaggio and Brooks Robinson, 5; Carl Braun and Lou Gehrig, 4; Babe Ruth and Jimmy Lynam, 3; Derek Jeter, Frank Crosetti, and Granny Hamner, 2.

"At Baltimore in 1978," Accorsi said, "we drafted this skinny punter from Richmond, Bruce Allen, in the twelfth round. Of course, David Lee was going to be our punter again, for about the hundredth straight year. Dick Szymanski was the GM then, I was his assistant, handling all of the low picks. I guess Bruce weighed about one-sixty. 'We're going to have a blocked punt drill now,' Ted Marchibroda tells Allen at practice. 'Don't let it bother you.' Well, we block fifteen straight punts on the poor kid, and whatever confidence he had was shattered forever. He couldn't kick the ball at all after that. He lasted about seven days."

Ernie was telling this story by way of explaining the final official transaction that had just come across his desk, forwarded by John Mara. It was from the Tampa Bay Buccaneers:

CONSENT FORM

Club Requesting Consent: Tampa Bay Buccaneers Employer Club: New York Giants Employee's Name: Ernie Accorsi Employee's Current Position: General Manager (motto: "God doesn't want me to be happy.") Position to be Interviewed for: TBA

We are looking for a talent evaluator (especially punters), friend, storyteller, NFL historian, Major League Baseball historian, negotiator, advisor, medical translator, scout translator, head coach's confidant, golfer, writer, PR advisor and, most importantly, we want someone who is loyal to his organization.

Signed: Bruce Allen, General Manager, Tampa Bay Buccaneers

Permission is granted:

Permission is denied: X

("Sorry," Mara wrote under the X, "but we do not have anybody here with these qualifications.")

Eddie Joost, 1.

Borrowing his exit line from DiMaggio, Accorsi said, "I want to thank the good Lord for making me a New York Giant," and left. Watching his mentor go, young Matt Harriss was interrupted in his reverie by capologist Kevin Abrams, who said, "Get yourself a plane ticket, Matt. You're going to the Senior Bowl." Harriss threw his arms in the air.

Ernie headed to baseball's spring training. ("I had a great day with Joe Torre Saturday," he reported via e-mail. "When Carl Pavano got hit with a liner, Joe said, 'Oh, shit.' They're just like us.")

Come late summer, when the Giants would be reassembling for the 2007 season, Ernie expected to be "zigzagging all over the country," looking for Rickey's grave in Ohio and Mantle's tin barn in Oklahoma. "I want to go to Fort Wayne, Indiana, to the arena where the Pistons used to play. It's still standing. I want to go see the Quonset hut where Bradley played its games during those great Missouri Valley Conference years. I want to go to the Eisenhower and Truman libraries, to Davenport, to Moline, to Quad Cities, to Yellowstone Park and Mount Rushmore and Squaw Valley, to see if that arena is still there where the first Miracle on Ice took place. I've been to Chavez Ravine before, but I've never seen a ballgame there. Then I'm going to go to Vancouver and take that Canadian railroad back to Montreal—it's a three-day trip through the Canadian Rockies. I'm going to get a compartment."

"Ernie is the last of his breed," said Pat Hanlon, who may be the last of his breed, too, a PR guy who speaks his mind. "Ernie represents the

Pete Rozelle era. Smaller organizations. Less specialization. Nobody else
is ever going to start as the PR director of the Colts and end up the general manager of the New York Giants. That's never going to happen
again. A lot of the fans are playing fantasy football and acting just like
GMs, but are any of them true believers? Will any of them end up the
real thing?"

Like Red Smith rattling off a pitching line, John Mara, sitting in his
office, ticked off the necessary qualities of a GM: "High degree of intelligence. Ethics. Courage. Trust. Respect. The ability to work as part of a
team. Someone who is willing to make bold moves that more cautious
people are afraid to make. Someone who will communicate with everybody in the office. When I was writing out this list," he said, "I realized I
was describing Ernie Accorsi. I think of Ernie as an executive as much as
a judge of talent, and I see an executive ability in Jerry Reese, too. But, as
the GM job continues to evolve in that direction, some element of the
scout will always be important to me. If the GM is going to be the last
authority on player decisions, before we commit millions of dollars on a
signing bonus, I want to know he's seen the player with his own eyes and
is capable of making his own judgment."

On the walls surrounding Mara's desk were black-and-white photographs of Tim Mara and Art Rooney at the racetrack, homburg hats,
binoculars, and cigars. "If you could name three people to have dinner
with someday," John said, "two of them would be my grandfather and
Mr. Rooney." Who can't name the third?

Walking me to the front office door, John asked, "Do you think
Ernie will ever come back?"

"To work?" I said. "No."

"I guess that's right. He always described Sundays as agony, and I certainly understand that. But do you think he'll ever come back just to see
the games?"

"Oh, yeah," I said. "I'm sure he will."

It's a fabulous game.

26

SUPER BOWL XLII

One year later, the Giants were in the Super Bowl. And won it.

The roster changed as it always does, though the marquee actors remained in place. The bigger change was in Tom Coughlin, hanging by that one-year extension. Justifying his hardest edges in 2006, Coughlin had insisted, "There are certain fundamentals I believe in, and that's just the way it is." But, under the prodding of John Mara and Accorsi's successor, Jerry Reese, Tom finally adjusted to modernity. "I may be a dinosaur," he said, "but I can change." Surviving by such a frayed thread, Coughlin may simply have been scared into changing. Had he been fired at age sixty, where in the game of football could he have gone? He might have landed at a small college. More likely he would have been interred forever in the assistant ranks of the NFL. Certainly the television networks would not have been competing to put Coughlin's personality in front of a camera. He was an old-school football coach who, as a matter of plain fact, got practically all of the big things right and practically all of the little things wrong. *The thing is, Tom doesn't make it very easy for you to like him,*" Michael Strahan had said for most of the players. *"He misses the human element. I think a coach has to show a human side."* When Tom started getting some of the little things right, everything at the Meadowlands improved.

In the off-season, Coughlin read a book about Johnny Unitas, a gift from Unitas's old friend, Accorsi. Out of it Tom gleaned a saying that would become a Giants mantra: "Talk is cheap; play the game." Before Unitas's Baltimore Colts took the field on Sundays, defensive captain

Fred Miller regularly heaped a few inspirational words on his team-mates, after which he invariably turned to the Colts quarterback, leaning against the exit door. "Do you have anything to add, John?" Unitas always added the same thing. "Talk is cheap; play the game."

Coughlin had T-shirts made up with that slogan and handed them out to the Giants on the first day of the new order.

The coach didn't alter his basic commandments, not even the measly ones. No ball caps, no cell phones, no crossed legs in the meeting rooms. But in the middle of one of the earliest sessions at training camp, Coughlin suddenly stood up and said, "C'mon everybody. We're going bowling." "Bowling?" Plaxico Burress said later. "So, here we are, the whole team, in an Albany bowling alley; I'm not kidding. And Coach is wearing those stupid shoes and pumping his fist up and down like a real bowler. I have to say, I enjoyed it." "We had a casino night, too," Coughlin said, held at the Meadowlands. "It was fun."

The most substantial thing Tom did was to appoint a committee of Giants leaders, among them center Shaun O'Hara, punter Jeff Feagles, Osi Umenyiora, Antonio Pierce, Michael Strahan, and Eli Manning. Coughlin let them in.

He didn't grant them a veto power, but he gave them a say. That's all they were waiting for. He was showing a human side. "There were nudges from us," Mara said, meaning himself and Reese (and Ernie, too, for more than a year), "but Tom did most of it on his own. 'We know what kind of person you are,' I told him. 'Why don't you let the players and public see that a little bit?' " The players saw it right away; the public took longer.

Before the regular season kicked off on a Sunday night in Dallas, Reese whispered to Mara, "This is going to be Tom's best year as a coach, because this year he's really going to have to be a coach." As Reese explained to me many weeks later, "We didn't get a lot done in free agency; number one, because we didn't want to get a lot done. We weren't going to overpay for a bunch of marginal guys." The Giants signed an inexpensive free agent, Kawika Mitchell, who performed handily as linebacker. But, still thinking like a scout, Reese jettisoned the most injury-prone veterans (Luke Petitgout, LaVar Arrington, Carlos Emmons) and tossed a legion of rookies into the fire.

"Do you know what drives player personnel guys crazy?" Reese asked. "Having a kid on your team for two or three years and still not knowing for sure if he can perform. We were resolved to play the young guys this time, and Tom and his assistants were just going to have to coach them." Traditionally, NFL head coaches oppose youth movements, but Coughlin embraced this one. "I had a good feeling from the start," Reese said.

Though the GM now, Jerry presided in the Giants draft room exactly as he had when he was the player personnel director the year before.

"The only difference was," he said, "Ernie wasn't sitting there. And I'll tell you what, I missed him." In the first round, New York selected defensive back Aaron Ross of Texas, counting on him to be a starter right away. "Ross made more plays in college than Leon Hall or Darrelle Revis," Reese said, mentioning the two corners picked earlier.

"The thing I liked most about Ross was just that fact—that he was a playmaker. He returned punts for Texas, too, which was a bonus." In the second round, the Giants took University of Southern California receiver Steve Smith. "Big-time program," Reese said. "Quarterback-friendly guy. QBs always have a special feeling for a receiver who knows what he's doing on third down."

On Accorsi's last scouting trip to Penn State, you may recall from Chapter 9, he took note of a defensive tackle named Jay Alford, who wore an unusual number, 13. Alford went to the Giants in the third round. "Developmental as a run stopper," Reese said, "but already a decent pass rusher. Alford had that explosive first step you look for in rushing the quarterback. We saw him as one of those 'get him in the game, get him in the game, get him in the game' guys, who a play here and a play there would eventually force his way into the pass-rushing rotation."

A rotation it definitely was, headed by Umenyiora, Justin Tuck, and Strahan, probably in that order. Blowing off the entire sweaty ordeal of training camp, Strahan threatened to follow Tiki Barber into retirement after fourteen NFL seasons. Actually, Strahan was hoping for a renegotiated contract, but Reese stared him down. "'Michael,' I told him when he finally came in, 'we're not going to ask you to play ninety plays a game. We want you to play in a rotation because we want you for sixteen games, not eight. We want you to be there at the end.'"

Returning to the New York clubhouse, Strahan discovered that he was still a captain but no longer a king. This had an agreeable and healthy effect on him and on the Giants.

Tiki, meanwhile, contributed more than anyone yet knew, not just by retiring but by ripping Manning for his new employer, NBC. Without screaming—still not a screamer—Eli stood up to Barber, and the Giants players cheered. It would take a committee of five different running backs to match Barber's 2006 yardage total almost to the foot.

But the team wouldn't miss Tiki.

In the fourth round, the Giants drafted linebacker Zak DeOssie. In the fifth, with the 153rd selection overall, they claimed tight end Kevin Boss. "Boss wasn't really on our list," Reese said. "He was rejected by the combine. But he was on what I call the scouts' grapevine. We kept hearing about this big kid, this two-hundred-and-sixty-pound pass catcher at Western Oregon, who might not be much of a blocker but had nice, soft hands. Jerry Shay was the first of our scouts who went to see Boss. Jerry liked him some. Then we had another scout, Steve Malin, go in to take a look. This is how it works. I watched Boss a bunch of times on tape. He was playing against a lot of little short guys, like me, towering over them, dominating his league. But he showed ball skills that had nothing to do with the level of competition. Unusual ball skills for a big man. And he could run."

("I not only never heard of Boss," Accorsi called Reese to tell him many weeks after the draft, "I never heard of the school he went to! Jerry, you're having the best rookie season since Fred Lynn!" Unfamiliar with the Boston Red Sox' Rookie of the Year in 1975, Reese could only presume that was a compliment.)

The Giants' sixth and seventh selections were Oregon State tackle Adam Koets and Arizona safety Michael Johnson. Deeper in the seventh round, Reese took a chance on a five-nine, 198-pound Marshall running back named Ahmad Bradshaw, who would soon become a celebrity.

"We had enough big backs," Reese said, "in Brandon Jacobs, Reuben Droughns, and Derrick Ward. In fact, we let Ryan Grant go to Green Bay, where he turned into a star. But late in the draft, we were still looking for that change-of-pace runner, and there was Bradshaw." The Giants had a mid-round grade on him. Only because of off-field issues was he still on the board. "We talked about that a bit in the draft room," Reese said. "There was an incident of underage drinking on a recruiting trip. Also, something about a stolen Nintendo set. 'That's all?' I asked. 'That's his whole blotter? Did anybody in this room ever have a drink when they were underage?' "

Come the morning of rookie camp, Reese called Bradshaw into his office. Like Accorsi reading the riot act to Kerry Collins, Jerry minced no words. " 'Do you know why you went so late?' I asked him. 'Yes sir, I know,' he said. 'Well, you're on a very short leash here.' He looked me dead in the eye. 'I won't let you down, Mr. Reese.' "

Not only did Ross, Smith, Alford, DeOssie, Boss, Koets, Johnson, and Bradshaw all play, they all helped. A ninth rookie, undrafted tight end Michael Matthews, joined in. Blocking fullback Madison Hedge-cock and kickoff returner Domenik Hixon were plucked from the waiver wire. They were useful, too. In what seemed a blink, the New York Giants looked up to find themselves the third-youngest team in the league. And, in the anomaly of the year, the more the young players played, the more seasoned the team seemed.

Still, the start was rocky. Yielding forty-five points at Dallas in the season opener, then being blown out by the Green Bay Packers at home, the Giants came from two touchdowns behind in Washington to fend off a third straight loss at the very goal line. Never mind second-half comebacks; the New York fans were ready to vote. Now they wanted Coughlin executed and Eli exiled. The most peculiar take on the season-saving victory over the Redskins came from *New York Times* columnist Selena Roberts, whose lead the next day was: "In one instant, quarter-back Eli Manning faked out the Giants' endemic inertia and duped their rooted dysfunction on a play that practically foiled management's grand design to set up this team for failure." *What?* According to a Coughlin confidant, Tom read that sentence three or four times, scratching his head. Blowing the whistle on "management's strategy of status quo," she unveiled the Giants' off-season "plot" to sit "passively on the sideline while the competition upgraded."

Coughlin was retained merely "to hold space, to be a body with a whistle until a superstar like Bill Cowher took his cue to swoop in and take over the scene." At that point, proving it was undeniably a new day, Tom threw back his head and laughed.

Winning the next five games, the Giants stood 6-and-2 at the midway point of the season, just as they had in 2006, when eminent players began tumbling like dominoes. But this time it wasn't until the four-teenth game that one of the stars collapsed: Jeremy Shockey. With Bar-ber retired and Strahan shuffled back into the deck, Shockey was the last remnant of the Me Generation in the Giants' clubhouse and hud-dle. As unkind as it sounds, Jeremy's broken leg may not have been the worst break for the Giants. "At the end of the regular season," a team executive said, "I was standing behind our bench and thought, 'Some-thing's different? What's different?' Then it dawned on me. Shockey wasn't there, calling attention to himself."

Shockey's teammates liked him; many of them loved him. But if the self-described "wild child" was to return to New York in 2008, he would have to be a slightly different kind of guy to fit in with this new team. Because that's what the Giants were now, above all. A team.

Concluding the regular season against New England's impeccable Patriots (15–0) in New York, the Giants (10–5) already were assured a playoff date with Tampa Bay. Whether they should risk injury in an all-out try to be a spoiler was a matter of citywide and even league-wide debate. At first Coughlin seemed inclined to be cautious. But in the last couple of days before the game, he stated emphatically that the Giants were playing to win. Maybe he had won an argument with himself. Or maybe the committee of players influenced him. But it was his best decision of the year.

Though Accorsi had dropped in on a few games at Giants Stadium, he kept the lowest profile. Even more quietly, he spent three weeks as a consultant to owner Arthur Blank in Atlanta, helping the Falcons find a new GM. Longtime scout Thomas Dimitroff got the job. "Tom's dad was a scout for me in Cleveland," Ernie said. "He died of cancer. After Tom was hired, he asked me what I considered to be a GM's priorities. I told him, 'I could write you out thirty-four pages, but I'll just give you three. Get the quarterback when you can, get the people to protect him, and get the pass rushers. Everything else falls into place.' "

On the day of the Giants' regular-season closer, Accorsi went to Baltimore to attend the wedding of Chad Unitas, John's youngest son. "At the reception, though," Ernie told Chad's mother, Sandy, "I'll be heading straight for the bar, to the TV set." Old Colts Tom Matte, Bruce Laird, and Sam Havrilak joined him. Trailing 28–16 in the third quarter, Tom Brady and the Patriots rallied to a 38–35 victory and an unbeaten regular season.

But early in the game, when a few customers in the bar were still arguing that the Giants should pull Manning at least, Havrilak whispered to Accorsi, "You can't pull him now. You just can't, Ernie. Players won't let you do that. Coughlin must have learned something this year about players."

Eli threw four touchdown passes in that springboard loss, almost offsetting the four interceptions he threw a month or so earlier against Minnesota (three for Vikings touchdowns). "Then I desperately wanted him to win the playoff game in Tampa," Accorsi said, and he did, 24–14. Next, a ninth consecutive road game was won in Dallas, 21–17, avenging, incredibly, the Giants' only out-of-town loss of the season.

Accorsi said, "When the Cowboys went ahead, 14–7, with forty-some seconds left in the first half, I went to church. St. Vincent Ferrer at 65th and Lexington. During the collection, I checked my BlackBerry. If they can break into the liturgy to collect money, I can check the score. It was tied at half, 14–14. I couldn't believe it." Eli had taken the Giants down the field in one of those defining drives that changes everything.

"I'll tell you something," Accorsi said. "Quarterback rankings don't mean a thing to me. They're stupid. Milt Plum had a better quarterback ranking than Unitas. They're passing rankings anyway. They aren't quarterback rankings."

At training camp with the Colts in 1970, Accorsi's first NFL stop, he watched the aging Unitas throwing flutterballs in practice and murmured to defensive back-turned-scout Milt Davis, "Do you think John has enough left?" "Ernest," Davis said, "the measure of a quarterback in the NFL is whether he can take a team down the field into the end zone with the title on the line." Baltimore won Super Bowl V that year.

Against the Packers in overtime, on a frigid day even for Green Bay (Eli gloved his left hand), the Giants intercepted Brett Favre's 9,479th and presumably last pass to reach Super Bowl XLII. *"You're good kids,"* *Accorsi had said. "Stay together. Trust each other and be good teammates to one* *another. I believe there is a championship in this room."*

At first Ernie wasn't going to go to Arizona, but Mara wouldn't take no for an answer. "You're going," John said flatly. Reese said, "I was afraid Ernie would stay away for my sake. I could tell he had laid low all year, for me. But I wanted him to be there."

Accorsi sat in the Arizona crowd with all of his children, together at an NFL game for the first time. An extra ticket in their row went to the pro golfer Billy Andrade, on the condition that he not cheer for the Patriots. Andrade grew up a Pats fan in Rhode Island.

At a team service on Super Sunday morning, the priest celebrating Mass delivered a pep talk of a homily. He recalled how Wellington Mara, the two-dollar betting son of a bookmaker, habitually coupled the numbers four and two in his exactas and daily doubles. Forty-two was the uniform numeral of the great Giants quarterback Charley Conerly, who, like Eli, played his college football at Ole Miss. Also, there were exactly forty-two Mara grandchildren. Was there any way the Giants could lose Super Bowl XLII? No, the chaplain answered his own question. It was a mortal lock.

Incidentally, one of the grandchildren, actress Kate Mara, spent the postseason games text-messaging her father, Chris Mara, Giants vice president of player evaluation, the same message over and over: "We Are Marshall!" She was in that movie. They all seemed to be in a movie.

To the dismay of a few in the organization, but not particularly Coughlin, Burress made a prediction, as opposed to a guarantee. He picked the Giants, of course, and pulled this odd score out of the air: 23–17. It probably had something to do with his jersey number, 17. *"Do you know why I wear seventeen?" he had said. "Because I signed as a free agent on the seventeenth of March. That's how much it meant to me to be a New York Giant."* Unwittingly, Plaxico hit upon the score of the fabled Colts–Giants Sudden Death Game of 1958, not an easy score to get to. When Tom Brady was informed of Plaxico's guess, he laughed and said, "We're only going to score seventeen points?" Eventually that would qualify as irony.

In New York's first stroke of indispensable luck, Methuselah the punter (Feagles) called tails, and tails it was. The Giants spent nine minutes and fifty-nine seconds on the most time-consuming possession in Super Bowl history just to chalk up a field goal. After waiting all day for the late kickoff, Brady was made to wait another half hour to touch the ball in what was now a shortened game. The Patriots answered with a touchdown, but as New England touchdowns went, it was unconvincing. The biggest play was a flagrant pass interference penalty committed by middle linebacker Pierce in the end zone on third-and-ten. By their standards, Brady and the Patriots' offense looked flat. On the orders of Steve Spagnuola, New York's cracking new defensive coordinator, the rotating pass-rushers started knocking Tom down. They kept knocking him down. They knocked him down about two dozen times. The score stayed 7–3 into the fourth quarter.

Manning began New York's first drive of the final period with a deep pass to Boss, the Western Oregon rookie with the ball skills and the soft hands. *"And he could run," Reese had said.* That opened up the game a little. The forty-five-yard gain pushed the Giants to the New England thirty-five, where reformed Nintendo player Ahmad Bradshaw of Marshall ("We Are Marshall!") made three tough runs to accompany two Manning passes. The first was a seventeen-yarder to rookie Steve Smith. Eli's second pass was for five yards and a touchdown to five-year veteran David Tyree, Tyree's lone TD of the season.

Accorsi said, "We decided—all of us—that Tyree was the best special-teams player any of us had ever seen. But every now and then he'd get in on the offense for a play or two, and Eli seemed to see him." At the end of Eli's rookie year, when Eli became a starter, it was Tyree who caught a bunch of passes to beat Dallas for Manning's first NFL victory.

With about eight minutes left in Super Bowl XLII, New York might have moved ahead by ten points if Manning and Burress hadn't wrong-footed each other on a maddening second-and-nine play at the Giants' thirty. Sprinting left, Eli saw Plaxico standing near the sideline so utterly open that the defenders weren't even in the frame. Plax didn't know whether to take off down the open field or stand in place. He didn't do either and Manning slightly overthrew him. A Giants fan seated in front of Accorsi screwed his head around and said, "Your quarterback just cost us the world championship."

Fielding the next punt at its own twenty, New England finally started a drive it would sustain.

PATRIOTS

1-10-P20 (shotgun) Brady passes to Wes Welker for 5
2-5-P25 (shotgun) Brady passes to Randy Moss for 10
1-10-P35 Laurence Maroney runs for 9

2-1-P44   Brady passes to Welker for 13
1-10-G43 (shotgun) Brady passes to Kevin Faulk for 4
2-6-G39   (shotgun) Brady passes to Welker for 10
1-10-G29 (shotgun) Brady passes incomplete
2-10-G29 Brady passes to Moss for 11
1-10-G18 (shotgun) Brady passes to Faulk for 12
1-G-G6   Brady passes incomplete
2-G-G6   (shotgun) Brady passes incomplete
3-G-G6   (shotgun) Brady passes to Moss for 6
    and the touchdown; Stephen Gostkowski's
    kick is good
Patriots 14, Giants 10

Fans of the Spygaters exhaled. Brady had done it once more. The 19 and 0 season was in sight again. First and ten at his own seventeen-yard line, Manning was left just two minutes and thirty-nine seconds to negotiate eighty-three yards. Accorsi thought of Milt Davis. (He would call Davis in Oregon right after the game, to thank him.)

Turning to son Michael, Ernie said of Eli, "If he's going to be what we thought he was going to be, he does it *now*." On his BlackBerry, the former GM tapped out the same message to me, mistyping just about every word.

GIANTS

1-10-G17 (shotgun) Manning passes to Amani Toomer
    for 11

"Sometimes I feel like I've been doing this eighty-five years," Toomer had said. "Other times it feels like I've just begun."

1-10-G28 (no huddle, shotgun) Manning passes incomplete
2-10-G28 (shotgun) Manning passes incomplete

Two-Minute Warning
3-10-G28 (shotgun) Manning passes to Toomer for 9 (1:59)
4-1-G37   Brandon Jacobs slams the line for 2 (1:34)
1-10-G39 (shotgun) Manning scrambles for 5 (1:28)
Giants time-out #1
2-5-G44   (shotgun) Manning passes incomplete (1:20)
3-5-G44   (shotgun) Manning passes to Tyree for 32 yards
   (1:15)

With his jersey being tugged at and strained like a bowstring, Eli somehow escaped a rush that would have defined "in the grasp" if that quasi-rule was still in even the unofficial book. It wasn't, and it hadn't been for years. In the NFL, you're either down or you're not.

Inexplicably, Eli wasn't down. "And then I saw Tyree," he said, that special team player he always seemed to see.

Outwrestling Rodney Harrison, the Patriots' strong safety in every meaning of the term, Tyree pressed the ball to his helmet. He basically caught it with his helmet. From the near-sack to the wild scramble to the catch, it was the most startling play in forty-two Super Bowls.

About a minute remained.

Giants time-out #2
1-10-P24 (shotgun) Manning sacked for -1 (:59)
Last Giants time-out
2-11-P25 (shotgun) Manning passes incomplete (:51)
3-11-P25 (shotgun) Manning passes to Steve Smith for 12
   (:45)

Many rookies might have kept going for the glory with no time-outs, but Smith made sure he reached the first-down stick before veering out of bounds to stop the clock. *As Reese had said, "QBs always have a special feeling for a receiver who knows what he's doing on third down."*

1-10-P13 (shotgun) . . . (:39)

What was Accorsi thinking then? "Only two times since about 1950," he said, "has an NFL championship been won on a touchdown pass. There have been a million runs, a lot of quarterback sneaks, and eight billion field goals. But Joe Montana to John Taylor [Super Bowl XXIII] and Bobby Layne to Jim Doran [1953] were the only two passes I could come up with that won titles. That's what I was thinking."

Doran was a defensive player by trade, for Detroit. But in the midst of the Lions' championship game against Cleveland, tight end Leon Hart wrenched a knee, and Doran moved over to the other side of the scrimmage line. After a couple of offensive series, he told Layne, "Bobby, I can beat this guy," meaning Browns cornerback Warren Lahr. Layne didn't know whether Doran could beat Lahr or not, but Bobby knew one thing. "Jim Doran wasn't no bull-shitter." All the same, the quarterback decided to wait.

Detroit was behind, 16–10, with the fourth quarter running out, when Layne called time to consult with head coach Buddy Parker at the bench. Rather, Parker consulted with him. "What do you think, Bobby?" the coach asked his whiskey-faced quarterback. Layne replied, "I think a cigarette would taste real good right now," and meandered back to the huddle. Bobby looked squarely at Doran and peeked across the line at Lahr. "Can you still beat that feller?" A few seconds later, Lahr was faked out and Doran was holding up the football in the end zone. Detroit 17, Cleveland 16.

"I can beat this guy, Hobbs," Plaxico had told Eli in the first half. He meant Patriots cornerback Ellis Hobbs, whose interception on a tipped ball in the second quarter was the only one Manning threw in the entire postseason. "This guy's a sucker for an inside fake," Burress said. "One quick move to the post and I'll be open in the left corner."

Manning looked hard at Plax, who had performed amazingly on a throbbing ankle all season and now had a tender knee to boot. "Let's save it," the quarterback said, "for when we really need it."

Manning passes to Burress for thirteen yards and the touchdown; Lawrence Tynes's kick is good.

"They finally came with an all-out blitz," Eli said. "I'd been waiting for it—hoping for it—all day." With an inside fake, Burress paralyzed Hobbs and slipped into the left corner. Looking up, he saw Eli's lob pass already on its way into his arms. The same play won an overtime game the year before in Philadelphia. It was Eli's and Plax's favorite play. *"Plax is smarter than what you think," Manning had said, "or what he shows you." "Eli and I have a long way to go," Burress had said, "but I think we're going to get there eventually. When Eli reaches his full potential, he's going to be much better than good. He's going to be absolutely great."* New York 17, New England 14

In the last half minute of the game, a fifth Giants sack reduced Tom Brady's options to seventy-five-yard prayers that were beautiful to look at but impossible to catch. At their own sixteen-yard line, the Patriots turned the ball over on downs. They were only a field goal shy of that seventeen-point mark that had made Brady laugh. The sacker, by the way, was Jay Alford, number 93. He wore 13 at Penn State.

As tough losses go, especially when it comes to head coaches, this one was almost enough to make Don Shula forget Joe Namath. In the days and years to come, the Patriots' relentless leader, Bill Belichick, will probably go as long as an hour and a half without thinking about it. New England's linemen were so gassed at the end that an obvious question turned into a moral. Mightn't the offensive linemen, in particular, have benefited from a few fourth quarters off when those 52–7 and 56–10 scores were being run up in October and November?

"My lasting memory," the golfer Billy Andrade said, "will be the way Ernie's kids looked at him the second the game ended. It's one of the most emotional things I've ever seen." During all of the subsequent embracing and jumping up and down, the fan who had said "Your quarterback just cost us the world championship" tried to kiss Accorsi on the lips. " 'No thank you,' I told him, pushing him away. 'I prefer the insult.' "

Later, the old GM said, "From now on, whenever I hear the words *The Drive,* I won't ever again think of John Elway."

"Make sure the office has your ring size," John Mara told Accorsi casually. Like Wellington, John has a way of saying a whole lot without saying very much. Accorsi came in with a ring and Johnny Unitas. He was going out with a ring and Eli Manning. "Ernie deserves as much credit for this as anyone," Mara said.

Arriving back at the Meadowlands, Accorsi got off the Giants bus to collect his luggage and saw a great hulking figure coming toward him in the dark. "It was Rich Seubert," he said, the walking miracle.

Seubert had worked his way back from "Number sixty-nine is reporting . . ." to a starting position again, at his beloved left tackle. "Neither one of us could speak," Ernie said. "We just stood there and hugged."

It was the perfect ending.

EPILOGUE

BY ERNIE ACCORSI

Nobody asked me, but . . .

- Baseball is the best game.
- Professional football is the best-*run* game.
- Unlike in football, basketball, and hockey, the baseball umpires don't determine the outcome of close games. The players do.
- That said, no professional sport has been managed as successfully as the National Football League.
- In primitive times, the NFL was more than blessed to have a blood-and-guts commissioner, Bert Bell.
- But looking back at the league's success, the indispensible person was very simply Pete Rozelle.
- I'm encouraged by the start new commissioner Roger Goodell has made.
- Rozelle's right-hand man, Jim Kensil, is the most underrated, most forgotten sports executive in the history of this country. Bill Granholm and Seymour Siwoff are close behind.
- The most thankless position is supervisor of officials. Art McNally and Jerry Seaman were the best.
- The two greatest-run sporting events in America are the Masters golf tournament and the Atlantic Coast Conference basketball tournament.
- The greatest pro football teams I ever saw were the 1975–79 Pittsburgh Steelers.

- In my lifetime, the second-greatest team was the 1962 Green Bay Packers.

- The Cleveland Browns teams of the first half of the 1950s were great, but twice they lost to what I consider to be the most under-rated team of the modern era, Bobby Layne's Detroit Lions.

- Not too many coaches have ever outsmarted the competition, but I think Bill Walsh did.

- Just as I think Bill Belichick does now.

- Chuck Noll, Vince Lombardi, and Paul Brown had superior intellects. Brown virtually invented the modern NFL.

- Tommy Henrich and Hank Bauer were the first players I idolized, but neither of them as much as Mickey Mantle. When Mantle limped, I limped, too.

- I still follow the Hershey Bears hockey team every day.

- My most heartbreaking losses weren't the 1986 and '87 AFC championship games between the Browns and Denver. Worse was a Little League play-off loss to the Harrisburg Suburban Americans.

- The first football team I ever fell in love with was the Hershey High School Trojans of 1952–53. They played two ties, 0–0 and 6–6, against their bitter rivals, the Milton Hershey Spartans, who had a single-wing tailback named John Elway.

- When Peter Gammons was inducted into the writers and broadcast-ers wing of the Baseball Hall of Fame, he said something that put my childhood in perspective: "My role models were already in place by the time I was fourteen years old." Me, too. My mom and dad, Tony DeAngelis, Flash Petrucci, uncles Ovidio and Tom, aunts Nardina, Margaret, and Lena. I was surrounded by character.

- Jim Brown was the greatest running back I ever saw.

- Gale Sayers was the greatest halfback. I haven't seen anyone yet like him; I have Lenny Moore a close second.

- In my opinion, we—the Giants, that is—never competed in the 2000 Super Bowl against Baltimore. I would love to criticize our offensive game plan, but I don't know that we had one.

- The best assistant coaches I was ever around were John Sandusky, Bobby Boyd, George Welsh, Jerry Sandusky, Lindy Infante, John Fox, Sean Payton, and Marty Schottenheimer before he became our head coach in Cleveland.

- It was obvious being around Jack Ramsay at St. Joe's and Joe Paterno of Penn State that I was around greatness. You didn't need to define it to know it.

- Being around Paterno turned on the electricity in my soul. I was lazy when I arrived there. I didn't know I was, but I was.

- One of the greatest joys of going to Wake Forest was befriending Pat Williams, ex-NBA GM, quite simply the most remarkable man I have ever known. Pat and his wife have nineteen children of all races and creeds. I have often told him, "Pat, you're going to heaven on the first ballot, but the good Lord is sending a private plane for your wife."

- The New York media are not only the best, they have as much integrity as any I've known.

- When I was a sportswriter with the *Philadelphia Inquirer,* I was lucky to be near George Kiseda, the all-around greatest newspaperman.

- Some of my favorite people in sports today are Tim Duncan, Joe Torre, Brian Cashman, Omar Minaya, Jim Leyland, Mark Shapiro, Terry Ryan, Albert Pujols, Derek Jeter, Joe Mauer, and Ryan Howard.

- Unitas and Paterno were the two toughest men, mentally and physically, I have ever been around.

- The best spaghetti sauce and pizza in the world come from Fenicci's in Hershey, formerly the DeAngelis Grill.

- The most breathtaking places I have ever seen are the birthplaces of my parents, in Paris, France, and Pitigliano, Italy. And the shores of Omaha Beach.

- I saw every shot of Jack Nicklaus' record-tying 64 on Saturday at the 1965 Masters.

- I saw Brown score five touchdowns, Unitas throw for 397 yards, and Raymond Berry catch twelve of John's passes, all in the same game.

- I saw Secretariat in the homestretch at Pimlico.
- I saw Jimmy Walker of Providence score fifty points to win the Holiday Festival at Madison Square Garden.
- I saw the University of Pennsylvania tie Notre Dame 7–7 before eighty thousand in Franklin Field.
- I saw Mantle hit a home run over the hedge in dead center field in Baltimore. In fact, I saw him hit eleven homers. Not bad for living in Hershey.
- The first time I saw the Phillies in the brilliant cherry-red pinstripes, playing the regal Dodgers in their gray away uniforms in 1950, it was over for me. Then, on a rainy Sunday in '51, I saw the great DiMaggio in his final season and the template was cut.
- It was important to my father that I see Jackie Robinson play.
- I saw live 140 of the 191 players in the Pro Football Hall of Fame, and I watched thirteen of the twenty-one inducted head coaches do their work.
- Of the twenty modern-day quarterbacks in the Hall, I saw nineteen.
- If Bert Jones hadn't hurt his shoulder, I believe he would have been there, too.
- Dammit, I never saw Sid Luckman play.
- I saw Yankee Stadium, Augusta National, Michie Stadium, Cameron Indoor, Wrigley Field, Roland Garros, Lambeau Field, Fenway Park, Saratoga Race Course, Pebble Beach Golf Course, Wembley Stadium, the Pit at the University of New Mexico, Camden Yards, Lamade Little League Stadium in Williamsport, Pennsylvania, the Old Course at St. Andrews, the Rose Bowl, the Boston Marathon course, and the Daytona Speedway.
- I also saw the Polo Grounds, Crosley Field, Forbes Field, Griffith Stadium, what's left of Braves Field, and old Comiskey Park.
- I saw the definition of leadership: Unitas getting on the team bus.
- I saw Henry Aaron hit his 399th and 400th homers in the same game.
- I saw Mays and Musial and Williams and Berra.

- And, of course I saw Eli Manning in Super Bowl XLII. A few days after the game, his father, Archie, called me. Just think of it: two Super Bowl MVPs out of one household in consecutive years. Both Peyton and Eli are just as humble as Archie, and as their mother Olivia, too. Laughing, Archie told me he had received a call from the president of Ole Miss about the 18 MPH traffic signs on campus that were put up to commemorate Archie's number 18. "The president told me, 'you've had it long enough,' Archie said. 'We've decided to change the speed limit to 10 MPH, for Eli.' " He and I laughed till we cried.

Will you tolerate an afterword now? The loves of my life, the most important people on earth for me, are my children and granddaughter. My oldest son, Michael, who graduated from the University of Pittsburgh, received his master's at Virginia while he was a graduate assistant coach under George Welsh and then became a coach at the University of Maryland. He got into high school coaching at Bishop McNamara High School in Maryland because he loved teaching young kids, and he is now teaching history at Archbishop Mitty High School in San Jose, California.

My daughter, Sherlyn, graduated from Penn State University and lives in Cherry Hill, New Jersey, with her husband, Jim, who is a career Air Force man, and my precious granddaughter, Alexandra. Sherlyn is a wife, a mother, and a sales executive.

My youngest child, Patrick, is currently living in Manhattan and giving me such an added joy of having a weekly dining partner. He is a sales executive with the Oxo Company in New York. Patrick graduated from the University of Maryland after attending the University of Kentucky first. I have always felt he is a Wildcat first, then a Terrapin.

The joy of my children at this point of my life is that they have now become more my advisors and someone for me to lean on. Life comes full circle.

—Ernie Accorsi

AUTHOR'S NOTE

The Giants' improbable victory was certain to combine with the fiftieth anniversary of the Colts–Giants Sudden Death championship to make 2008 a rough year for trees. "I guess this will inspire another barrage of New York books," said a non–New Yorker in the press box as Super Bowl XLII wound down.

"Afraid so," a member of the Giants' regular press corps replied. "In fact, our beat guy is nearly finished with his."

"*Really?* When did he start?"

"The first quarter."

But one football book will be missing—the best one.

In the spring of 2006, a few weeks before he died, David Halberstam phoned me to talk about the '58 game. He had seen my book, *Johnny U,* about its Most Valuable Player, Baltimore quarterback Johnny Unitas.

David was as kind and funny as always, but of course I knew what he was calling for really: home numbers for old Giants and Colts, Sam Huff and Gino Marchetti. I gave him all I had. He intended to make that storied game his "in-between" book after Korea and before the next heavy subject. For Halberstam, sports served as a sort of R & R.

I met him in Washington during the 1970s, when I was a sports columnist for the old *Washington Star.* To meet David once was to know him forever, because he insisted on staying at least in ragged contact with everyone he knew, and he did all of the work. New England Patriots coach Bill Belichick, not a man anyone would take for a social animal or reader, cherished his connection to Halberstam and read all of David's books. "I like the one he wrote on the firehouse," Belichick said, "the best."

The sportswriters never thought of Halberstam as a poacher or slummer. Those bow-tied laureates who rhapsodize about the "emerald greensward" of baseball and find metaphorical lessons in the infield fly rule make the sportswriters laugh out loud. When historian Doris Kearns Goodwin called back her detailed recollections of the 1949 Brooklyn Dodgers, one couldn't help but smile. She was six at the time.

But Halberstam was different. He was one of us.

Though he brought a fan's passion to games, he didn't forget the reporter's restraint born of good taste, and he had a big advantage over clubhouse regulars: fresh eyes. He could see things we had stopped looking at long ago. Admittedly, in his devotion to thoroughness, Halberstam was inclined to repeat himself. I used to tease him with this rattle: "The coffee was black. Utterly black. Without cream or sugar. We're talking black here. Blacker than half-past midnight. Blacker than the other color besides red on a roulette wheel. Blacker than Shirley Temple's married name. Black City. Black Junction. New paragraph." He would laugh and say, "Well, it was pretty black." He forgave me, I think, because I told him how, years ago, Red Smith, Jack Murphy, and I went together to a Connecticut bookstore to buy three copies of *The Powers That Be*. You needed a car with a strong suspension to carry three of those babies home. Red was one of David's heroes.

When it came to sportswriting, Halberstam knew his stuff, all right.

He wasn't at all interested in the NBA ref who bet on the games, the track star who en route to jail had to return her Olympic medals, or the baseball slugger who was a stick figure in Pittsburgh but ballooned into the Michelin Man in San Francisco. Halberstam was much more intrigued by the fact that Michael Jordan could fly. "What do you think of Eli Manning?" David asked me. "Seriously, what do you make of him? Up close, is there more to Eli than meets the eye?" What he meant was: Did Manning have at least a chance to be great? Halberstam was taken with excellence. Though Joe DiMaggio declined several invitations to sit

down with him (Joe ducked most interviews, presuming the third question would concern Marilyn Monroe), David never held it against him.
He loved Joe D's famous reply to why, near the close of his career, he still
tried so hard in every game. "Because there might be someone in the
ballpark who had never seen me play."

"Jimmy Cannon made that up," I told Halberstam.

"There's no hope for you," he said.

David mentioned a quote from *Johnny U,* actually from Yvonne
Ameche, fullback Alan Ameche's wife, who said, "I remember when
Alan and I bought our first row house in Baltimore. We paid $8,000 for
it. John Unitas came over and laid our kitchen floor." So, even to Halberstam, $30 million ballplayers were cutting into the fun. "One of the
things I love about these old Giants and Colts," he said, "is that they all
had real jobs in the off-season, selling paint and working construction."

In the smallest footnote to 9/11, retired batting champion Carl
Furillo—one of Ms. Goodwin's beloved Dodgers—had been a construction worker on the Twin Towers, installing Otis elevators. Today's pro
athletes won't be installing any elevators.

Signing off, I told Halberstam he better hustle. More than a few
others were on the same case. When Halberstam was killed in a car accident in California, he was on his way to see Y.A. Tittle ("Yelton Abraham
Tittle," he would say), who ended up a Giants quarterback but in 1958
served the San Francisco 49ers. The 49ers beat the Colts just a couple of
weeks before the Sudden Death game. Tittle's phone number was one
of the ones I gave David.

INDEX

Aaron, Henry, 278
Abrams, Kevin, 132–134, 187, 228, 257
Accorsi, Ernie, 1–4, 5–14, 16–22, 25–27,
    29–37, 40–42, 48–63, 65–91, 93,
    95–101, 104–111, 113, 115, 118,
    119, 122, 124, 127–132, 134–135,
    137–139, 142–145, 149–153, 155,
    158–163, 169, 171, 174–188, 190, 191,
    197, 199, 202, 203, 205, 206, 209–212,
    216–223, 225–227, 231, 232, 234–235,
    237, 240–245, 247–253, 255–258,
    260–263, 265–266, 268, 269, 271–273,
    275–279
Accorsi, Ernie, Sr., 8, 9, 11–13, 222, 234,
    276, 278
Accorsi, Mary Nardi, 76–77, 81, 234, 276
Accorsi, Michael, 37, 50, 269, 279
Accorsi, Patrick, 279
Accorsi, Sherlyn, 279
Adcock, Joe, 250
Agnew, Tony, 131
Aikman, Troy, 43, 129
Akers, David, 44, 215, 216, 240
Alexander, Brent, 143
Alexander, Shaun, 113
Alford, Jay, 108, 261, 263, 272
Ali, Muhammad, 3
Allen, Anthony, 149
Allen, Bruce, 256, 257
Ameche, Alan "the Horse," 54–55, 217
Anderson, Gary, 197
Anderson, Ken, 214
Andrade, Billy, 3, 4, 266, 272
Angelos, Peter, 81
Armstead, Jessie, 95, 144

Arrington, LaVar, 2, 42, 112–115, 130, 139,
    140, 142, 144, 187, 233, 261
Ashenback, Eddie, 30
Atkins, Tom, 218
Atlanta Falcons, 26, 125–129, 186, 265
Austin, Ocie, 53
Awasom, Adrian, 169

Bahr, Matt, 183
Baltimore Colts, 5, 36–37, 47, 49–63, 81,
    153, 154, 217, 219, 225, 258, 259–260,
    265–267
Baltimore *Evening Sun*, 1, 29
Baltimore Orioles, 59, 81
Baltimore Ravens, 15, 74, 86–87, 99, 175
Baltimore Stars, 152
Banks, Chip, 69
Banner, Joe, 48
Barber, Marion, 140, 200
Barber, Ronde, 101–102, 164
Barber, Tiki, 21, 22, 26, 41, 43–47, 94,
    101–102, 111, 112, 125, 126, 128–130,
    140–142, 164, 165, 167, 169, 170, 172,
    178, 179, 189, 190, 193, 199–202, 209,
    210, 214, 229–235, 237, 239, 241–242,
    244, 248, 249, 262
Barnes, Ronnie, 83, 117–124, 143, 180,
    185, 205, 234, 235
Basilio, Carmen, 185
Bauer, Hank, 247, 250, 276
Bavaro, Mark, 117, 154, 172
Bednarik, Chuck, 115
Belichick, Bill, 79–80, 89, 252, 272, 276
Bell, Bert, 50, 275
Bell, Jason, 130, 201

Bell, Upton, 50–52, 188
Bengston, Phil, 34
Benjamin, Guy, 214
Bennett, Drew, 193
Benson, Brad, 154
Berger, Mitch, 197
Berra, Yogi, 10, 251, 278
Berry, Raymond, 40, 217, 253, 277
Berwanger, Jay, 60–61
Betts, Ladell, 228–231
Bielski, Dick, 54
Bironas, Rob, 192, 193
Bishop, Keith, 75, 76
Blackburn, Chase, 144
Blank, Arthur, 265
Bledsoe, Drew, 140, 141
Bledsoe, Terry, 68–70
Bolden, Ricky, 150
Boras, Scott, 70
Boryla, Mike, 221
Boss, Kevin, 262, 263, 268
Boyd, Bobby, 20, 277
Bradley, Mark, 177, 257
Bradshaw, Ahmad, 263, 268
Bradshaw, Terry, 25
Brady, Dave, 218
Brady, Tom, 43, 106, 252, 265, 267–269, 272
Branca, Ralph, 78
Branch, John, 157
Braun, Carl, 256
Brees, Drew, 174, 255
Brennan, Brian, 74, 77, 150–152
Britt, Wesley, 17
Brookhouser, Frank, 33
Brooklyn Dodgers, 5, 8, 10, 78, 278
Brown, Alex, 179
Brown, Dave, 83, 138
Brown, Jim, 105, 116, 128, 276, 277
Brown, Levi, 108
Brown, Mike, 105
Brown, Paul, 55, 65, 66, 68, 69, 105, 276
Brown, Reggie, 215, 240
Brown, Roosevelt, 180
Brown, Sheldon, 47
Brunell, Mark, 111, 226, 231
Bryant, Bear, 183, 184
Buchanon, Phillip, 95, 99
Buckhalter, Correll, 44, 215
Buffalo Bills, 68, 70, 71

Bugel, Joe, 138, 226
Bulluck, Keith, 195
Burgess, Smoky, 80
Burns, Curry, 149
Burress, Elijah, 42
Burress, Plaxico, 2, 21, 25, 39–43, 45, 47,
    112, 113, 139, 164, 165, 168, 170, 179,
    182, 189–192, 201–203, 208, 229, 237,
    239, 242, 260, 267, 271–272
Burt, Jim, 154
Bush, Reggie, 169
Bussert, Joel, 68, 69, 71, 81–82
Butler, James, 143
Byner, Earnest, 77, 78, 134–135, 150
Byrum, Dion, 208, 210

Callison, Johnny, 250
Campanella, Roy, 247
Campbell, Jason, 228–231
Cannon, Jimmy, 218–219
Capitani, Frank, 250
Carolina Panthers, 25, 84, 85, 107, 207–212
Carr, David, 98, 168, 169
Carson, Bud, 79
Carson, Harry, 154, 251
Carter, Chris, 86
Carter, Drew, 208
Carter, Tim, 22, 45, 46, 126, 130–132, 239,
    242, 243
Carter, Virgil, 214
Casares, Rick, 143
Cashen, Frank, 29
Cashman, Brian, 277
Casper, Billy, 3
Casper, Dave, 98
Cassady, Howard "Hopalong," 33, 247
Casserly, Charley, 162
Castille, Jeremiah, 77–78
Chamberlain, Wilt, 31, 250
Charlotte Hornets, 29–30
Chernoff, Michael, 61, 62
Chester, Raymond, 219–220
Chicago Bears, 154, 170, 175–183, 191,
    214, 232, 251–252
Christensen, Jeff, 149, 150
Cimoli, Gino, 250
Cincinnati Bengals, 191
Cincinnati Reds, 6, 69, 150
Clark, Dallas, 21

Clemente, Roberto, 249
Cleveland Browns, 1, 5, 49, 55, 65–80, 81,
    88, 105, 107, 150, 243, 271, 276, 277
Cleveland Indians, 11, 122, 123
Colbert, Bobby, 219
Colbert, Keary, 107
Cole, Trent, 46, 216
Collier, Gene, 218
Collins, Kerry, 84–87, 89, 91, 263
Conerly, Charlie, 118, 267
Cook, Carroll "Beano," 87, 108
Cook, Jameel, 168
Cooley, Chris, 226, 229, 231
Cosell, Howard, 52, 61
Coughlin, Judy, 107
Coughlin, Tom, 1, 2, 15, 17, 25, 26, 40, 41,
    47, 89–91, 94, 100–104, 106, 107, 109,
    111, 112, 114, 121, 127–130, 132, 137,
    141, 145, 147, 153, 165, 169, 175,
    180–183, 189, 191, 193–196, 199, 200,
    202–204, 210, 222–223, 225–227, 233,
    234, 237, 241, 244, 247–250, 252, 254,
    259–261, 264, 265, 267
Cowher, Bill, 183, 264
Cox, Fred, 55
Crayton, Patrick, 201
Crennel, Romeo, 89
Crosetti, Frank, 10, 256
Csonka, Larry, 90
Cunningham, Randall, 43
Cuozzo, Gary, 151
Curry, Bill, 55
Curtis, Mike, 53, 55

Dallas Cowboys, 26, 54, 124, 128, 139–142,
    153, 198–204, 231, 254, 256, 263,
    265–266, 268
Dalton, Harry, 29
Danielson, Gary, 150–151
Dark, Alvin, 55, 250
Davidds-Garrido, Norberto, 84
Davis, Al, 98
Davis, Jeremiah, 158–159
Davis, Milt, 266, 269
Davis, Stephen, 181
Dawkins, Brian, 241
Dawson, Len, 105
Dean, Dizzy, 10
Dean, Paul, 10

DeAngelis, Tony, 276
DeBartolo, Eddie, 57
DeBerg, Steve, 214
Delhomme, Jack, 207
Demps, Will, 45, 130, 143–144, 177, 202
Denver Broncos, 61, 74–78, 99, 124, 276
DeOssie, Zak, 262, 263
Detroit Lions, 271, 275
Devaney, Bob, 34
Dickey, Bill, 247
Dickey, Lynn, 35
Diehl, David, 190, 208, 209, 238, 239
DiMaggio, Joe, 10, 256, 257, 278
Dimitroff, Thomas, 265
Ditka, Mike, 83, 218
DiTrani, Vinny, 250
Dixon, Hanford, 69
Dockery, Kevin, 141
Dolson, Frank, 31–32
Donovan, Art, 217
Doran, Jim, 271
Droughns, Reuben, 243, 263
Druckenmiller, Jim, 214
Drysdale, Don, 135
Duckett, T. J., 230, 231
Duncan, Tim, 277
Dunn, Warrick, 125

Earl, Glenn, 170
Egan, Edward, 122
Eich, Art, 62
Elway, Jack, 58, 59
Elway, John, 25, 43, 58–63, 75, 76, 79, 87,
    150, 273, 276
Emmons, Carlos, 130, 144, 261
Engle, Rip, 34, 36
Ewbank, Weeb, 217

Farley, Dale, 52
Fassel, Jim, 85, 87, 89, 102, 106, 137–139
Faulk, Kevin, 269
Favre, Brett, 43, 132, 162, 186, 238, 266
Feagles, Jeff, 130, 139, 152, 153, 155,
    162–163, 178, 182, 192, 193, 242,
    260, 267
Feagles, Michelle, 163
Feely, Jay, 21, 43, 45, 46, 93, 112, 126, 127,
    131, 141, 164, 165, 168, 179, 197–200,
    202, 209, 210, 215, 229, 230, 239, 242

Feller, Bob, 219
Finks, Jim, 218
Finley, Charlie, 55
Finn, Jim, 20, 45, 127, 130, 142, 164, 239, 243
Fisher, Jeff, 196
Fitzgerald, Larry, 88
Flutie, Doug, 43, 66–68, 90
Foley, Glenn, 90
Ford, Whitey, 247, 250
Fouts, Dan, 214
Fox, John, 86, 181, 212, 277
Francis, Joe, 25
Franks, Bubba, 113
Freeman, Bobby, 54
Frick, Ford, 7
Fryman, Travis, 11

Gabriel, Roman, 221
Gallery, Robert, 88
Gammons, Peter, 276
Garcia, Jeff, 213–215, 240
Garland, Ozella, 158
Garman, Francis, 12
Garman, Terry, 12
Gastineau, Mark, 98, 111
Gautt, Prentice, 222
Gehrig, Lou, 256
Geletka, John, 68
Gettleman, Dave, 147–149, 161
Gibbs, Joe, 226, 227
Gifford, Frank, 170, 232
Gilbride, Kevin, 20, 223, 227
Gilliam, "Jefferson Street Joe," 25
Gillman, Sid, 225
Gilmore, John, 178
Glenn, Terry, 140, 141, 200, 201
Goldberg, Joel, 138
Goldstein, Al, 59
Goodell, Roger, 275
Gostkowski, Stephen, 269
Gould, Robbie, 177
Grabowski, Joe, 250
Gradkowski, Bruce, 164
Graham, Archibald "Moonlight," 30
Graham, Kent, 84, 86
Graham, Otto, 105, 151, 250
Gramatica, Martin, 199–202, 204
Gramigni, Ron, 12

Granholm, Bill, 275
Grant, Bud, 73, 103
Grant, Ryan, 130, 263
Gray, Earnest, 170
Green Bay Packers, 66, 152, 185, 186, 197, 263, 266, 276
Griese, Bob, 55
Grossman, Rex, 170, 176–179, 182, 251
Grout, Jack, 8
Groza, Lou "the Toe," 55
Gruden, Jon, 164
Guglielmi, Ralph, 55
Gunsel, Austin, 220
Guokas, Matt, 247

Haas, Jay, 3
Halas, George, 61, 218, 221
Hall, DeAngelo, 125–126
Hall, Leon, 261
Ham, Jack, 34, 35, 244
Hamner, Granny, 256
Hanlon, Pat, 2, 103–104, 203, 248, 258
Hannah, John, 60
Harper, Nick, 22
Harris, Franco, 34, 244, 247
Harris, James, 161
Harrison, Marvin, 21, 22, 24
Harrison, Rodney, 270
Harriss, Matt, 187–188, 257
Hart, Jim, 221
Hart, Leon, 271
Hasselbeck, Don, 93
Hasselbeck, Matt, 93, 94
Hasselbeck, Tim, 93, 130
Havrilak, Sam, 265
Hayes, Woody, 103, 172
Hedgecock, Madison, 263
Hemond, Ollie, 81
Hendricks, Ted, 53, 244
Henrich, Tommy, 276
Henry, Travis, 192
Herrmann, Mark, 61
Herron, Mack, 35
Hershey, Milton Snavely, 8, 9, 13
Herzeg, Ladd, 69–71
Hester, Devin, 176, 179, 180, 182, 183
Hill, Marquise, 107
Hilliard, Ike, 86
Hillsman, J. C., 157

Hinebaugh, Gary, 12, 13
Hinton, Chris, 61
Hixon, Domenik, 263
Hobbs, Ellis, 271, 272
Hogan, Ben, 9
Hogeboom, Gary, 151
Holmgren, Mike, 197
Hornung, Paul, 33, 109
Houston Oilers, 69–71, 98, 150, 173
Houston Texans, 167–169
Howard, Elston, 247
Howard, Ryan, 277
Howe, Gordie, 250
Hufnagel, John, 25–26, 111, 182, 223, 227
Hull, Bobby, 250
Hulmes, Henry, 49–50, 82, 187, 188
Hummer, Paul, 11, 12
Hunt, Lamar, 221

Imhoff, Darrall, 31
Indianapolis Colts, 15, 20–22, 27, 54,
    62–63, 129, 151, 240
Infante, Lindy, 138, 277
Ionni, Ed, 77
Irsay, Robert, 49, 54, 55, 59–62, 249
Irvin, Michael, 140
Isenberg, Jerry, 29

Jackson, Keith, 52
Jackson, Mark, 75, 76
Jacobs, Brandon, 45, 46, 102, 112, 126, 128,
    143, 164, 165, 168, 176, 179, 182,
    189–191, 196, 200, 209, 210, 242, 263,
    270
Jefferson, Roy, 53–54
Jennings, Kelly, 17
Jennings, Michael, 167
Jeter, Derek, 256, 277
John-Baptiste, Peter, 2
Johnson, Chad, 40
Johnson, Johnny, 117–118
Johnson, Keyshawn, 40
Johnson, Michael, 263
Jones, Adam Bernard "Pacman," 191–193,
    242
Jones, Bert, 55, 219, 278
Jones, Brandon, 193
Jones, Homer, 170
Jones, Julius, 140, 200, 201

Jones, Sean, 107
Jones, Thomas, 113, 175, 177, 178
Jones, William "Puddin' Head," 256
Joost, Eddie, 257
Joseph, William, 178
Jurgensen, Sonny, 33
Justice, Charlie, 115

Kaline, Al, 256
Kanell, Danny, 83–84
Kansas City Chiefs, 15, 105, 107
Karlis, Rich, 76
Kellett, Don, 37
Kelly, Jim, 43
Kennedy, Walter, 32
Kensil, Jim, 218, 219, 275
Kilroy, Bucko, 48
Kiseda, George, 277
Kiwanuka, Benedicto, 17
Kiwanuka, Mathias, 17, 168, 176, 193–195,
    200, 202
Klein, Gene, 60
Klosterman, Don "Duke," 37, 49–54, 82,
    220
Knox, Chuck, 221
Koets, Adam, 263
Koppett, Leonard, 32
Kosar, Bernie, 1, 67–74, 77, 78, 80, 150, 250
Koufax, Sandy, 135
Kraft, Bob, 137
Kuehl, Ryan, 130, 242
Kush, Frank, 58–61, 63
Kuzava, Bob, 249
Kwalik, Ted, 22

Lahr, Warren, 271
Laird, Bruce, 265
Landeta, Sean, 152–156
Landry, Tom, 103
Lansky, Meyer, 49
Larsen, Don, 250
Lauer, Matt, 101
Lavelli, Dante, 151, 152
Layne, Bobby, 10, 271, 276
Leaf, Ryan, 254–255
Leahy, Marshall, 220, 221
LeBaron, Eddie, 54
Lee, David, 256
Lemon, Cleo, 241

Lewin, Leonard, 32
Lewis, Barry, 148–149
Lewis, Eli, 148
Lewis, Jamal, 113
Lewis, Tim, 91, 249
Leyland, Jim, 277
Lindsey, Dale, 113
Little, Floyd, 90
Logan, Jerry, 17
Lombardi, Vince, 14, 35–36, 50, 66, 218, 276
Lopat, Eddie, 219, 247
Lorenzen, Jared, 130, 237
Los Angeles Rams, 48, 49, 54, 65, 152
Louis, Joe, 2, 31
Luckman, Sid, 278
Lundy, Wali, 168
Lurie, Jeffrey, 48
Lynam, Jimmy, 256
Lynn, Fred, 262–263
Lynn, Mike, 69

Mack, Connie, 6
Mack, Kevin, 134–135
Mackey, John, 54, 244
Madden, John, 221
Madison, Sam, 130, 141, 142, 178
Mahe, Reno, 240
Malin, Steve, 262
Manning, Archie, 15–16, 19, 22–24, 194,
        221, 238–239, 252
Manning, Cooper, 23
Manning, Eli, 2, 15, 17–26, 29, 39–40,
        42–47, 87–89, 91, 93, 94, 99, 111, 112,
        115, 118, 124–127, 139, 141–143, 164,
        165, 167, 168, 170, 173, 176, 178, 179,
        182, 183, 188–190, 193–194, 199–203,
        208–211, 214–218, 222, 225, 229, 234,
        237–239, 241–243, 250, 252–256, 260,
        262, 264–273
Manning, Olivia, 15, 16, 19, 217–218, 252
Manning, Peyton, 15, 19–25, 129, 238,
        251–253
Mantle, Mickey, 6, 57, 256, 257, 276, 278
Mara, Chris, 161–162, 251, 267
Mara, John, 2, 89, 90, 95, 122, 124,
        137–139, 142, 159, 161, 190, 191, 196,
        202, 203, 206, 217, 225, 226, 228, 232,
        234, 235, 247–249, 251, 256–258, 260,
        266, 273

Mara, Kate, 124, 162, 165, 267
Mara, Steven, 216
Mara, Tim, 232, 258
Mara, Wellington, 2, 27, 57, 91, 106,
        115–116, 120–124, 137–139, 159, 161,
        162, 187, 199, 206, 218, 232, 266, 267,
        273
Marani, Galiano, 77
Marchetti, Gino, 217
Marchibroda, Ted, 56, 256
Marino, Dan, 25, 43, 60, 61, 110–111
Maroney, Laurence, 268
Marshall, Jim, 162, 195
Marshall, Leonard, 154
Marshall, Willie, 251
Mason, Larry, 150
Matte, Tom, 265
Matthews, Michael, 263
Mauer, Joe, 277
Maynard, Brad, 175
Mays, Willie, 247, 278
Mazur, John, 220
McCafferty, Don, 220
McCauley, Don, 55
McConkeys, Phil, 110
McCree, Marlon, 252
McDonald, Paul, 65
McDonough, Will, 17, 137
McDougald, Gil, 250
McGann, Dan, 30
McGraw, John, 30
McGuire, Frank, 34
McHan, Lamar, 25
McKay, John, 186
McKenzie, Kareem, 46, 168, 169, 190, 238
McKenzie, Reggie, 209
McKinnie, Bryant, 95, 99
McMahon, Jim, 170
McNabb, Donovan, 43, 44, 47, 48, 213
McNair, Steve, 195
McNally, Art, 275
McQuarters, R. W., 130, 178
Meredith, Don, 52
Miami Dolphins, 55, 170
Miller, Fred, 260
Minaya, Omar, 277
Minnesota Vikings, 58, 69–73, 86, 99, 162,
        195, 197, 212, 265
Mitchell, Kawika, 260–261

Mitchell, Lydell, 34–36, 247
Modell, Art, 62, 65, 67–69, 71, 72, 76, 79–80, 150–151
Monk, Art, 40
Montana, Joe, 20, 214, 271
Moon, Warren, 69
Moore, Lenny, 217, 247, 276
Morgan, Cy, 6
Morrall, Earl, 33
Morris, Joe, 154
Morris, Larry, 54
Morton, Chad, 43, 130, 143, 214
Moss, Randy, 40, 86, 268, 269
Moss, Santana, 228, 229, 231
Moss, Sinorice, 44, 209, 242
Motley, Marion, 143
Mueller, Don, 249
Muhammad, Muhsin, 84, 177, 178
Munson, Thurman, 250
Musial, Stanley (the Man), 7, 256, 278
Mutscheller, Jim, 217
Myers, Billy, 11, 12

Namath, Joe, 253, 272
Nardi, Joe, 8–9, 11–12, 32
Naval Academy, 33–36, 110
Nelson, Andy, 247
New England Patriots, 15, 17, 80, 89, 106, 107, 137, 150, 219, 240, 252, 264–272
New Orleans Saints, 15, 83, 84, 174, 222, 255
New York Giants, 1–3, 5, 10, 15–17, 20–26, 30, 39, 41–48, 56–57, 66, 78, 82–91, 93–108, 110–135, 149–156, 158–183, 185–212, 214–217, 222–223, 225–235, 237–245, 247–273, 276
New York Jets, 15, 74, 106, 186, 217
New York Mets, 29
New York Yankees, 10, 56, 59, 102
Newsome, Ozzie, 74, 150, 161, 244
Nicklaus, Barbara, 8
Nicklaus, Jack, 8, 277
Nieman, Bob, 59
Noll, Chuck, 25, 276

Oakland Raiders, 25, 88, 89, 91, 98, 99, 219
O'Brien, Jim, 153, 154
Odom, Antwan, 107

O'Hara, Shaun, 47, 94–95, 111, 125, 144, 163, 165, 169, 180, 208–211, 234, 24?, 260
Ohio Wesleyan, 6, 32
O'Hora, Jim, 36
Okeafor, Chike, 207
Orr, Jimmy, 247
Osborne, Tom, 34
Owens, Terrell, 40, 43, 140, 200, 201

Packer, Billy, 247
Palmer, Arnold, 3, 13
Parcells, Bill, 80, 89, 109, 137–139, 141, 150, 199, 202–203, 226
Parilli, Babe, 105
Parker, Buddy, 271
Parker, Jim, 217
Paterno, Joe, 22, 34–37, 65–67, 84, 85, 108, 115, 181, 183–184, 277
Paterno, Sue, 184
Pavano, Carl, 257
Payton, Sean, 15, 174, 277
Payton, Walter, 170
Pearson, Preston, 53
Penn State, 22, 32–37, 65–67, 68, 84, 85, 95, 108, 110, 113, 115, 174, 183, 243
Pennington, Chad, 113
Peppers, Julius, 208
Pereira, Mike, 27
Perkins, Ray, 220
Perry, William "the Refrigerator," 170, 207
Petitgout, Luke, 20, 47, 94, 125, 130, 176, 178–181, 233, 253, 261
Petrino, Bobby, 225
Petrucci, Flash, 276
Philadelphia Eagles, 10, 26, 43–48, 61, 86, 128, 142, 152, 165, 212, 214–216, 221, 231, 237–240, 278
Philadelphia Inquirer, 29, 31–32, 277
Philadelphia Stars, 152
Picard, Henry, 8
Piccolo, Brian, 13–14, 221, 247
Pierce, Antonio, 26, 94, 141, 144, 163–164, 169, 177, 188, 196, 200, 202, 210, 260, 267
Piersall, Jimmy, 29
Pinchbeck, Val, 221
Pioli, Scott, 131, 162
Pisarcik, Joe, 193

Pittsburgh Steelers, 10, 40, 41, 53, 69, 80,
    105, 162, 183, 188, 255, 275
Plum, Milt, 266
Plunkett, Jim, 17, 25
Ponzoli, Gary, 11, 48
Pope, Mike, 94, 96, 244
Portis, Clinton, 95, 99
Posluszny, Paul, 108
Posner, Roy, 227–228, 234–235, 242
Powell, Shaun, 250–251
Pujols, Albert, 277
Puzzuoli, Dave, 75

Quinn, Brady, 109

Ramsay, Jack, 33, 277
Randle El, Antwaan, 228, 230, 231
Raschi, Vic, 250
Ratterman, George, 105
Reed, Ed, 95, 99
Reese, Gwen, 160, 161
Reese, Jerry, 17, 106, 130, 157–161,
    250–251, 258–263, 266, 268, 270
Reeves, Dan, 25, 75, 76, 137, 138
Reid, Andy, 48
Reid, Mike, 34
Revis, Darrelle, 261
Reynolds, Allie, 249
Rhodes, Dominic, 22
Richard, Maurice, 250
Richards, Paul, 98
Richardson, Bobby, 247
Richardson, Willie, 53
Rickey, Branch, 5–8, 29, 32, 257
Riggins, John, 226
Rivers, Philip, 87, 88, 255–256
Rizzuto, Phil, 10, 250
Robbie, Joe, 55
Robbins, Fred, 111, 130, 141, 228
Roberts, Selena, 264
Robinson, Brooks, 256
Robinson, Frank, 81, 249
Robinson, Jackie, 8, 10, 31, 247, 278
Rockne, Knute, 51, 196
Rodgers, Johnny, 105
Roethlisberger, Ben, 88, 183, 255
Rollins, Bill, 12
Romo, Tony, 141, 200–202, 204, 255
Rooney, Art, 26, 50, 69, 188, 218, 258

Rooney, Dan, 40, 218
Rosenbloom, Carroll, 49–54
Rosenhaus, Drew, 41, 82, 95, 98
Ross, Aaron, 261, 263
Rote, Kyle, 42, 170, 217
Rozelle, Pete, 29, 48, 56, 61–62, 70–72, 218,
    220, 258, 275
Rucker, Mike, 208
Ruegamer, Grey, 211
Rumph, Mike, 95, 99
Ruth, Babe, 221, 256
Rutigliano, Sam, 65, 66
Ryan, Terry, 277

Saban, Nick, 148
Sain, Johnny, 250
San Diego Chargers, 23, 88, 89, 240, 243,
    252, 255
San Francisco 49ers, 57, 99, 107, 140, 207,
    213, 214
Sanders, Deion, 176, 179
Sandusky, Jerry, 277
Sandusky, John, 277
Sauer, Hank, 250
Sayers, Gale, 13–14, 247, 276
Scaife, Bo, 192, 195
Schaefer, William Donald, 81
Schlister, Art, 103
Schnellenberger, Howard, 55
Schobel, Matt, 240
Schottenheimer, Brian, 76
Schottenheimer, Marty, 66, 73, 74, 76–79,
    88, 90, 151–152, 227, 240–241, 252,
    254–255, 277
Schramm, Tex, 220
Schubach, Fred, 52, 59
Schulberg, Budd, 53
Schwartzwalder, Ben, 90
Scott, Clyde "Smackover," 247
Seaman, Jerry, 275
Seattle Seahawks, 26, 93–94, 204
Sehorn, Jason, 86
Sellers, Mike, 228, 230, 231
Sellers, Ron, 17
Seubert, Rich, 205–211, 243, 273
Sewell, Steve, 75, 76
Shantz, Bobby, 247
Shapiro, Mark, 277
Shaw, George, 55

Index

Shay, Jerry, 262

Shiancoe, Visanthe, 164, 209, 237

Shockey, Jeremy, 2, 22, 46, 47, 93–100, 104, 112, 119, 126, 127, 129, 141, 167, 168, 170, 189, 190, 199, 200, 206, 209, 222, 243, 247, 248, 264

Shockey, Lucinda, 97, 98, 129

Shofner, Del, 40, 170

Short, Brandon, 128, 144, 165, 174, 243

Shula, Don, 51, 253, 272

Sigel, Jay, 13

Simms, Phil, 83

Simpson, O. J., 57

Singletary, Mike, 170

Sipe, Brian, 65, 74

Siragusa, Tony, 87

Sisler, George, 7

Siwoff, Seymour, 275

Skowron, Bill (Moose), 250

Slaughter, Webster, 78, 152

Slusher, Howard, 70–71

Smith, A. J., 88, 240–241, 252

Smith, Al, 232

Smith, Bruce, 68, 69, 71

Smith, Dean, 34

Smith, Emmitt, 128

Smith, Holden, 58

Smith, Jason, 233

Smith, L. J., 44, 215

Smith, Lovey, 89

Smith, Robert, 86

Smith, Steve, 208, 261, 263, 268, 270

Smith, Walter Wellesley "Red," 7, 219, 258

Snee, Chris, 44, 47, 107, 169, 208, 209, 239

Snee, Cooper Christopher, 107

Snee, Dylan, 107

Snee, Katie, 107

Sollinger, Bobby, 256

Songin, Ed, 116

Spagnuola, Steve, 267

Spahn, Warren, 65

Spanos, Dean, 252

Spencer, Shawntae, 107

Spinney, Art, 116

Springs, Shawn, 113

Spurrier, Steve, 55

Stagg, Alonzo, 51

Stallworth, Donté, 215

Stanky, Eddie, 79

Starr, Bart, 25

Staubach, Roger, 110, 250

Stautner, Ernie, 116

Steinbrenner, George, 59

Stengel, Casey, 56, 150

Strahan, Michael, 26, 43, 56, 101, 102, 111, 128, 130–132, 141–142, 152, 159, 165, 169, 202, 210, 216, 233–234, 244, 248, 259, 260, 262, 264

Stram, Hank, 105

Strange, Curtis, 3

Suisham, Shaun, 228, 230, 231

Sullivan, Chuckie, 60

Summerall, Pat, 218

Super Bowl, 51, 53, 54, 74, 78, 80, 86, 87, 106, 137, 153, 212, 255, 259, 266–272, 279

Swink, "Swanky Jim," 33

Szymanski, Dick, 52, 56, 256

Tampa Bay Buccaneeers, 152, 162–165, 186, 256–257, 264

Tarkenton, Fran, 221

Tarman, Jim, 33–35, 108, 183

Tarman, Louise, 108

Taylor, Jamaar, 130

Taylor, John, 271

Taylor, Lawrence, 154, 196

Tennessee Titans, 98, 107, 189–196, 254

Testaverde, Vinny, 68

Texas Rangers, 79

Thomas, Joe, 54–57

Thomson, Bobby, 78, 249

Tisch, Jonathan, 161

Tisch, Preston Robert, 91, 137–139

Tisch, Steve, 161

Tisch family, 228

Tittle, Y. A., 151, 232

Toomer, Amani, 21, 22, 43, 45–47, 112, 130, 142, 168, 170–173, 233, 253, 269, 270

Toomer, Donald, 172

Torre, Joe, 102–103, 257, 263

Towler, "Deacon" Dan, 48

Tressman, Mark, 73

Trotter, Jeremiah, 47–48

Tuck, Justin, 142, 180, 262

Turley, Bob, 247

Tynes, Lawrence, 272

Tyree, David, 179, 190, 193, 210, 229, 242, 268, 270

Umenyiora, Osi, 88, 111, 128, 142, 168, 233, 243, 260, 262
Unitas, Chad, 265
Unitas, Johnny, 1–2, 10, 20, 21, 49, 52–54, 59–61, 74, 80, 99, 144, 151, 217, 219, 225, 238, 244, 249–250, 259–260, 266, 273, 277, 278
Unitas, Sandy, 265
Urlacher, Brian, 113

Vanderjagt, Mike, 199, 204
Vick, Michael, 125, 127–129
Vinatieri, Adam, 21, 22
Volk, Rick, 17

Wade, Bobby, 191, 192
Wadkins, Lanny, 3
Wake Forest University, 3, 13, 29, 51, 255, 277
Walker, Frank, 144–145, 192
Walker, Jerry, 98
Walker, Jimmy, 278
Walsh, Bill, 57–58, 150, 213–214, 222, 228, 234, 251, 252, 276
Walsh, Steve, 213
Walsh, Whitey, 106
Ward, Derrick, 263
Ward, Hines, 40
Warfield, Jimmy, 11, 12
Warfield, Paul, 40, 151, 152
Warner, Kurt, 89, 131–132
Washington, Gene, 161
Washington Redskins, 26, 111–113, 114, 124, 134, 142, 149, 225–234, 264
Watson, Courtney, 107
Watson, Steve, 75, 76
Way, Charlie, 85

Weaver, Earl, 79
Webb, Tom, 250
Webster, Corey, 142–143, 168, 192
Weinke, Chris, 207–210
Weis, Charlie, 89, 109–110, 225, 252–253
Weiss, George, 5, 56, 57
Welker, Wes, 268–269
Wells, Lloyd, 105
Welsh, George, 33–36, 51, 90, 102, 233, 250, 277, 279
Wepner, Chuck, 185
West, Jerry, 145
West Point, 33, 34, 110
Westbrook, Brian, 44, 45, 215, 239–241
White, LenDale, 191
White, Mike, 79–80
White, Patty, 56
White, Stan, 56
Whitfield, Bob, 130, 168–170, 179–180
Wiegert, Zach, 169
Wilkinson, Gerrit, 144
Williams, Doug, 251
Williams, Mario, 169
Williams, Pat, 277
Williams, Reggie, 119
Williams, Ted, 278
Wilson, Gibril, 143, 196, 209
Wilson, Kris, 107
Winder, Sammy, 75
Witten, Jason, 202
Wolf, Ron, 132, 185–188
Wyche, Sam, 214

Young, George, 50–52, 57, 82–83, 129, 132, 137–139, 147, 150, 152, 158–159, 161, 171, 187
Young, Steve, 43, 214
Young, Vince, 169, 189, 191–196, 238

Zellers, Rob, 218

ALSO BY TOM CALLAHAN

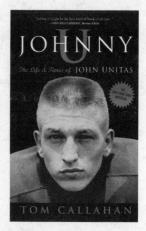

JOHNNY U
The Life & Times of John Unitas
$13.95 paper (Canada: $17.95)
978-1-4000-8140-0

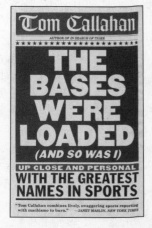

THE BASES WERE LOADED (and So Was I)
Up Close and Personal with the
Greatest Names in Sports
$12.95 paper (Canada: $17.95)
978-1-4000-8156-1

IN SEARCH OF TIGER
A Journey Through Golf with Tiger Woods
$14.95 paper (Canada: $16.95)
978-1-4000-5140-3